The
STREET SMART
PSYCHIC'S
GUIDE TO
GETTING A
GOOD READING

About the Author

Lisa Barretta is a psychic reader, artist, and certified Reiki practitioner who lives in Philadelphia. After receiving her first set of tarot cards at the age of fourteen, Lisa began studying divination and astrology while honing her own innate psychic skills. Over the past thirty-plus years she has developed her client base strictly by word of mouth, and her many clients live throughout North America, Europe, and the Middle East. Please visit her website, http://thestreetsmartpsychic.com.

LOVE · HEALTH · MONEY

The
STREET SMART
PSYCHIC'S
GUIDE TO
GETTING A
GOOD READING

LISA BARRETTA

Llewellyn Publications
Woodbury, Minnesota

First Edition
First Printing, 2009

Book design by Donna Burch
Cover design by Kevin R. Brown
Editing by Brett Fechheimer

Llewellyn is a registered trademark of Llewellyn Worldwide, Ltd.

Tarot card from the *Universal Tarot* by Roberto De Angelis © 2000 by Lo Scarabeo and reprinted with permission from Lo Scarabeo.

Library of Congress Cataloging-in-Publication Data
Barretta, Lisa, 1956–
 The street-smart psychic's guide to getting a good reading / Lisa Barretta. — Ist ed.
  p. cm.
 ISBN 978-0-7387-1850-7
 1. Psychic readings. I. Title.
 BF1045.R43B37 2009
 133.8—dc22
                          2009025943

Llewellyn Publications
A Division of Llewellyn Worldwide, Ltd.
2143 Wooddale Drive, Dept. 978-0-7387-1850-7
Woodbury, Minnesota 55125-2989, U.S.A.
www.llewellyn.com

Printed in the United States of America

Dedication and Acknowledgments

This book is dedicated to my parents, Marie and Fred D'Amico; my talented son B. J.; my daughter, Alison (with one *l*), who was a tremendous help in editing my work and taking my initial author photos; and my brilliant son Nicholas (Delta Tau Delta).

I also want to thank my family, the Galzo (Gallagher) clan, and my amazing posse: Aunt Rose, who keeps me laughing; Alex, a true-to-the-bone friend; and Bob, a very cool musician.

A big, big thank you to Carrie Obry, who believed in me enough to see a "reader" become a writer; Brett Fechheimer, for his sharp eye when editing my book; and to the rest of the awesome staff at Llewellyn, who collectively made this book happen.

To all of my wonderful, crazy, kooky, interesting clients who have been a true source of inspiration for this book: each and every one of you has been my teacher.

A very special thank you to Kim Renk, my biggest promoter.

I want to pass on to the reader of this book the energy with which it was written. Read it and smile. Laugh while you are learning. Keep your vibration high and attract all that is good. We are only sojourners passing through this life, for the universe holds our next destination.

Yo, Philly! This one's for you.

Contents

**Chapter 4: How Much Should You Pay
for a Psychic Reading? . . . 129**

Chapter 5: The Psychic-Reader Care and Use Guide . . . 159

Chapter 6: Psychic-Reader Risks 101 . . . 187

Chapter 7: Psychic-Reader Match Dot Com . . . 219

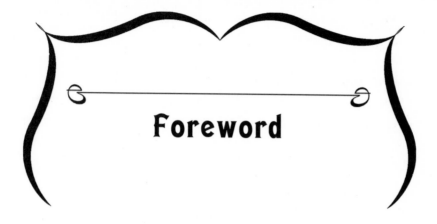

Foreword

What is it like to be a psychic reader? How does it feel to peek into the very private—and at times painful—lives of people who come looking for advice in the hope that their problems will somehow be straightened out by the turn of a tarot card?

I have been giving psychic readings since I was fourteen years old, the year I received my first deck of tarot cards. I somehow instinctively knew that by opening that box of tarot cards, I would also be taking on a responsibility to provide and translate, with the utmost integrity, the information I received through those cards.

After I became familiar with reading tarot cards, I loved to sit in amazement watching my aunt Rose give tarot-card readings for my family and our friends. I was drawn to psychics; I would often scan the personals section of the local newspapers looking for psychic readers. Each psychic I went to not only gave me a psychic reading but was also a mystical teacher who provided me with unique knowledge about the art of divination.

I experimented with the different methods of doing psychic readings, and I expanded my *psychic tool shop* to include divination by using regular playing cards, black mirror scrying (which is similar to using a crystal ball), and astrology. I eventually developed my third-eye and crown chakras enough to be open to doing psychic readings without the props. I became psychically open enough to feel and read energy imprints.

I was born and raised in Philadelphia, which gives me a bit of an edge when it comes to being street smart. Philly is a city where if you talk the talk, you better know how to walk the walk. It's a city of neighborhoods, with an eclectic mix of people embracing many ethnic and cultural traditions. I believe that almost every neighborhood in Philly has at least one resident psychic shop, botanical store, Reiki share group, or holistic medical practice. Some of the psychic establishments in and around Philly offer a mystical mix of tarot readers, palm readers, aura readers, candle-magick experts, energy-balancing professionals, and sometimes some spicy stuff such as Voodoo. The local psychic shops are loaded with enticing flavors of mystery—just like a famous Philly cheesesteak with the works, complete with hot peppers on top.

The first "psychic-hopping" experience that taught me to be street smart about psychics occurred in my late teens, when I went downtown to check out a tarot/palm reader. The old woman inside the shop was lying on a hospital-type bed, hooked up to an oxygen tank, and her raspy voice revealed a very gripping, exotic, foreign accent. She told my fortune for the sum of $10 by reading some tattered tarot cards. The reading was very good. She had me hooked. The only thing standing between me and all of my foretold good fortune was the standard jealousy curse.

She told me that the only way to remove the dreaded curse was to bring her a loaf of bread, a box of pasta, a bottle of ginger ale, a bag of sugar, and an additional $30.

A few days later I brought her some of the requested food items and the required money for curse removal. The old woman insisted that she look at my palm before I left her shop. It seems that my "jealousy curse" had become more lethal, and the fee for getting the curse off of me was now $60, which would include prayers and candle lighting. This is when I got street smart. At that point I had already been reading tarot cards for friends for a few years, so I basically knew the procedure for doing readings. What was all this "curse" bullshit? Why the escalating price tag?

I got an attitude with the woman when she objected to the brand of ginger ale I'd brought her and complained that I'd forgotten the bag of sugar. I bitched about the increased price for the curse removal and made innuendos about her hospital-bed setup; with that, she kicked me out of her shop. I was afraid that she would really put a curse on me now because of my street-smart, smart-ass manner!

I immediately went to another local psychic to get a second opinion, and I was assured by him that I was just fine. No curse was on me. He told me that in the future when I get a psychic reading, I should drop imaginary roots into the earth to ground out my own energy field and keep safe energetic boundaries. At that point I learned respect for psychic energy and the precautions to take to avoid getting *shocked*. That was excellent advice, and I will pass information about energy grounding on to you throughout this book.

The city of Philadelphia has a very distinctive, historical, and edgy vibe. It is a city known not only for its cheesesteaks, water-ice (if you're from Philly it's pronounced *wooder*-ice) sports teams, music, and urban attitude, but also for historical events built around the practices of a secret society. Philadelphia, the birthplace of the nation, was a meeting spot for many prominent founding fathers of the United States who were allegedly Freemasons familiar with esoteric symbols and rituals. The founding fathers supposedly used astrology when planning the dates for certain events. It is a long-standing belief that the date of the signing of the Constitution of the United States of America, in Philadelphia, was chosen because the planets Venus and Mercury were rising in the sign of Virgo on September 17, 1787, making for the right astrological aspects to ensure this country's destiny. Interestingly enough, the courtyard of Philadelphia City Hall has a large zodiac wheel imprinted onto the main walkway.

Philly is also known for its famous ghosts and many haunted places around town. If you walk through a potter's field such as the one at Washington Square near Independence Hall, you can feel the ghost energy of Revolutionary War soldiers, yellow-fever victims, and other people who were buried there during the early years of the city's history. A potter's field is a cemetery in which all the unclaimed bodies from war, disease, and murder are buried, usually without proper services and in shallow or mass graves.

Philly boasts many haunted sites, such as Saint Peter's Church cemetery, City Tavern, Eastern State Penitentiary, Fort Mifflin, Powel House, and Independence Hall, just to name a few. Philly even has its own ghost tours, which take people around to these haunted places. In addition to the local ghosts, there are also plenty of psychic-reader shops scattered throughout the streets of Center City. For me, growing up in this city has definitely contributed to my fascination with "things that go bump in the night," magick, and all forms of psychic divination.

I learned through "baptism by fire" that a psychic reader must protect herself from the often erratic energy of a client. We are all energetic forces, and even though the exchange of energy between us is invisible, the intense energy exchange can result in negative effects, causing headaches or worse; in extreme instances, there can be a transference of the client's problems into the psychic's life. The universe works in balance, and when a psychic reader taps into a client's energy, the energy exchange is sometimes turbulent.

Not all energy exchanges are negative, of course. I have had many clients who elevated my energy flow because the exchange of energy was upbeat and equalizing.

Over the years I've had a few past-life psychic readings, and I was told by various past-life psychics that I have brought my past-life knowledge of divination into this current incarnation. Growing up, I was an artistic child who would sit for hours and draw pictures that would somehow wind up depicting past-life experiences and also future events in my life. Creative visualization helped me tap further into the mystical arts, and I began to hone my skills at doing psychic readings. While other children my age were playing tag, I preferred to play *psychic self-defense*.

I am not only a psychic reader but also a *psychic junkie*. I am therefore able to give you a clear picture of what, exactly, a client expects from a psychic reading, and also how a psychic expects clients to behave in order to get the most from the reading.

Psychic junkies love to get psychic readings. They embrace anything mystical, and I bet if you look in their wallet the "in case of emergency" phone number is most likely the number of a favorite psychic. A psychic junkie seeks out psychic fairs, psychic phone-line services, and neighborhood psychic readers in a quest for the ultimate psychic reading. I even used to wish that there was a standardized and reliable rating system for psychics, so I would know which ones to go to for a reading. Yes, I admit it. I am guilty of scouting out super psychics.

As a psychic reader, I have learned over the years to deal with many different types of clients. I owe a lot of my initiation into the psychic-reader world to my first clients, my proverbial "training-wheel" clients. My client base is a mix of old clients, some who are new, some I share with other psychics, and some who are blue. The blue ones don't stay blue very long, because it is my job to get their energy levels up and running so they can get out of their funk and get moving.

Most people start their day with a cup of coffee. I usually start my day with a call from a client who is *in need of a read*. I have to admit that I have tightened up my boundaries over the years. At one time I would accommodate anyone at any time, but I found out that doesn't produce the best results. I like my clients to make appointments so I can better schedule my time. My clients know that I prefer to do readings in the evening, as that time of day is more mood-enhancing for me. I also love to read on rainy days. There is something about the water element in the air that fuels my intuition.

My clients are a revolving, assorted mix of people who are very interesting, entertaining, and basically nice people. I have learned to weed out the type of energy that I can't deal with, which is *nasty-people energy*. Nasty-energy clients put me in a low energy mood, which sometimes has an effect on my reading sessions with other clients. I am very understanding when it comes to being aware that some clients may be having a bad day and are in need a reading, but I will not tolerate clients who are looking to take out their frustrations on me. Control-freak clients who will only settle on what they want to hear during a reading are quickly reminded that they have to be open to other possibilities, and be aware that maybe a better-than-expected outcome is in the cards for them. My job as a psychic reader is to keep my clients informed and on track, so they don't get caught up in energy-zapping situations.

Sometimes I laugh to myself, because this really is a unique profession. I love what I do. I get to fill my days with tarot, astrology, and psychic energy. How fitting for a double Pisces like me. I am like a fish in the best water!

I have been to almost every type of psychic reader, and as a seeker what I want most from a reading is the confirmation that I am staying on my path, as well as an awareness of life's pitfalls and the knowledge of when to connect with the right opportunities. I want to leave a psychic session with an energy boost and the hope that tomorrow will be better than today. I go to get an energetic high because like attracts like, and if my energy is spinning in a positive direction, then I will be more in tune to drawing the positive things that I need in my life. Low energy leads to depression and the creation of a series of negative, depressing situations.

As a psychic reader I want my clients to approach the session seriously and understand that often the outcome they desire isn't always the best outcome for them.

To get a good psychic reading, the client needs to realize that there are certain conditions that, when met, will provide the best atmosphere for both the psychic and the client, so that they can each get the most out of the session. As psychic readers, we can only ask that clients come to the session with respect for what we do. I've had to deal with clients who have tried to badger me into getting the answer they want instead of the truth.

I want my clients to be open to the surprises of life, and I want them to trust that the information I give them during a psychic reading is for the good of their higher self.

This book will inform you of the proper preparations for getting a good psychic reading, and it will also remind both psychics and clients about the importance of energy grounding before getting or giving a reading.

If you're seeking a psychic reading, you'll get an inside view of what it's like to be a psychic as well as street-smart advice on harnessing your energy and clicking with a psychic so that your reading is successful. The mystique that veils the psychic profession will be peeled back, and you'll be able to understand how a psychic reading is given.

Psychic readers are enigmas. We are perceived at times to be mystical channelers of untapped events, but we must also deal with the negative connotations about us in popular culture—that we're nothing more than carnival soothsayers. When people ask me what I do for a living and I reply that I do psychic readings, I sometimes have to deal with scaredy cats who think they need to put a garlic necklace around their neck for protection when dealing with me. I've also experienced the other extreme: being held captive by people who corner me with their questions, asking me what I see for them in the future.

It is an interesting profession, to say the least.

What do clients expect from psychic readers? As someone who has been on both sides of the cards, I feel that clients want the truth, and they don't want to be judged for the situations in which they find themselves. Most of all, clients don't want to have their problems exploited for nothing more than financial gain.

This book will help psychic-reading seekers get a bird's-eye view of what is expected during a psychic session. Linking into someone's energy field invites that person's vibration into your own life. Clients have to be cautious and discerning enough to make sure that they aren't dealing with an unbalanced psychic. Psychic readers have to be diligent about energy clearing between clients. Responsibility is necessary when working with energy.

Neither Benjamin Franklin nor Mary Shelley's fictitious Frankenstein discovered energy, but they both tried to harness it as electricity. Franklin made great strides working with energy in positive ways, and Frankenstein made a monster. So, you can see that working with energy, especially the unbridled energy of psychic forces, can have both positive and negative results. Respect for tapping into someone's energy is necessary, because no one wants to get shocked.

You will find out what type of psychic-reading skills are the most appealing for you, as well as learn about the sometimes quirky personalities of psychics and how to cope with them. As you'll discover, psychic readers live in this world but work in the outer limits.

You will also become familiar with the types of clients that the psychic often deals with; and if you are a psychic reader yourself, then you will appreciate the validation that the job of being a psychic is not as easy as it looks.

In short, this book is for anyone who has ever had, given, or wants to get a psychic reading.

My most sincere desire is to provide you with information on how best to set things up to ensure that you get a good psychic reading. Remember that psychic readers deal with your energy, and if your energy is out of control, then you are starting your session with a built-in handicap.

Our job as psychics is not to become your best friend, psychiatrist, lawyer, doctor, or conscience. Our purpose is to tap into your past to see where you are coming from, look into your future to show you possible outcomes, and help you deal with the present so you can navigate through life's labyrinth. Consider the psychic reader as a GPS system for your soul's journey.

CHAPTER 1

The Evolution of Psychics and Divination

Humanity has always had a need to know what the future holds. People used to look to the heavens for signs, noting eclipses and the movement of planets. Folks would interpret their dreams, looking for symbolic answers to their concerns. What spurs the need to know what tomorrow holds for us? The ancients readily sought out different forms of divination, and some of their methods of looking into the future are still practiced today. If it's true that time is the test to see if something has value, then the naysayers who discount different forms of divination should take note of how long mystical arts like crystal scrying, astrology, numerology, psychic oracles, and other practices have existed.

Some people believe that the caveman was once a prehistoric psychic junkie who would predict things by casting lots, reading the ripples in water, and watching the birds in flight. The solar and lunar eclipses were ominous signs to the primitive psychic seeker. As man became more civilized, the art of scrying grew more refined. The birth of astrology is equivalent to the birth of the wheel in that it shaped destiny. Ancient humans may have looked to the stars just as modern folks read their daily horoscopes. How far have we come along in divination practices? Is curiosity for the future part of our psychic-seeker DNA?

Psychic readings at one time were only meant for monarchs and people of high standing, because knowledge is power and it was as well guarded as gold. Over the years, different religions have tried to suppress human curiosity about the future, and psychics were readily tried as heretics or locked away in prisons and labeled as crazy. Those at the top of the societal hierarchy wanted to be the only ones privy to ancient, cosmic information and would dissuade common people from using their natural birthright of all six senses.

We are all born with a sixth sense, but we are taught to develop our logical mind in the belief that logic will override intuition. We are taught to put our gut feelings, the seat of our intuition, second and approach problems "logically." But some things have no logic, such as love. Psychic readers have honed their skills of perception, developed their psychic abilities, and have learned how to override the logical mind and tap into the quantum universe, where the past, present, and future are all happening simultaneously.

Psychics, Sibyls, and Sages

The practice of looking into the future by astrology, scrying, and animal omens had its historically recorded start in ancient Babylon. Ancient scryers were considered important, especially by kings. The first seers would burn offerings to the heavens in an effort to receive omens for the future.

From Babylonians, the art of divination found its way to ancient Greece, where the famed Oracle of Delphi was seated. The legend states that there was a large chasm on Mount Parnassus that gave off intoxicating vapors. The vapors were thought to be of a divine source, and people would come from all over to inhale the vapors and thus have the gift of prophecy. Some people were so overcome by the vapors that they fell into the chasm. To avoid the fate of falling into the chasm, a tripod was built and a woman called a *Pythia* was appointed as the seer. She would sit upon the tripod and prophesy. The Pythia held a cauldron of Kassotis water taken from the Castalian Spring, a sacred site to Apollo, and a handful of laurel leaves that were believed to induce prophecy when chewed.

News of the oracle spread, and people came from all over to have a psychic reading. Consultants brought a black sheep to be sacrificed, branches of laurel leaves, and money for the oracle.. Priests were trained to attend the oracle and translate the cryptic messages of the Pythia. A large temple was built for the oracle, which soon became a booming business. Initially, a young virgin was chosen and appointed to be the Pythia. Only men could receive psychic readings from the Pythia, and having a young virgin as the Oracle of Delphi proved to be a mistake. There was a high turnover of Pythias because the men found the virgins attractive and interesting, and they would run off with the youthful oracles. It was later decided to appoint an older, more mature woman, preferably married, as the Pythia. The Pythia sat on the tripod for hours on end, answering questions posed by farmers to the famous leaders of the day. Gifts were brought to the oracle, and the Delphic temple became one of the largest banks in Greece.

The Oracle of Delphi lasted well into the fourth century AD but was abolished when Christian beliefs became more widespread. This ancient oracle seems to be the precursor to today's popular psychic phone lines. One can only imagine how the Pythia felt after a long day of sitting on a tripod, answering question after question. She was probably relieved to see the last client come into the temple so she could wrap up her day and go unfry her brain. The Pythia would go home and crash after a day of chewing laurel leaves. I wonder if the Pythia got the munchies and snacked on feta cheese fries while she was doing her job of magickal mystery trippin'?

Another sought-after psychic was the sibyl. The sibyls were prophetesses who would give divine revelations while they were in a frenzied state. Being a psychic reader myself, I can only imagine the types of clients that the sibyls must have been reading to put them in such a rattled condition. There were supposedly ten sibyls who dwelled in different places. The sibyls would make predictions, which were recorded in books, and their collection of predictions were gathered and guarded in the temple of Jupiter Capitolinus. The sibyls were very influential and played a big part in shaping the religious views of the day. Unlike the Pythia, who gave personal psychic readings as well as political psychic readings, the sibyls made prophecies regarding historical events about nations and kingdoms. Collections of these oracular utterances consisting of cryptic and chaotic writings are still in existence. They are not the same as the Sibylline books of the Greeks and Romans, which were lost in antiquity. The artist Michelangelo painted five sibyls on the ceiling of the Sistine Chapel, giving credence to their place in prophecy.

Early civilizations seem to have had an amazing fascination with psychics. I often wonder who the psychic junkies of those times were. Most everyone is aware of the biblical story of Joseph and his ability to interpret dreams for the Pharaoh. The Pharaoh got hooked on his dreams being interpreted. I wonder if the Pharaoh took daily naps so he could have both his daytime and nighttime dreams deciphered by Joseph?

Another psychic seeker was Cleopatra, Queen of the Nile. Cleopatra called for her *augur* (ancient hip street term for fortuneteller) so the condition of Julius Caesar's political standing in Rome could be divined. If Cleopatra was a typical female psychic seeker, she probably wanted to know if Caesar was also going to leave his wife and move to Egypt. Caesar's wife also consulted a seer to check on Caesar's political career. Hence the phrase "Beware the Ides of March" was born when it was given as a warning to Caesar's wife that he should not attend the Senate on March 15th. (Caesar's wife, I'm sure, had further questions for her psychic, especially concerning the fidelity of her husband.)

That fated day of March 15, 44 BCE, proved to be deadly for Caesar. Legend has it that he was on his way to the Senate when he passed the seer who had predicted his fate. Caesar supposedly said to the seer, "The ides have come," *ides* being the word for the fifteenth day of a month. The seer replied, "Yes, Caesar. But gone not." The seer was definitely spot-on, and the rest of the story is history. Caesar was murdered on the steps of the Senate that fated day.

In sixteenth-century England a fascinating man named John Dee practiced astrology. He was also well versed in the supernatural and alchemy. John Dee made the A-list because of his skills, and it wasn't long before Queen Elizabeth I made Dee her astrologer. Being an astrologer and a conjurer had some pitfalls. Dee was imprisoned for a short time for heresy and also for being a magician. His political connections paid off because he never stayed in prison for very long. Dee's knowledge of the heavens was respected, and he was asked to choose the date for the coronation of Queen Elizabeth I. He is also well known for his dealings with angels and his interpretation of Enochian, the angelic language.

Another well-known psychic of the same era is Nostradamus, a French homeopathic doctor and astrologer. In those days, one had to have knowledge of astrology in order to become a doctor, since it was believed that certain parts of the body were ruled by certain planets. Nostradamus is like the rock star of psychic readers. His groupies and fan club are still active. He is best known for writing prophetic quatrains, which contained cryptic prophecies applicable well into the new millennium. His quatrains foretold the rise of the Nazi regime hundreds of years before Hitler came to power.

Nostradamus is also given credit for predicting both world wars. The quatrains of Nostradamus are popular to this day.

The ever-growing curiosity about fortunetelling prevailed throughout the ages, and men and women alike had a fascination for the unknown. One of the most famous card readers of all time was Marie Anne Adelaide Lenormand (1772–1843). Mademoiselle Lenormand said that she received her first deck of cards from gypsies when she was fourteen years old, and that the gypsies taught her how to do card readings. Empress Josephine was a total psychic junkie. She frequently sent for Mademoiselle Lenormand and put great faith in her predictions. Napoleon also got hooked on psychic readings and consulted the cards. However, in the Restoration period following Napoleon's rule, psychic card readings could land one in jail, and Lenormand was imprisoned for fortunetelling several times throughout her life.

The menu of psychics, sibyls, and sages is endless, and with such a varied and interesting group of psychic readers to choose from, it is no wonder that people can form an addiction to finding out what the future holds in store for them.

Victorian Parlor Games and Mediums

The Spiritualism movement began in Hydesville, New York, in 1848. Two sisters, Catherine and Margaretta Fox, claimed to have made contact with spirits in their home by using a tapping method to communicate with the dead. The showman P. T. Barnum took the sisters to New York and made them into stars. They were billed as famous mediums for several years, even as some people thought the sisters were frauds and nothing more than a "carny act." In any event, the Fox sisters became as popular as the sword swallower and the two-headed goat, and are responsible for trend-setting séances.

The Spiritualism movement made its way to England, and séances became very popular there during the Victorian era. Crystal balls, bells, automatic writing, and hypnotic trances were all methods used to contact the spirits of the dead. Psychic junkies of that era couldn't get enough of this new form of entertainment.

The Ouija board is another method used to make spirit contact. In the early twentieth century, the interest in séances was growing, and William Fuld, who owned a novelty company, developed the Ouija board. The Ouija board is a flat-surfaced board displaying printed letters, numbers, and other symbols. A small movable planchette is placed on the board, which is used to indicate words and sayings. The seeker touches his or her fingers to the planchette and spiritual forces are believed to communicate by spelling out messages.

The superstitions and legends of the Ouija board live on to this day. Users of the board are warned never to play alone, and there have been reports of people contacting negative spirits that attempt to possess the user of the Ouija board.

I remember a story that I heard years ago from a very intelligent, reliable person, who told me of a friend who had encountered a dark force through the use of a Ouija board.

Three people got together to have some fun with a Ouija board. One of the participants was a psychic who wanted to see how accurate the board would be in answering some questions. The psychic and one of the participants placed their fingertips on the planchette and watched as it seemed to fly effortlessly from letter to letter. After a series of questions were answered and the participants were relaxed, the negative energy that had been playing Ouija with them suddenly turned into a raging bolt of unbridled terror.

The Ouija board supposedly flew across the room, and the smell of sulfur filled the air. The psychic knew enough to continuously scream, "Go back to where you came from! Leave us alone!" After a few minutes of havoc the smell subsided, but one of the participants had what appeared to be unexplained, burn-like welts on his arm.

Crystal-ball scrying and black-mirror scrying are also methods used to make contact with the other side. Mirror scrying goes back to ancient times, and it is recorded that John Dee, the astrologer to Queen Elizabeth I, used mirror scrying as a means to make contact with angels.

When you use these tools for divination purposes, keep in mind that you could also be summoning darker forces that can come through your scrying tools. You don't want to disturb these negative entities, because they can be quite dangerous and play all kinds of games with your subconscious mind.

Some cultures don't like mirrors due to a fear that they can act as portals for nasty spirits to come forth or that they can allow one's doppelgänger access to this world. A doppelgänger is your negative ghostly double. People in some cultures cover up mirrors in the home of someone who has recently died so that a malevolent spirit won't come through the mirrors and trap the deceased person's soul.

Black-mirror scrying is another form of divination. Black mirrors are made on the Full Moon, anointed with oils, and charged with energy. The mirror is made through an observed ritual with the Moon and left in a protective circle for a day; then it is coated in black to seal in the energy charge. Black scrying mirrors should always be on a wooden stand for grounding purposes, since the wood acts as a natural ground for any extreme entity energies.

By looking into the black mirror, one can access the Akashic records, where all knowledge of the past, present, and future is held. Some find these records useful for astral travel and past-life psychic readings, but at all times they are also convenient openings for unwanted spirit visitors.

Mirrors are very deceiving because when you look in a regular mirror, you see a backward reflection of your perceived physical self; the true energy essence of who you are can't be seen. Unlike a mirror, your sixth sense will tune you in to the true reflection of the energetic image of someone. If you pay attention to your sixth sense, you can detect the auric field around any person or object, and sometimes a physical reaction will follow. Feeling sick tells you something is bad, just as feeling giddy tells you that something is good.

Crystal scrying also has to be done cautiously, since crystals will tune in and amplify any nearby energetic disturbances. Crystal scrying aids in tuning in to spirit energy and also acts as a tool to be used in a semi-trance state so your own astral body can experience the vibrations coming from the other dimensions outside of the current earthly one that you are now in.

Venturing into the multidimensional world inhabited by all kinds of energy entities and cosmic debris is never to be taken lightly. Rubbing two sticks together will produce an energetic spark, so imagine the electricity generated when humans take their own energy and amplify it with crystals, a group séance, or a one-to-one psychic reading.

Even experienced psychics and mediums can get into trouble with the calling of spirits. Grounding and protection are just partial insurance that you won't get snagged by playing these parlor games.

Séance: The "Happy" Medium between Worlds

At one time attending a séance was as fashionable as going to happy hour at a new, hip nightspot is today. Queen Victoria (1819–1901) was very supportive of Spiritualism and was known to attend séances along with her husband, Prince Albert. An entry in the queen's personal journal recalls a vision that Princess Feodora, the queen's older half-sister, had while on her death bed. Right before she died, Feodora saw the spirit of her child who had preceded her in death.

Queen Victoria was curious why, at the point of death, the veil between the worlds becomes transparent enough to allow one to see the spirits of the dearly departed who wait on the other side. For help, the queen sought out the services of Robert James Lees, a well-known medium.

The popularity of séances also opened the doors for some skeptics to try and debunk the legitimate psychic mediums of that time. Famed escapologist Harry Houdini (1874–1926) attended séances in disguise, hoping to expose fraud. I guess Houdini didn't realize that spirit is known for being a "trickster" and takes umbrage at being tested and exploited. Houdini's attempts to debunk spiritualists ended up destroying his friendship with Sir Arthur Conan Doyle, the creator of Sherlock Holmes and a devoted believer in Spiritualism.

For ten years after his death, Houdini's widow, Bess, held a séance for her late husband on Halloween, which is when the veil between the worlds is at its thinnest and also happens to be the anniversary of Houdini's death. Harry Houdini never appeared. Bess supposedly said, "Ten years is long enough to wait for any man." I wonder if some of my own clients who get love-life psychic readings might eventually take note of that phrase.

To this day, Houdini's spirit seems to be a favorite invite to séances at sleepover parties, college frat parties, and spooky gatherings on Halloween.

The word *séance* is French, meaning "session" or "sitting." How is a séance conducted? A séance is usually held in a quiet room where there is limited noise. The number of people needed to have a séance can be as low as two, or the group can be made up of a larger number of people. It is suggested that the group be limited to no more than seven people, because the energy and mindset of the participants needs to be focused—and a smaller group is easier to keep on the same path.

The séance begins with the group sitting on chairs around a table. Usually a lead person called a *trance medium* will conduct the séance, although when contact is made with a spirit the information can come through any one of the participants. There have been instances when someone at a séance who has no knowledge of a foreign language suddenly begins to speak in another tongue.

During the séance the medium will instruct all participants to first make sure that everyone's feet are firmly touching the floor and that all cell phones, iPods, and other electrical equipment are off. This is very important because working with spirit energy can be extremely dangerous. You must be grounded; putting your feet on the floor will provide some necessary grounding protection. It is not uncommon to have electrical malfunctions when spirit energy is around, because the interplay of energy can really blow out some appliances and make technical gadgets go schizoid. Calling in the swirling energy mists of those residing on the other side is really not a game. Some beings who belong to our multidimensional universe can be quite hostile. Calling them in is like touching a live wire.

The next step is for everyone in the group to join hands. In this way the collective consciousness and electrical contact will be established, and the group as a whole will send out a stronger signal into the outer realms and possibly make spirit contact. Think of it like trying to string Christmas lights together. The contacts have to be plugged in concurrently in order to light up the lights, and one bad bulb may shut down the whole display. Also, if you don't know what you are doing, you may get shocked and possibly start a fire. Same thing goes for contacting spirit energy.

The medium may place a quartz crystal on the table. The quartz crystal is used to amplify the thoughts and energy of the group much in the same way that they were used in crystal radios. Sometimes a bell is also placed on the table and used as a method for the spirit to reply to questions by making the bell ring. The room is usually dark except for maybe a lit candle. This setting adds atmosphere, and helps scare the crap out of you.

The medium leading the séance begins by telling all of the participants to close their eyes and relax by taking deep breaths, in then out, and to concentrate fully and solely on bringing through the spirit.

Now, here is where the danger lies. Say, for instance, that the purpose of conducting the séance is to make contact with a deceased loved one, a dead rock star, or some other desired person from the other side. Once you allow the doors to the spirit world to be open, you may unknowingly invite hostile, wicked, or mischievous spirit energy into your life. Errant, negative energy swirls will sometimes pose as deceased loved ones and play head games with the participants in the séance.

Most spirits pass through a tunnel and go toward the light; once there, they are reluctant to return to the hollow dimension between the worlds. The spirits that do stay trapped between worlds are usually angry, confused, and mean. No one has sent them to the light, and they stay locked in a dimension that is like an overcrowded airport during a holiday in which all the planes have been grounded because of bad weather. They are pissed-off spirits that are bored and looking for trouble. Once this spirit energy is let back in through a séance, it may be reluctant to go back to where it came from, and in some instances it will attach itself to someone. If the spirit attaches to a person, it is called a *possession*; if it attaches to a place, it is called a *haunting*.

What about the mediums who make contact with friendly spirits? Where do the friendly spirits come from, you may wonder. The friendly spirit information comes more from a good vibration or energy imprint left behind. A skilled psychic medium can sometimes focus and project her psychic linking cord far into the light at the end of the tunnel. It is the equivalent to a psychic medium long-drive hole-in-one. The medium may be picking up on an energy imprint that a spirit left in a room. Keep telling yourself that we live in a multidimensional universe, so you will understand how this works.

Energy leaves an imprint where things take place, especially when attached by strong emotions, which in themselves are energy frequencies. If you press your finger to a window your fingerprint will stay put, marking exactly where you were long after you have pulled your finger away. Now layer someone else's fingerprint over the original and you will have a compound fingerprint that is basically an accumulated energy imprint. That explains why multiple spirit energies can come through in one séance sitting.

The job of the medium is to psychically read the energy left by the print, as the energy imprint holds all of the recorded data of the person who once was physically around.

Mediums who bring forth friendly spirits are basically reading the recorded data lingering around your own energy field that are still attached by the frequency of emotion left by your deceased loved ones. Liken it to a spiritual tape recording of your deceased loved ones' energy. The medium may tune in to a name, date, or happy event, all of which are recorded in the energy imprint either within your own energy or auric field or that of the location of the séance. Spirits who have passed through the tunnel to the light will find ways to get messages to loved ones via spirit-guide messenger services.

Spirit guides are like the FedEx of the outer limits, and the psychic medium is the one who signs for the package. Spirit guides are not necessarily the energy of your deceased loved ones. A deceased loved one who is in the light will sometimes feel the pull of the mourner's emotions and the attached frequencies may pull them back into the gray area, but it is often very temporary.

Spirit guides are mists of benevolent protective energy that police the ether waves and help deliver positive energy to those in need. The spirits are not the same as the Ascended Masters because they have not yet reached perfection, which is nothing more than pure, uninhibited love and happiness.

Spirit guides are the lower octave of angels and Ascended Masters. They have chosen to remain and help humans in their physical form.

If you could shed your body, you would be nothing more than a mist of energy. Your thoughts create and materialize your physical form along with the *thought memory* encoded into your DNA. Believe it or not, we hold many lifetimes in our DNA, because it is like the soul's hard drive and every experience is downloaded into the memory.

Now that you are aware of what can happen at a séance, the big question is: "How the hell do you end a séance?"

The medium conducting the séance will usually decide to wrap up the session after everyone present has been sufficiently scared, because of someone speaking in a weird voice, loud unexplained noises, funky odors, or some random electrical malfunction. If contact has been made with an unfriendly spirit, the medium may instruct the participants to quickly cross their feet at the ankles or to cross their legs. This practice cuts off any invasion of intimate space, sort of like what you do on a date when the other party tries to get fresh. The medium will instruct the contacted entity to return home and go back to where it came from. Some spirits listen and some don't. If a spirit chooses to stay, the next step is to call in someone experienced in exorcisms or house clearings.

Another way a séance can end is when some chickenhearted participant begins to scream and cry while everyone unlocks hands and runs to put on a light. Even if your intention at the beginning of the séance was to make positive contact with friendly spirits, there is always a chance that the party will be crashed by some negative uninvited beings.

Psychics of the Twentieth Century

Some twentieth-century psychics are sure to be forever included in the Oracle of Delphi Hall of Fame. Edgar Cayce, the Sleeping Prophet, was very popular in the early to mid-twentieth century. Cayce would lie down on a couch and go into a trancelike sleep. Questions would be posed to Cayce while in this state, and his answers, especially to medical questions, were remarkably accurate. Cayce never had any formal medical training but the answers seemed to come to him from channeled sources. Psychic seekers would flock to him for readings, and most of the time the psychic readings would be freebies. Cayce is said to have suffered severe headaches from giving so many psychic consultations. I wonder if he was really sleeping, or posing some ruse so he didn't have to deal with all of the crazy clients?

Another popular psychic reader was Jeane Dixon. Dixon is best known for her prediction that President John F. Kennedy would be assassinated in office. She was also consulted during the Nixon presidency and was referred to by Richard Nixon as "the Soothsayer." Dixon consulted for President Ronald Reagan and First Lady Nancy Reagan for some time. But Mrs. Reagan preferred to consult with astrologer Joan Quigley because she felt that Dixon was losing her powers as she grew older. (Wow! I guess even psychics can be forced into retirement.) President Reagan's schedule was mapped out by the stars, and the use of astrology to set the President's day was often frustrating to his staff. During the era of the Reagan presidency, it was chic to know or use an astrologer, and having your own psychic reader was like having the latest hip accessory. This interest brought on the birth of the 1-900 psychic phone lines.

It is hard to believe that in this day and "new" age, some places still consider fortunetelling to be a misdemeanor crime. Certain old-school people still think psychic readers are all scammers and carnies, yet the police use psychics to help solve crimes and the CIA has been using psychic remote viewers for years. Fears that psychics would rip people off and get them to invest their life savings in false hopes led to these archaic laws all those years ago. But I think that the outdated laws against fortunetelling are now more suited for investment bankers and subprime mortgage lenders. Those guys are guilty of *fortune selling*.

The Popularity of Psychics, Culture to Culture

It seems that every era has its psychic source of the moment, and almost every culture embraces some form of fortunetelling skills. The New Age movement is really just a more modern version of Old Age beliefs. The Chinese have the I Ching, face reading, and the Chinese zodiac. Folks in the Middle East read coffee grounds. Lots of people in India strongly believe in Vedic astrology and the power of wearing certain gemstones.

Europeans delight in tarot-card readings. In Italy the Strega, which is the Italian word for "witch," are revered for their skills with herbs and divination. Eastern Europeans peer into the future by reading tea leaves and palms. In Romania the fortunetelling skills of the Roma people are well advertised. Plenty of people in Britain and Ireland hold strong to the *Olde Celtic* ways, and mediumship is a favored method of ghost hunting.

The Native Americans all had their shamans, or medicine men. The Hopi Indians are known for the famed Hopi prophecy, which predicts coming events. Practitioners in traditional African cultures told fortunes by casting bones, stones, or pieces of leather. Communication with spirits is still very popular, as is the reading of animal omens.

The Central American people have the Mayan calendar; people in the Caribbean Islands, especially Haiti, still use the invocation of Voodoo gods to guide them through the future. The Polynesian people practice Huna, which is a method of manifestation techniques, and the United States seems to be a melting pot for all forms of psychic abilities.

Some cultures respect fortunetellers, considering them to be wise men and women gifted with the ability to see the future. For example, Chinese businesspeople consult with fortunetellers, especially when looking for an auspicious date to conduct important business meetings. I have personally consulted with my share of business professionals, CEOs, and politicians who strongly believe in astrological and psychic consultations as a way to further enhance their dealings.

1-900 Psychic

At one time I worked on a 1-900 psychic line. The stint lasted a full three months. I worked for one of the first 1-900 psychic lines in existence. My interview consisted of me reading a tarot-card spread over the phone to my future boss. I was hired immediately but was reluctant to take the job. I was so used to the old-school method of sitting face to face with a client, making contact by shuffling and cutting the deck and letting the client pick her selected cards. I initially turned down the job offer, but two days later the company owner called and asked me to try it for one night since he was so busy and had a shortage of psychic readers.

The staff of psychic readers was small, but the six people employed by the company were all amazingly gifted. The first night I worked, I could not believe the number of calls I received. The callers were automatically cut off after fifteen minutes, and they would feverishly call back and try to continue the reading for additional time. I hardly had time to clear my energy space from one caller before the phone would ring again. The 1-900 psychic line made getting a psychic reading available to anyone with a telephone. The usual way of finding a psychic reader before the advent of the 1-900 psychic line was to ask around and see if anyone knew of good psychic readers in the area. Going to a psychic before the telephone craze began was limited to going to gypsies with neon signs in the window; seeking out the low-key, unadvertised neighborhood woman who knew how to read tarot cards or regular playing cards; or visiting a psychic fair if one happened to be nearby at some point.

The 1-900 psychic phone lines provided complete anonymity for the client. No longer did clients have to fear that the psychic reader might see them on the street and remember all the intimate details of their problems. Now with complete abandon, callers into the 1-900 psychic lines can spill their guts, tell their darkest secrets, and get a psychic reading to foretell the outcome of the issues going on in their lives.

How do you know if the psychic reader on the other end of the line is legitimate? There has been some bad press about who gets hired for these positions and one can't help but wonder, since it now seems as though there are just as many psychic readers as there are clients. Can you mass-market psychics? Just as with any big business, corruption can slip in, so the seekers of a psychic reading needs to be careful not to let their desperate need to know be exploited by the few non-legitimate psychic readers who give the rest of us a bad name.

It is so easy to become a psychic junkie now. With the click of a computer mouse you can schedule a psychic reading with psychics all around the world. The psychic phone lines are still booming with business, and the availability of psychic readers to anyone, anywhere, is unbelievable. Some psychic readers on the phone lines develop followings of fans who will book psychic readings days in advance. To get a reading with the psychic of your choice can be like scoring center-ice tickets to game seven of the Stanley Cup final.

Where do all of the telephone psychic readers come from, you may ask. The shifting of the energy of our collective consciousness has allowed more people to be open to psychic abilities. We are all born with a soft spot on the top of our head, which is where our crown chakra is located. The crown chakra is the energy center of our body, which allows us to experience connection with the universe. This chakra governs our beliefs and our spirituality. The crown chakra is highly developed in psychic readers, because they have achieved raising their vibration high enough to keep this chakra open. The crown chakra connects with the energy of the universe, in which knowledge of the past, present, and future all are recorded in the Akashic records. The Akashic records are basically the universal database that contains knowledge about everybody and everything.

How do you know if the telephone psychic you have just picked from the recorded carousel of available psychic readers is a legitimate psychic? Most good psychic phone lines will conduct an interview with potential psychic-reader employees, and part of the hiring process involves the potential psychic-reader employee giving a sample of what they can do. It's a bit like an audition for *Psychic Star Search* or *Psychic Idol*.

The psychic phone lines keep track of which psychic readers get numerous callbacks, and they will usually give their top psychics a high-priority rating, which means that most calls are fielded over to the top psychic readers. The psychic readers who are just starting out and have not had a chance to build up a following may sit by the phone for hours waiting for a call to come in. For not-so-busy psychic readers, the wait can sometimes feel as though they are the last people to be asked to dance.

The hierarchy of psychic readers can be compared to the system in a big-city hospital, only in this case it's spiritual ailments being treated. There are top doctors as well as residents or interns. All have knowledge of psychic abilities, but some have practiced longer and are more adept at doing psychic readings. If your need for a reading goes beyond what can be achieved from an emergency-room visit with your favorite psychic phone line, then you can always seek out specialists who have their own psychic practice and who do private readings.

As you read this book I will tell you firsthand what you, the seeker, need to know in order to have an inside track on how to get a good psychic reading.

Guidelines for Psychic-Energy Consumers

Energy efficiency and conservation are big issues of the day. Everywhere you look there are reminders that we need to protect our natural resources and be mindful of how and when we use the energy extracted from them. We all want efficiency without waste when it comes to our power sources, and that should also include our abundant and often unacknowledged psychic energy.

You might be familiar with the term *energy vampire* and the phrase *suck the life out of me*, both of which refer to people who drain others of their own energy or *chi*, which is life-force energy. Some people aren't even aware that they are not properly insulated, grounded, or protected when it comes to their own personal energy or power. How many times have you given so much of yourself to others only to be drained and energetically depleted afterward?

People who go to psychics for readings have to understand that they are exposing their energy to that of the psychic's; educating yourself about psychic energy is in your own best interest if you are a novice when it comes to psychic-energy consumption.

Unfortunately, just as in any profession, the psychic field has its share of charlatans to avoid. People who go to psychic readers are usually having a life issue, are vulnerable, and if they are not careful they risk having their problems exploited. Any psychic reader who encourages you to come back repeatedly for constant psychic updates and insists on receiving large amounts of money before offering any help is definitely someone to avoid. They are no better than drug pushers who promise a quick fix to ease your pain.

Don't think that just because psychics seem to be all about energy balance, karma, and spirituality that they are not above being psychic sorcerers, out to manipulate your energy for a sometimes heavy price tag. Some psychic phone lines charge over four dollars per minute, and if you get hooked up with a psychic scammer, you can end up in severe credit-card debt. Imagine getting a psychic reading at four dollars per minute for a total of sixty minutes. That is $240 per hour, and if you become a psychic junkie, get hooked, and reach for the telephone each time you have a problem, then you will find yourself in deep financial trouble.

When people are desperate and need answers, they will basically pay anything and even put up with professional arrogance. Some psychic readers are like psychic shylocks, in that they nearly want a pound of your flesh. They can promise you results, for a price. They can sense your anxiety, smell out your fears, and if you are willing to shell out enough money, they will give you a reading. The psychic taxi meter starts running from the initial introduction and runs until the last frantically asked question of the psychic-reading session. They are like the high-priced lawyers of the mystical world: getting you out of trouble, advising you, and helping you maneuver through the cosmic energy—all at an exorbitant cost.

A good psychic realizes that her skills are not to be exploited like a carnival act and will not encourage you to complicate your life further by creating financial problems along with whatever else may be troubling you. Psychic readings are addictive because they concern everyone's favorite subject: themselves. Avoid any psychic reader who crosses the line of advising and tries to dictate your every move. Any psychic reader who begins to trespass on your free will to make choices, trying to program you to do certain things, is not a good person. Remember that you are the consumer; be street smart and don't let an unscrupulous psychic reader take advantage of your free will.

There are psychic readers who want you to become dependent on them, and they will encourage you to get numerous psychic reading because they would love to try and sign you up for the lifelong psychic-seeker program. Don't give your personal power over to any psychic just because they have the ability to tap into the cosmos. You know how some doctors drag out the treatment of an illness, or the way an attorney shuffles around legal papers in order to ensure additional billable hours? Some psychic readers like to give their clients a cliffhanger at the end of a psychic reading in order to guarantee a return visit from the client. A shifty car mechanic may forget to tighten a belt on your car so you have to return for additional repairs, and some psychic readers resort to the same type of tactics—only they mess with your energy.

Be wary of the psychic readers who have "God complexes" and try to convince you that they have supreme knowledge about what is right for you. Also be on the lookout for the psychic lecturers, who prefer to *psychically analyze* you instead of read your cards, palm, astrology chart, or whatever else they're *supposed* to do.

Don't be intimidated by the cranky, arrogant demeanor of some psychic readers, who want you to be submissive to them so they can more easily manipulate you into spending more money to get more readings. I knew one psychic reader who was so nasty that I swear she could get a second job hiding under a bridge and scaring billy goats. Even though this woman was a *psychic-reader bully*, she was a very good and gifted psychic. I truly believe that her clients, of whom she had many, were afraid of her, but because she was such an accurate psychic her clientele faithfully came back. I think she used to get off on being a bitch because doing psychic readings was the only area of her life in which she had total control.

Be careful of the nasty psychic readers, even if they are accurate readers, because when you are energetically open during a psychic reading you could possibly allow some of the psychic's arrogant energy in. That transference of energy can put you in a bad mood or even affect your energy field to the point that you start to have electrical problems with your car, appliances, or lights. Sometimes a psychic germ can even cause a headache or some other vague ache or pain. I am not kidding. You are dealing with high-voltage energy, and you need to be careful who you let tinker with you auric grid. Always ground yourself by dropping roots into the earth, or carry a piece of hematite for protection.

Another thing to keep in mind is that grounding before a psychic reading is very important. (I have actually had clients who were so grounded and protected that it took me a while to get into their psychic area and make a good connection.) You have to find your own personal mix of grounding and openness, and if a psychic reader appears to be crossing too far into your personal space, then just cross your arms or legs. That will usually work to cut the juice off of the reading. Once you find a psychic whom you trust and who has proven to be legitimate, then you can approach the reading with the proper amount of grounding and not feel that you have to wear a lead apron before your psychic session. Know who and what you are dealing with. There are energy predators out there.

Do not be taken in by a psychic reader in angelic sheep's clothing. Just because a psychic may punctuate every sentence with a positive affirmation, tell you to have a blessed day, or appear to be virtuous and sweet, it's no guarantee that they are aboveboard. Use your street sense and your own intuition to *feel* if the psychic reader is a good person or possibly as fake as a knockoff Fendi bag being sold by a guy on the subway.

I did use the word *feel*, because your own intuition or protective energy field will signal your physical body if something isn't quite right. The feeling usually occurs in the solar plexus or stomach area, the proverbial gut feeling. When you sense that someone is looking at you or following you, it means that your perception safety mechanism is working. You must also tune in and get a feeling for the psychic energy worker that you will be letting into your very personal and private energetic aura area. It is like letting someone go into the hard drive of your computer. They better know what they are doing or you will *crash*.

There is no real regulatory index for psychic readers to follow, except for some local laws throughout different communities. Some places ban psychics from doing readings and still consider readings to be witchcraft or demonic practices. Such archaic rules are still in existence because of the psychic readers who pull scams and give the truly gifted lightworkers a bad name. Know who you are allowing to operate on and in your energy zone. Get references or just be street savvy, and know to exit as soon as you smell a scam. Believe me: no matter how desperate you are for answers, you can still smell a scam.

I'm surprised that many clients seem disappointed if a psychic reader looks too normal. Such clients think they are getting a better psychic reading if the psychic looks a little offbeat. Look around at a psychic fair. The psychic readers who look like soccer moms sit and shuffle their tarot cards or play around with their crystal ball waiting for someone to approach them. The psychic readers wearing three to five necklaces, a few rings, and bohemian-looking clothes, and who reek of patchouli and amber, have clients waiting in line. You can't stereotype psychic readers by their looks, just as you can't judge a book by its cover. It's often the person who looks least like a stereotypical psychic reader who turns out to be an amazingly gifted psychic.

The next chapter will take a look at the diverse ways a psychic reader taps into a client's energy and some of the interesting and unusual types of psychic readers.

CHAPTER 2

The Psychic-Reader Smorgasbord

Anyone interested in getting a psychic reading will discover an almost unlimited variety of skills from which to choose. There is more to psychic readings than tarot cards and palms. Choosing the right type of psychic reader for you is like trying on shoes. You have to find the right fit and be comfortable. A psychic who is amazing for your friend may not be the right type of psychic reader for you. You need to become familiar with the types of psychic readers out there and find one who clicks in with your particular energy field.

Some people don't feel they are getting a good reading unless they go in person to visit the psychic, and yet there are people who prefer to get their reading via the telephone because it is more convenient than traveling to see the psychic in person. Most psychic readings can be done over the phone, whether you choose to call a private psychic reader or call a psychic phone line. There are psychic readings that do require you to visit the psychic in person—such as aura reading, when it is necessary to be in front of the psychic so that they can see the color of your energy and tap into your aura. Tea-leaf reading also requires a personal visit to your psychic reader.

Some clients find their favorite psychic reader right away while other clients go psychic hopping in hope of finding their *soul doctor*. The *card-side manner* of the professional psychic is also a big factor for the client to consider when choosing a psychic reader. There are psychics who baby their clients, and then there is the other extreme: psychics who are blunt and right to the point with their clients. Whatever works for you is definitely out there for you to choose.

What exactly are you looking to get from a psychic reading, and what are you looking for in a psychic? As you read through this book you will see how to get the information you want by being a *part* of the psychic reading and not just a bystander. You will learn how to connect your energy with that of the psychic reader and how to ground your own energy so you get a clear psychic reception without picking up any static or interfering energy that is floating around out in the ether waves.

Seek out a psychic who specializes in what you want. Most psychics can pick up on any situation, but some are better at love readings or are, for example, strictly medical intuitives. Finding the right psychic reader is like power dating; you'll know when to stop after you find the right one.

Along with taking a look at the different methods of divination, this chapter will also describe some of the psychic-reader personality types that you, as a client, may encounter.

Psychic-Reader Specialties and Personality Types

Every profession has its specialists, and the psychic profession is no exception. Just as there are many types of psychic skills, methods used, and psychic tools, there are also just as many psychic-reader personality types. The usual stereotype is that all psychic readers are gypsies (see previous chapter). When looking for a psychic reader, the client has to make sure that the personality and card-side manner of the psychic is agreeable; the chemistry has to be right in order to make a good psychic connection.

I have had experiences with psychics who are extremely gifted, but their client care leaves a lot to be desired. Dealing with the public on a regular basis can be very intense, and some psychic readers get cranky, just as those in other people-intense professions do. Some psychics wake up on the wrong side of the cards and can be difficult to deal with at times.

I am a psychic reader and I know plenty of other psychic readers. No matter how normal we look, we are also, let's face it, somewhat unconventional. I think nothing of calling up a psychic peer and telling them that I felt an energy shift while in a multidimensional meditation, or that I had an out-of-body experience. It's definitely not your typical coffee talk.

Clients first have to determine just exactly what they are looking to get out of a psychic reading. Most clients usually seek out a psychic reader when they have a big decision to make or are looking for a direction in life. There are psychics who specialize in almost every area of life: love specialists, financial specialists, medical intuitives, astrological daily planners, pet psychics, and your general practitioners—just to name a few.

The following is just a sampling of the many different specialty skills and personality types you may encounter when looking for and working with a psychic.

Tarot-Card Readers

As a psychic reader myself, I can tell you that tarot-card readings are the most requested method of divination from clients. There are many different tarot decks to choose from, and the psychic may have a preferred and favorite tarot deck. It is also possible to do psychic readings by using a regular deck of playing cards, but most clients request the tarot cards.

A session usually begins with the client, either in person or over the telephone, being asked by the psychic to silently focus on any concerns and clear her mind from other distractions. The tarot cards are shuffled by the psychic if the tarot reading is being conducted over the phone, or the client may be asked to shuffle the tarot deck if the reading is conducted in person.

I would like to clear something up that seems to be a concern for people getting a tarot-card reading over the telephone. It is not necessary for the client to touch the tarot cards in order to get a good reading. I personally do not like anyone touching my tarot cards except me. I am careful of the energy that goes into the cards, and I make sure that after a tarot session I clear my deck by passing the cards through the smoke of burning sage. I like conducting psychic readings over the phone, because then I am not being influenced by the client's body language or distracted by their fidgeting in the chair across from me.

Energy is energy, and you are going to make a good connection as long as the proper condition is met—the proper condition being that you give your full attention to the psychic reading and shut off distractions in the background, such as the TV or friends prompting you to ask a question for them.

A tarot-card reading, whether in person or over the phone, will begin with the psychic reader laying out the tarot in a chosen spread that the psychic feels most inclined to use. The interpretation begins. Skilled tarot readers do not go strictly by the book in interpreting tarot cards, but instead use their psychic abilities to tap into the symbols on the cards, in combination with the prevailing energy of the client, to give a good and unique psychic reading. I was told by a psychic card reader years ago not to be overly influenced by the book meaning of the tarot cards when giving a reading, but rather to use the cards as a tool to tap into the energy of a situation.

The Tower card, for example, when explained solely by its book meaning, means destruction, undoing, devastation, and sudden, unexpected events. But a proficient tarot reader knows that the surrounding cards will influence the meaning of the Tower card either by softening some of the effects or by further complicating the results. Another feared card is the Death card. It doesn't necessarily mean the death of a person but rather a change or transformation of a given person or situation.

A good tarot reader uses highly developed intuitive skills to tap into the complete spread and thread the meanings of the tarot cards into a coherent explanation and potential resolve to whatever is being queried. Keep in mind I said *potential* resolve. We are all energy, and we respond as energy. When getting a tarot reading you are in an active energy state, but the predicted outcome lies in the resting energy state because you have not yet had the opportunity to act on it. A tarot reading is not meant to dictate your fate, but rather to show you the possible and probable outcome should you not make certain adjustments in the path you are on.

Usually at some point during the tarot reading, the psychic will ask the client if there are any questions. Keep in mind that if you ask an ambiguous question, you will get an ambiguous answer. Ask viable questions that have a root because hypothetical situations do not yet exist, and you are basically asking the psychic reader to spell out some fantasy for you.

I will give you an example of what not to do, so you can get the most out of your tarot reading.

A client made an appointment with me for a tarot reading. The session was done via telephone, and the client knew the procedure because she had called me before for a tarot session. Doing a tarot reading for this particular client is challenging to begin with because her approach to the service is at times a little frivolous. I feel that everyone should have the services of a psychic made available to them if they so wish, but I do request that clients behave with me the same way that they would behave when conducting business with any other type of professional.

The reading began with me shuffling the tarot cards and laying out the spread. The client was watching television and simultaneously holding a conversation with a friend on her cell phone while having a tarot reading with me on her landline. Not a good mix! I tried to keep my cool, but my personal feeling of animosity toward this client's behavior was building.

She asked me a question about a man who has never shown any interest in her. I pulled some tarot cards, which revealed there was no possibility of the two of them getting together. Between talking to a friend on her cell phone and half-listening to me, she managed to respond that she felt I was wrong because she knows that this guy is her soul mate. I tried to keep my professionalism, but I had to let her know that I felt her anticipation of this man getting together with her is wishful thinking, 99 percent wishful and 1 percent thinking.

I later asked this client why she continued to get psychic readings from me and other psychics if she refused to acknowledge what we revealed to her during tarot sessions. She was missing out on information about better possible outcomes, because she persisted in her fixation on a fantasy love relationship. I also told her that by inviting other energy into the tarot-reading session, she was complicating things. We are all electrical beings, and when you play around with electrical or charged gadgets during a session, you ultimately interfere with the energetic connection between you and the psychic reader.

Tarot-card readings do not necessarily have to be conducted in a somber mode. They are meant to be informative and uplifting experiences, in which you feel more in charge of your life because you have been given some personal and useful information with which you can better navigate through a difficult situation.

If you really want to tune in to a psychic reading, then turn *off* any distracting devices or noises and stay in the moment of the reading.

Mediums

There seems to be an ever-growing popularity with regard to psychic mediums. Psychic mediums can be *clairvoyant* (meaning that the medium sees the spirit), *clairaudient* (meaning that the medium hears the spirit), or *clairsentient* (meaning that the medium senses the presence and thoughts of the spirit). Some mediums encompass all of the above-mentioned skills. Psychic mediums make connections with deceased loved ones and can possibly connect you with your spirit guide. The results of making a connection are never guaranteed, but a truly gifted psychic medium is able to provide you with uncannily accurate information and messages from the other side.

The psychic medium can successfully relay information from the spirit world that will help you become aware of certain outcomes to situations you may be experiencing. Psychic readings with mediums do not need to be conducted in person. Mediums can and often do conduct sessions over the telephone. This type of psychic reader seems to be a favorite for law enforcement officers, as many psychic mediums have helped solve crimes that otherwise would have remained cold cases.

Your session with a psychic medium will usually begin with the medium asking you to be still, to clear your mind and relax. Most psychic mediums will make a connection with spirit within a few moments. The information coming through the medium may include anything from certain smells that they smell, tastes that they are picking up, or personal information the medium may be given about you that only a loved one would know. Some psychic mediums seem to talk really fast, as if they are reading to you the subtitles of a foreign film.

The spirit information coming through the medium during a session may at times be like playing psychic charades, because the medium is trying like hell to convey all the channeled information with the hope that it will make sense to the client. The medium doesn't want to lose anything during the translation.

As with any psychic reading, you are required to be respectful of the spirit coming through; questions about trivial things such as winning lottery numbers are frowned upon because the purpose of the psychic medium session is for guidance, not ego-based nonsense. Is it possible to get a lucky number through a psychic medium session? Yes, but only if the spirit feels that you are meant to have the information.

Some sessions with psychic mediums can be very emotional, especially when a loved one comes through during the session. Some mediums can tell the client what a loved one died from, and even give confirmation of important dates such as birthdays. Clients wishing to connect with deceased loved ones are the most common type of client, but people looking for guidance from the other side also employ psychic mediums.

Years ago I went to a psychic medium. The woman I went to was not well known, but she was amazing. The session began with me sitting across from her with nothing on the table except a glass of water, which served as a means to conduct the electricity between the veils of the spirit world and the earthly world. The medium closed her eyes briefly. She knew that I had attended art school. The spirit told her that. The medium connected with the spirit of a guide, not a loved one, but the information being provided to me was accurate.

The medium picked up that I would soon be moving and that the street where I would move would begin with the letter *V*. At the time of the psychic reading I had indeed purchased a home, but because it was new construction the street names were not yet designated. I moved into my new home six months later, and sure enough the street name did begin with the letter *V*! Looking back on the experience, I can truly appreciate how gifted this woman was.

As with any psychic reading, you are expected to approach the psychic without arrogance or frivolity but with a sense of respect. That is the only way to get the most out of your experience. A truly professional psychic medium will conclude a session early if she feels that a connection cannot be made at the time of the appointment. Many things factor in to the success of a good session with a psychic medium since mediums are so very energy sensitive. If a medium is battling a personal problem, it is very possible that the medium will reschedule your appointment. You will get your best results if you can approach the psychic-reading session with your own energy field intact, and with an open mind that the information and messages coming through are usually comforting and pertinent.

Aura Readers

Aura reading requires a face-to-face visit with the psychic reader. Some trained and skilled psychic aura readers may pick up your energy vibe over the telephone and sense if your energy is low or high, but a meeting in person works best to get the most from your session. This type of psychic reading seems to work best with medical intuitives and healers.

An aura reader starts the session by doing an energy scan of your body. The aura is scanned first to see if there are any holes in it resulting from either illness or drug and alcohol abuse. Holes in the auric field can lead to illness if not addressed and properly closed. Some psychic aura readers will assess your condition by reading the colors of your aura, while other aura readers will measure the condition of your aura by feeling for hot and cold spots. The temperature variations in the aura will let the aura reader know where the energy is high, low, or even blocked.

The psychic aura reading is really not predictive of future events, but it gives clients a clear and concise picture of their energetic body. For example, if you are in a bad relationship or have a job that you hate, your aura's color will likely be muddy or dull. The aura reader may get a sense of a lower vibration coming from you. The aura reader will be able to identify the problem and suggest ways to raise your vibration to make the necessary corrections. A quick scan of the energetic body will identify where any deficiencies are. Homeopathic therapy or aromatherapy will be recommended to help bring the aura back into balance.

I was told by a very proficient aura reader that we can raise our vibration by wearing pure rose oil when we feel that our energy is low. The normal vibration of the human body is about 78 hertz, and pure rose oil has a vibration frequency of 320 hertz; therefore, by applying pure rose oil to your body you can help raise your vibration. We are energy and like attracts like. If you want to keep good things coming your way, you need to take care of your auric field. Psychic aura readers are not medical doctors, but consultations with them can be incorporated into your traditional medical regime.

Aura readers are also skilled at detecting if a client has come into contact with a negative entity or thoughtform. Sometimes your own negative way of thinking or negative "energy arrows" being flung at you by someone else may also affect your aura's condition. Negative thoughtforms or entities can be picked up by dealing with a nasty, jealous person or by being in a negative relationship or situation.

The aura reader may ask you if you get high or drink a lot, because drugs and drinking to excess will negatively affect the aura and thin it out making it easy for dark-energy thoughtforms to slip in. Aura readers will perform a clearing ritual on you if your problems are caused by an uninvited entity. Often, clearing out the aura will suddenly result in the client feeling a lot better.

I know of an aura reader who came into contact with a very violent thoughtform while she was clearing out a client's energy field. The client had gone to the aura healer because of unexplained body aches and pains along with unjustified outbursts of anger. Medical doctors thought that the woman was bipolar or mentally ill and medication didn't seem to help her. The woman tried a more holistic spiritual approach to her problem, and sure enough it worked.

This woman had a difficult past, suffered from depression, and *always thought negatively*. The cumulative effects of her negative thinking had lowered her vibration and allowed mean thought-forms to inhabit her energetic field. What you think, you shall create! The aura reader recognized this client's symptoms because she had seen similar dispositions in past clients. The aura reader cleared the client of her low-lying negative influences and helped her strengthen her auric field so as not to fall victim to this problem again. The aura reader actually had things fly off her office shelf and felt sick to her stomach as she worked on the client to dispel the negativity. It is important to always be aware of your energetic interaction with others and to stay grounded. The chemistry of energetically connecting with people has interactions and reactions, just like any other chemical mix.

Aura readers will recommend routine maintenance of your auric field by suggesting that you get into the habit of grounding and clearing your energy. Grounding can be done in a number of ways, but the most traditional way is to visualize a silver cord or roots dropping deep down into Mother Earth. You can also carry around a piece of hematite or black tourmaline as a way to ward off negative vibes. Since the left side of your body is the female side, or *drawing side*, you can carry a protective stone on your left side to bring in protective forces. The drawing side of your body pulls, or *draws in*, energy that is around you. That is why it's important to be aware of what and whom you deal with. The right side is the male side of the body, and by keeping the protective stone on your right side you will release any negative energy that you may be carrying around due to having had a bad day. Remember: the left side receives, and the right side releases.

Always clear and cleanse your protective stones. Run the stones under water or cleanse then by passing them through the smoke from burning white sage. Sage, especially white sage, is great for clearing out negative energy, and aura readers sometimes start and finish a reading session by burning white sage in a bowl and passing it over and around the client.

Aura readers know the importance of telling clients to cut the cords at the end of the day before going to bed, and especially after having any negative experiences. Cord-cutting is a way of releasing any negative thoughtforms that may try to attach themselves to you as a result of you having a nasty experience. Thoughts are the most powerful energy generators around, and they can zap you harder than a live wire. You can cut the invisible energetic cords of the day by tapping yourself on the right shoulder and asking archangel Michael to take his sword and cut the cords that bind, or you can visualize a large machete cutting through the cords of the day.

The practice of cutting cords is especially helpful when you are ending a relationship or a job situation that didn't work out. Cutting cords ensures that you don't bring any negative vibes into a new experience. Remember that it is all elemental, and the elements make up the energy. The word *electricity* originates from the Greek word *elektor*, meaning "beaming sun." In essence, we are all star children originating from the light, although some choose the dark side of the sun.

Medical Intuitives

Medical intuitives are a very interesting and specialized field of psychic readers. They are like the chiefs of staff of aura readers. These psychics are not crazy faith healers who disregard traditional medicine in favor of New Age methods of healing, but rather they embrace the teachings of the ancient shamans.

Our bodies are energetic, and any negative vibration can upset our normal energy balance. Stress, anxiety, and difficult relationships—to name just a few factors—all have adverse effects on us. When our vibration is low we can become susceptible to all types of bodily discomfort.

The medical intuitive's little black bag usually contains crystals and stones to aid in healing along with a drum, because drumming will raise your vibration. Bodywork, such as massage and Reiki, is the medical intuitive's equivalent to chicken soup. The medical intuitive pays special attention to the chakra centers, which are the energy centers of the body. A quick scan by a medical intuitive can tell which chakra is in a low spin cycle. An energy attunement is usually done in an attempt to get the flow of energy back to its optimum state.

Medical intuitives work on the premise that every thought has a vibration, and negative thinking is the root of most problems having to do with the physical body. The skilled medical intuitive can tell psychically where there are energy blocks in the body and make a diagnosis of the condition. More and more people are incorporating medical intuitives and holistics into their traditional medical regimen.

I know a very gifted woman named JoAnn Ward who does bodywork. She has successfully cleared me of numerous aches and pains. Being a psychic reader myself leaves me wide open for catching a *psychic-energy cold*, which is basically caused by not fully clearing off client energy after doing psychic readings. Because my chakras are open during a psychic-reading session, I may inadvertently let in some errant energy. The chakras, or energy centers, of your body can be compared to the spark plugs in your car. If one is misfiring, then the ride will be on the rough side and you may even stall out from time to time.

You can tell when a tune-up is necessary because your body may begin to give you clues such as headaches, anxiety, clumsiness, or other unexplained aches and pains. This signals that your energetic body is in need of a medical-intuitive tune-up and a treatment like Reiki, chakra balancing, or crystal healing

(just to name a few), which can be successfully administered before the unattended negative vibration turns into a disease. Look
at the word *disease*. It is really dis-EASE, the uneasiness toward
something or someone. Medical intuitives see what is going on
in the energetic body, just as medical doctors deal with the physical body.

One morning I woke up and my left sinus was so clogged that
I developed a severe headache. The pressure from my sinus problem radiated down into my left shoulder as well. I heard my phone
ring and contemplated picking it up. I lifted the receiver to my ear
and heard JoAnn's voice on the other end of the line. JoAnn has a
very soothing way of speaking, and her healing energy immediately
began to settle me down. I couldn't believe that she called at a time
when I needed some immediate relief from my sinus problem.
She told me that she was picking up on me and decided to give me
a call.

I told JoAnn how I was feeling, and she went right into my
energy field like a skilled doctor. JoAnn is also a Reiki master,
which means that she has abilities to heal from a distance. Since
my problem was on my left side, which is the female side of the
body, JoAnn determined that my intuitive, feeling mechanism
must be overstressed. She started to do an energy clearing for
me, and within twenty minutes of talking with her my severe
sinus problem was nothing more that a slight ache in the corner
of my eye. JoAnn told me that the ache would subside in a few
hours, and it did.

I had been doing a lot of psychic readings in the few days that
preceded my sinus flare-up, and so I had completely drained
my intuitive side of all its energy. I also did not allow myself the
necessary time between psychic readings to fully recover my own
energy, and I basically gave all my energy away by doing the readings. I know better than to go on a psychic-reading binge, be-

cause I have had the *psychic-reader hangover* before and it sometimes takes me days to recover.

One of my favorite examples of psychics and healing concerns Madame Helena P. Blavatsky. Madame Blavatsky was a spiritualist who resided mostly in New York after many years of traveling the world. However, in 1875 she temporarily lived at 3420 Sansom Street in my hometown of Philadelphia. While in Philadelphia, Madame Blavatsky became ill and the doctors wanted to amputate her leg. She refused to have her leg leave this world before she did, so she determined that she would do her own healing. Some say that she placed a white dog across her leg for a healing, while others say that she saw an apparition of a white dog lying across her leg as it was healed. In any case, when the doctor came by to check on her he was amazed that she had managed to heal herself.

Madame Blavatsky's illness inspired her to start the Theosophical Society, an organization committed to spreading awareness of the spiritual principles known as Theosophy. The house where she resided has since been turned into a cute little café called the White Dog in honor of her healing.

It is amazing how closely linked our minds and our bodies are. Patients can consult medical intuitives along with traditional doctors in order to get a full scope of what is going on with their health. A combination of body, mind, and spiritual treatments will give you the full spectrum of healing.

Tea-Leaf Readers

One of the oldest forms of divination is tea-leaf reading. Some believe that the skill developed in China, while others believe it originated in the Middle East.

A visit to a psychic tea-leaf reader begins with the reader brewing some tea. The tea used is usually green, black, white, or oolong. Only the loose leaves are used. The leaves form the symbols in the cup, and the meaning of the shapes is read to reveal one's fortune.

Once the tea is brewed it is poured into a light-colored cup because the patterns of the tea leaves will show up better that way. The psychic tea-leaf reader will ask you to sip your tea and think of your wishes. Don't completely finish your tea; leave a small amount of liquid in the bottom of the cup to be swirled around. The tea-leaf reader will ask you to turn the cup upside down on a saucer to drain out any remaining liquid, and will also ask you to turn the cup around and around clockwise on the saucer three times and make a wish. The psychic will then pick up the cup and read the patterns in the tea leaves, intuitively interpreting the patterns and symbols of the remaining leaves in the cup and telling your fortune.

Leaves close to the rim of the cup indicate events that are close at hand, and leaves on the bottom of the cup show situations that are in a state of flux and likely to change. Symbols are carefully interpreted by the tea-leaf reader. Once the symbols are all interpreted, the tea-leaf reading is done.

I remember my first experience with a tea-leaf reader. A friend of mine had told me about a woman who lived in a small house off a country road. We went to see her, and she was all that I had envisioned her to be. The woman was about eighty years old. Her gray hair was short and permed, and she wore a simple, green-print house dress. The inside of her home was as neat as a pin, and I felt like I was a visitor to a bygone era. Her antique tables were covered with lace doilies, as were the arms of her overstuffed chairs and big blue sofa. An old black-and-white cat followed her from room to room, then settled on a nearby windowsill.

The old woman led my friend and me into her kitchen and told us to have a seat at her Formica kitchen table. She went to her stove and boiled some water. She approached the kitchen table where I was seated, and she handed me a cup with some tea leaves in it. After the water on the stove had come to a boil, the woman brought the tea kettle over to the table and poured some of the boiling water over the tea leaves. The cup was only about a third of the way filled with water, which made me happy because I couldn't imagine drinking the weird-looking tea. Hey! I'm a city girl. All of my tea comes in little tea bags.

The tea brewed for a few minutes, and then the old woman told me to drink the tea but not to finish it. She also told me to be careful not to swallow any tea leaves if I could help it. I took a sip of the tea and was very nervous about swallowing some tea leaves. What if I accidentally swallowed the tea leaves that could possibly symbolize some important event for me? The tea-leaf reader next told me to hold the cup in both hands, make a wish, and turn the cup upside down onto a nearby saucer. Once the cup was on the saucer, she instructed me to think of my wish, turn the cup around and around clockwise three times, and say, "In the name of the Father, the Son, and the Holy Spirit."

The old woman turned over the teacup and began to read my fortune. She told me that I was beginning a new cycle, and that there was another child for me. She also told me that she saw a "horse" in my cup, which showed her that I liked beautiful things and that I had artistic ability. She saw two people moving away, but that I would still have contact with them. She also told me that someday I would be dealing with people in a foreign country. She accurately picked up on things that were going on in my life and even gave me names of people I was associated with.

I had that tea-leaf reading twenty-two years ago, and I can tell you with certainty that everything that the old lady told me came true. At the time of the reading I didn't experience the full impact of her predictions, but as I look back I can see how her tea-leaf predictions all came to pass.

Unlike tarot-card readings, which can be done over the phone, a tea-leaf reading must involve a personal visit to the psychic reader. Keep in mind that there are also other forms of cup divination.

Reading coffee grinds is a method used mostly in Turkey and the Middle East.

Astrologers

Since Babylonian times, astrology has been recognized as one of the oldest forms of prediction. An astrologer does not necessarily have to be psychic to give a good astrological reading, but the astrologers who have honed their intuitive skills and combined them with the interpretation of an astrological chart are extremely accurate. There is a saying that astrology is the golden key and the tarot is the silver key, and when combined the integrated method of divination will unlock the unknown to the seeker. J. P. Morgan, one of the greatest financiers of all time, was quoted as saying, "Millionaires don't have astrologers, billionaires do."

There are different types of astrology: Western, Vedic, and Chinese, just to name a few. Almost every major newspaper runs a daily astrology column, and daily horoscopes are regularly sent to millions of e-mail addresses. Astrologers can do various types of charts for clients, including birth charts, progressed charts (which show you where you are currently headed), and horary charts (which give you an answer to a specific question). I find horary charts to be the closest thing to out-and-out fortunetelling. The horary chart is cast for the moment that the question is posed to the astrologer, and the answer is derived from the placement of the planets in the chart.

Most people will make an appointment with an astrologer to get a birth-chart interpretation and maybe a current planetary transit report. Astrologers usually make their clients aware of upcoming planetary trends such as a Jupiter return (which can be fortunate), a Saturn return (which can be trying), and the ever-so-annoying Mercury retrograde (which occurs a few times a year and sends all forms of communication and transportation into a state of frenzy). The void-of-course Moon phase (the period when the Moon is between zodiac signs) is carefully watched by astrologers, because plans made during that phase of the Moon will not have the desired results. Astrologers study their skill for years, and they must constantly be aware of the ever-changing sky and eclipses, both solar and lunar.

In scheduling an appointment with an astrologer, you will have to provide your birth information. You need the date and exact time you were born, along with your city of birth. Some people don't know their time of birth, and in that case a solar chart using 12 noon as a time of birth is used. I have seen solar-chart readings that are very accurate, but there is nothing like having a chart done for your specific time of birth. The astrologer will cast your chart and see how the current planetary transits are affecting your horoscope. When you arrive for your session or receive your phone consultation, the astrologer will make predictions based on his or her interpretations of the planetary aspects.

An astrological chart can reveal many things. It can show how many marriages you may have, the condition of your employment, and the type of work you are best suited for. A well-trained astrologer can view your birth chart and read it as if reading the newspaper. You can hardly hide who you are from an astrologer. During a consultation you may ask the astrologer questions based on your chart, and if you are in a relationship the astrologer can even do a synastry chart for you and your intended in order to look at the relationship as a whole.

Being both an astrologer and a tarot-card reader, I can honestly tell you that men prefer astrological consultations over tarot-card readings. Most people who seek psychic readings are women, but men seem to like the bit of mathematical logic that is involved in a chart reading.

Astrologers also take note of the eclipses for the year, usually two lunar and two solar eclipses, which are very foretelling of change. Special attention is also given to the ascendant or rising sign, because it will show the outward temperament of the client. The MC, or Midheaven, is the high point of the astrological chart, and any planetary activity going on in that area of the chart usually highlights one's current standing at work or in the community.

The astrological chart is divided into twelve houses, and each house represents an area of your life. For example, the fourth house will show what your home is like, whereas the seventh house will give information about partnerships, a first marriage, friends, and even enemies. The planets that are posted in the different houses at birth will influence the nature of what goes on in that part of the astrological chart. For instance, say the planet Mercury, which rules communication, is in your first house. An astrologer would be able to see that you are the type of person who has no problem communicating about yourself. The sign that the planet Mercury was in at birth will also influence the nature of that house. Imagine that Mercury in the first house was in the sign of Aquarius; that would mean that you're witty and open to a wide range of ideas, but at times you can be very stubborn. You would be inclined to be very verbal and enjoy expressing your views to anyone who listens. Writing would come easily for you.

I like to tell my clients to imagine the wheel of their astrology chart as a community made up of twelve houses. Some houses have planets living there and some houses are empty. Throughout the year different planets that are transiting will move into the houses of the chart. You can consider them to be *renters*, because they will only stay in that house for a while. The chart houses that already have planets living in them may take in a transiting or visiting planet, and some of the vacant houses will, at times, take in a temporary transiting resident planet. The nature and aspects of the planets will tell if the planetary stay will be harmonious or lead to an astrological street brawl.

Say, for instance, that the planet Venus is transiting through town and decides to stay in your second house of money. That would mean that all of the benevolent gifts of Venus would be bestowed into that house. Now, what if the planet Uranus, known for the unexpected, was already a permanent resident of the second house? The two roommates, Venus and Uranus, could wind up in trouble because the sudden erratic nature of Uranus would mean that the normally refined Venus might suddenly start to act like a drunken sailor on a spending spree. On the positive side it could also mean a sudden, unexpected windfall. A lot depends on the activity and nature of the whole chart. After the temporary lease of Venus runs out and she moves into another house, the condition of the second house will either be better off because of the visit from Venus or, in a worst-case scenario, would leave the second house upside down and in a financial free fall.

Astrology readings are good for pinpointing the timing of an event, because the movement of the planets can be looked up online or in an ephemeris, a table that lists the positions of the planets. When astrology is combined with a tarot reading, I find that the ever-so-elusive bull's-eye for getting timing right becomes a bit more accurate. The two forms of divination work together like threading a needle.

The Love Psychic

The *love psychic* is probably one of the most popular psychic readers around. These psychics specialize in giving readings concerning relationship problems.

The temperament of the love psychic can be that of your best high-school girlfriend or more like the disposition of a pit bull. The high-school-girlfriend type of psychic reader will pull out her tarot cards and hang on your every word as you explain how your date stood you up. She will empathize with you as you tell her that you caught your then-boyfriend cheating, and if she is the ultimate love psychic reader, she will take your tearful phone calls even if it is two o'clock in the morning. What more could you ask for in a psychic reader? This love psychic will not only tell your fortune, but she will boy-bash along with you, too.

The high-school-girlfriend type of love psychic has most likely heard every type of relationship problem around, and she finds her clients' love lives to be better than the daytime soaps. This love psychic's advertisement promises to reunite loved ones, tell you what your lover is thinking, remove all obstacles, and help where all else fails. How can you possibly go wrong? She will hand you tissues to dry tears from your eyes as she lays out the cards to reveal to you the description of your boyfriend's new love interest. This particular love psychic is always careful when revealing news to the heartbroken client about the new replacement girlfriend. Should your boyfriend's new girl toy be a thin, leggy blond, this type of love psychic will describe the new girlfriend as an anorexic giraffe with bleached-out hair.

This type of love psychic is often considered part of the family. She is invited to wedding showers (for all of the couples she has reunited), and some clients even promise to name their first-born child after her. She will get you through all of your relationship problems, help you pick a good day for your wedding, and flip some tarot cards to help you find hidden assets during your divorce. The high-school-girlfriend type of love psychic usually has a long, sustained relationship with her clients throughout the years.

Keeping professional boundaries can be tricky at times for the high-school-girlfriend type of love psychic, however, since her clients really do grow to love her as a true friend and confidante. Payment for her psychic services can sometimes cause sticky situations, because some clients think that their pledges of loyal friendship and invites to family parties and weddings are payment enough. Please remember that psychics have to pay their bills. Think of payment for this type of psychic service in this way: you get good, friendly vibes and dynamite psychic insight, all for one price.

The pit-bull type of love psychic is not for the tenderhearted. This type of psychic reader will verbally rip you apart if you even *think* of calling back your boyfriend after a huge fight. The pit-bull love psychic will insist that her clients retain their power at all times during the course of a relationship. If you call this type of love psychic for an appointment, be prepared for some boot-camp-style love lessons.

The pit-bull love psychic always makes a point to tell you not to fall apart during a love crisis. This type of love psychic is like a first-response team sent out to the site of a broken heart. The first mission of the pit-bull love psychic is to get you breathing again. I must tell you from my own experience that this type of psychic reader really doesn't encourage you to be *needy*.

I had an experience with a pit-bull love psychic back when I was about twenty years old. I went to see her because I had broken up with a boyfriend and I *thought* that I might want him back. She was a woman about forty years old who did psychic readings out of her apartment. She looked more like a gangster's gun moll than a psychic reader. I liked her energy, even though she seemed a little rough around the edges.

She welcomed me into her three-room apartment, which was on the third floor of a converted brownstone. The inside of her place was shabby chic, decorated with odds and ends that somehow seemed fitting for her personality. There was a tough black-leather sofa softened by a leopard-print, faux-fur throw that had been flung over the cushions. Hanging spider plants served as curtains for her front bay window, and the centerpiece on her coffee table was an empty Mateus wine bottle with a half-burned red candle plugging up the opening.

She brought me into her kitchen, where she conducted her psychic readings, and began to complain about her downstairs neighbors as she lit a cigarette. She told me that the neighbors always gave her strange looks because of all the people traffic in and out of her *crib*. She assumed that the neighbors thought that she was dealing something other than tarot cards.

This pit-bull love psychic told me to shuffle the cards, cut them into three piles, and pick only one pile to be read. I was warned not to use the term *soul mate*, because she was tired of hearing it. She threw down some cards and immediately as well as correctly described my situation with the former boyfriend. While looking me straight in the eye, she firmly told me that if I took him back he would ruin my life and try to hold me back.

I was shocked! I thought that I was going to hear the desired out-come that was floating around in my head: the one where the guy comes crawling back, begging for another chance. No way was this pit-bull love psychic going to tell me that! She warned me to for-get about him. She recounted a story about her old boyfriend, who she somewhat endearingly called *the creep*. She told me that after nu-merous breakups with him and a recovery from a walking nervous breakdown, she had finally decided that he wasn't worth it.

She told me that if I went back with my boyfriend, I would have to deal with someone who was always competing with me and who was very jealous of my abilities. She picked up the tarot cards from the table, put them into a full pile, then firmly banged them down and said, "Get over him. He's no good. Just another rat."

I paid her for the reading and left her place feeling like I had just been lectured by a Marine drill sergeant. The uncanny truth of the matter is that she was absolutely right. She gave it to me straight on. No games. No handholding. Just the facts. It truly was one *bitchin'* tarot reading.

Love psychics will deliver the truth; it is just a matter of whether you want the facts sugarcoated or straight up like a shot of tequila.

The Money Psychic

Next to love comes money as the object of most people's desires. Psychics who tout themselves as financial genies are sure to have plenty of clients. The psychic financier sometimes uses a combination of astrology and psychic abilities to help predict everything from the possibility of a client getting a raise to the condition of the stock market.

The money psychic is a right-brained intuitive with a renegade gene activating a left-brained, logical mind. There are two strains of money psychics; the first is the *hedge-fund Houdini*, who is a more conservative psychic financial counselor, dealing mostly with big corporate executives. The hedge-fund Houdini advises companies on how to be more profitable and is sought after by those making serious investments. Stockbrokers have been known to consult with psychics who specialize in money matters. Strategic astrological planning has been behind many a successful business deal, and it is no secret that psychic advice has been sought out on Wall Street and in major foreign markets.

The second strain of money psychic is the *psychic bookie*. The telephone of the psychic bookie rings off the hook with clients seeking street-smart psychic financial advice. The psychic bookie deals with everything from which horse will win in the fifth race at Belmont to pulling a few cards to find out if a client's requested credit-card limit increase will go through. The psychic bookie is often consulted to give the winning score for a major sporting event so that clients can bet on the game's winner. Clients want everything from lucky days to lucky numbers.

Here is the big question: How come psychics don't always win the lottery if they can predict the future? The answer is simple. If psychics won the lottery, they would stop working, vacation in the south of France, and there would be no psychics left to help you with your financial dilemmas.

The famed psychic Edgar Cayce was often asked by his clients for lucky numbers, but such questions gave him headaches. Psychic abilities are meant to help you as you go through your soul's training period, called *life*, and money lessons are just like love lessons. You have to learn them well, and there is no cheating. Every experience has a purpose in your life. The psychic reader who is looking into the energy of your financial situation may be able to pick up the best direction to take with your finances. Remember that psychics work with energy, and money is just another form of energy. Psychic readers have to get the client's energy up and running in order for the client to be able to transmute their own energy into earning power—with the final result being more money. The money psychic doesn't pull a tarot card and make money materialize for the client, but instead looks at the psychic reading as a way to steer the client in the most profitable direction.

I have helped many a client get through lean times, and the experience of transcending tough financial issues helped them evolve spiritually. Money definitely doesn't buy happiness. Money buys things to fill the void where happiness should be.

Sometimes the money psychic is asked by the client to become a *psychic money bloodhound*. Clients going through a divorce often seek psychic advice in locating missing assets. I had a client going through a divorce who was trying to locate some missing financial documents. I told her that they were in the trunk of her husband's car—and sure enough, they were.

I like to tell my clients about ways in which they can help bring better financial situations into their lives. Clients have to realize that they actually have more control over money than they do over love. You can't make someone love you, but you can create opportunities to make money. Fear of not having money is what holds you back. You have to stay in the moment, live in the moment, and the only plan you need for tomorrow is to have a good attitude about looking for opportunities to make money. You are more resourceful than you know, and you have to go after what you want to have in your life.

I think Reiki is an amazing way to remove energy blocks and get the energy going and flowing into the areas of your life where it's most needed. Reiki isn't just for bodywork. When I took my Reiki class, we learned that you can Reiki everything from your food to your wallet.

I gave a client a reading that concentrated primarily on her finances. The stock-market drop had obliterated her portfolio, and she desperately needed some psychic insight to see if she would survive financially. Her astrological chart did show some temporary financial upsets, and the accompanying tarot reading confirmed that it would be a blessing in disguise. I suggested that she try some Reiki to get her energy going and balance her out. She found a Reiki class in her area and took the course. I thought it would be a good idea if she did Reiki on her wallet every day to get her money energy up.

As it turned out, my client found a love for Reiki and decided to take additional Reiki classes. She is also giving Reiki treatments as a way to make some extra money, and she is considering a complete change of career suited more toward massage and bodywork.

Money is another form of energy, and we are all energy. It is all *elemental*.

Gypsy Scams and Cold Readings

A *cold reading* occurs when you are approached by someone, usually a stranger, who strikes up a conversation with you that at first may seem harmless. The scam begins when the stranger tells you that you look sad. The cold reader will say something to you that seems comforting, something to the effect of, "Life will be getting better soon" or "Something good is about to happen for you; I can see it in your eyes!" Before you know it, you are given a piece of paper with the cold reader's phone number on it.

The cold reader is often a gypsy who has unassumingly solic-ited you for a gypsy scam. I want to be clear right off the bat: the word *gypsy*, as I'm using it in this book, does not refer to, and is not meant to be derogatory toward, any ethnic group, but rather it's a reference to some street-slick psychic readers.

In the fifteenth century a nomadic group of people started to show up in Europe. This group of people had darker skin and were immediately linked with the people of Egypt, who for cen-turies were associated with the ability to tell fortunes. Because this nomadic group of people wandered from place to place, they often made money by telling fortunes; they didn't stay in one place long enough to establish themselves in businesses.

A large faction of this nomadic group came from India, Tur-key, and other places east of Europe. As an ethnic group they are called the Roma and their root language is Romani. Their root language shares many similarities with Sanskrit, the histori-cal language of the Hindus of India. The Roma were known for their remarkable fortunetelling gifts and psychic abilities. We are all born with this gift, but the Roma culture allows and encour-ages these abilities to develop. Even though this ethnic group was nomadic and tribal for centuries, they somehow managed to hold on to and preserve a great deal of ancient knowledge about psychic abilities, crystal scrying, and even curses.

It wasn't, and often still isn't, easy to be a Roma in Europe, because prejudice and cultural differences made it difficult for them to find good jobs. They resorted to using their fortune-telling skills as a way to make money. The fear of a *gypsy curse* also made it easy for some desperate fortunetellers to exploit their customers and ask for large sums of money or goods.

The Roma sometimes get incorrectly confused with the con-temporary use of the word *gypsy*, meaning one who chooses to live a carefree, nomadic lifestyle while making a living with trick-ery. As I mentioned, I use the word *gypsy* not to refer a particular ethnic group, but rather to describe street-slick hustlers and psychic-service hucksters. I am using the word to describe any scammer who takes your money and makes false promises and predictions while also exploiting your fears.

How do gypsies know who to approach? They know just by observing. I know a gypsy who is a very talented and gifted psychic reader, but she uses her talents as a lure to pull in desperate people looking for help. The gypsy cold reader has a talent for knowing who to approach. Usually young women or women shopping alone are the preferred targets. Chances are that there is a love-life issue going on, and the cold reader can hone right in and exploit it.

A visit to a gypsy may start out as a novel experience, but it can turn into a financial disaster if you are not aware and discriminating. The lure of a neon palm in the window beckons you to come in for a psychic reading. The gypsy parlors are usually a funky mix of a psychic reading room and the gypsy's personal living quarters. It isn't uncommon to see religious statues mixed in among the clutter of crystals, hanging beaded curtains, unpacked boxes (gypsies are always ready to move), and usually a television on in a back room that is entertaining an older relative or a group of children.

The psychic reading begins with the gypsy reader telling you that she will tell you everything, both the good and the bad of the psychic reading. Next, you are given a choice of a palm reading or tarot-card reading. The choices are expanded to either a short overview reading or a whole-life reading. The funny thing is that no matter which type of reading you pick, the predictions all have one thing in common: "Someone is jealous of you and has wished you bad luck." You are instructed to place your money on the table so the gypsy can bless it and then take it. Now the scam begins.

The gypsy looks you straight in the eye, and in a serious tone she tells you how she is going to help you but you must follow her instructions carefully or risk carrying the dark cloud of bad luck around with you for the rest of your days. The scam of choice is to promise to light some special candles for you so that the gypsy can read the wax drippings, pray for you, and begin to chase the bad luck away. She will size you up by looking at your clothing and general appearance, and through a series of carefully phrased questions she will begin to randomly state facts about the condition of your life. The gypsy will say that she can sense a relationship problem. If you respond by telling her that you aren't having a relationship problem, she may tell you that one is about to come up, but it can be avoided if you come in for a special spiritual cleansing and the ever-so-popular gypsy candles.

The person who enters a gypsy establishment intending to pay $20 for a psychic reading can be scammed into paying hundreds, even thousands, of dollars. Once hooked, the client develops a fear that if she doesn't do as the gypsy asks, then a curse may be placed on her. The gypsies have an innate skill for picking potential victims of their scams, so if you are a novice at getting psychic readings, it is in your best interest to avoid the gypsies.

Not all gypsies have storefronts with glowing palms and crystal balls strategically placed in the window. Beware of the so-called *designer gypsies*, who do not fashion themselves after the stereotypical fortunetelling gypsies of folklore. These designer gypsies wear stylish clothing and sit in fashionably decorated office suites, but they are just as manipulative, dangerous, and money-oriented as their lower-end counterparts. The high-end gypsy scams are similar to the street-style gypsy scams, in that they both require escalating fees and frequent visits with the gypsy in order to turn your luck around. It's like signing up for a "lifelong gypsy curse removal" plan, in that it is never-ending. There is a touch of larceny interwoven with their psi abilities.

I have gone to gypsies for psychic readings and they were talented, but as soon as the candle conversation starts I know to make my exit. One time, my visit to a gypsy just for fun turned into a session of me reading the gypsy's tarot cards. The session started with some brief conversation as the gypsy handed me the tarot cards to shuffle. A card fell from the deck as I was shuffling it, and I picked it up and noted the meaning out loud. The gypsy asked me if I knew how to interpret the cards. I replied that I was very familiar with tarot cards and that I was a tarot-card reader and astrologer.

I asked the gypsy her birthday, made some quick astrological predictions for her, and allowed her to pick a few cards for confirmation of what I had just told her. She was impressed. My psychic reading consisted of some vague information and intermittent questions about what I had picked up about her life.

It seems that gypsies are psychic junkies, too. I paid the gypsy for the brief tarot reading, and as I drove home it dawned on me: I didn't get paid by the gypsy or get offered a free reading in exchange for reading her tarot cards! The gypsy not only got a free tarot-card reading from me, she also got paid for being my client!

The Wise Witch and the Goth Energy Vampire Slayer

I will admit that, personally, my favorite type of psychic reader is the *wise witch*. First of all, a witch is not a satanic demon or the devil's disciple. Quite the contrary. The wise witch is someone who practices or has some knowledge of Wicca, a belief system that embraces nature. The word *witch* can also mean "wise one." These days more and more women and men who embrace Wicca as a method of self-empowerment are coming out of the broom closet, so to speak.

The wise witch is into herbal remedies, divination, and the transformation of energy by using candles, herbs, oils, and rituals for empowerment. The casting of spells or intentions is done in accordance with the Moon, and the wise witch heeds the

Wiccan Rede, or moral code: *An it harm none, do what ye will.* Or in more modern English: *If it harms none, do what you will.*

Modern witches are skilled in divination. Astrology, tarot cards, and rune stones assist the wise witch in giving psychic readings. The wise-witch psychic reader believes in magick and the power of intention, and she can look for guidance from the astral realms.

Witches have gotten a bad rap over the years, due to widespread fears and ignorance about Wicca. Sure, there may be a few negative witches who give the rest of the group a bad name, but truthfully I fear politicians more than I do witches.

Wise-witch psychic readers are like shamans: they both have psychic powers, yet are also skilled healers and knowledgeable about herbs. The crazy thing is that telling someone you are a shaman commands respect, but the word *witch* brings to mind for too many people an image of a stereotypical, devious, spellcasting wench.

As a teenager my curiosity and interest in Wicca led me to become somewhat of an urban witch. I frequented the local occult stores (stores that sell tarot cards, herbs, candles, and magickal supplies), and I'd *psychic-reader hop* the way some people bar or club hop. The occult store was my Macy's. Every visit provided me with over-the-counter knowledge and essential info, such as how best to ground myself during a psychic reading and the protective uses of stones like hematite. The fragrance counter of my metaphysical mecca sold divination-enhancing oils, and the tall, balding man behind the counter took my orders for candles inscribed with my desired intentions. The occult store had its resident psychic reader, as well as regulars who volunteered to do psychic readings if the house psychic was busy. It was pure magick!

The wise witch who worked at one of my favorite occult stores would give tarot readings when she wasn't busy filling orders for gris-gris bags, love candles, and magickal brews.

She was a woman in her late fifties, slightly round with shoulder-length red hair that fell to one side and nearly covered the black-rimmed glasses she wore low on her nose. Her manner of dress was sixties hippie meets J.Crew. Her conservative slacks were usually topped with some far-out peasant top, which she adorned with multiple strands of beads, peace signs, pentagrams, and crystal points on a chain.

The reading room was a converted closet that still had the top shelf in place, and the doorway was kept private by a dusty tan curtain that hung from a tension rod. Inside the room two mismatched folding chairs and a small table covered with a dark tablecloth decorated the *psychic suite*.

The wise witch would enter the reading room, filling the small space with the scent of the magickal oils she wore. After plopping down on one of the folding chairs, she'd give me a choice of a card, crystal-ball, or channeled-spirit reading. She started each session by ringing a small brass bell in order to call in her spirit guides, and she'd light a charcoal filled with some *psychic-powers incense*.

I loved getting psychic readings from her, because not only was she accurate, she was also a real witch who shared her knowledge of oils and herbs with me. Each reading session usually ended with her recommending herbal-bath soaps, magickal oils, and a protective stone. She instructed me to carry a piece of red jasper around as a protection from psychic attack, because she felt that energy vampires would recognize my psychic abilities and try to drain me. She was so cool!

The little occult store where she worked has since changed hands, but the same tingling doorbell rings as you enter the store, which still smells of her oils and incense.

Another variation of the wise witch is the urban *goth psychic reader* who has an interest in Wicca. The goth psychic reader is extremely popular with the younger generation. Their mindset and verbiage are influenced by the goth subculture and are familiar to the new wave of street-smart psychic junkies. Goth psychic readers are usually under the age of thirty, have strong intuitive qualities, and are very aware of *prana*, or chi life energy. They are savvy about vampires, but they keep in mind that not all vampires suck blood. The new strain of vampires are the energy vampires, the *chi juggers*, who are the bona fide Draculas of the New Age.

Anyone who goes to a goth psychic reader will be warned about energy vampires, both psychic and psychological. The goth psychic is knowledgeable about the ways in which psychic vampires use and misuse telepathy to get results. His reading style is dark, and his favored divination tools are runes as well as tarot cards.

The goth psychic reader is either a dark, industrial type or the more empathic, dramatic "emo" type. The emo goth has a more emotional style of doing psychic readings; when you hurt, he also hurts, and when you cry, so does he. This psychic reader feels energy imprints and will read the vibes given off by an individual.

Goth psychic readers, whether dark goth or emo, will not tolerate anyone who is a poseur. A poseur is someone who really isn't into the goth style of thought or dress, basically a *wannabe* goth. Every now and then you may come across an urban old-school psychic witch who will dress in an industrial or Renaissance fashion in order to attract the younger subculture psychic seekers. Forget about it! A poseur can't pull it off, no matter how much eyeliner she wears.

One day I was in a mall bookstore, lingering in the New Age section. A young guy with multiple body piercings around the age of twenty struck up a conversation with me as we both reached for the same book on psychic attacks. There was no doubt that he was a goth. He had on black pants, black boots, a black jacket with heavy chains on it, and a black-and-gray-striped top hat.

His hair was obviously dyed black, and he wore black eyeliner and black nail polish.

We struck up a casual conversation, and he told me he is a psychic and has a complete library of books on Wicca, tarot, psychic abilities, shadow people, and vampires. He told me that he telepathically connects with his small group of friends and can tell when someone needs his assistance. This Man in Black also claimed to be empathic; if someone he knows cuts himself, he can feel it too, even if he isn't anywhere near the cutter. Interesting!

Contrary to what you may think, goth psychics are more than dark personas sporting multiple body piercings, imprinted with gothic cross tattoos on their arms and neck. They are not just ornamental mall dwellers or part of the industrial music scene. They are totally aware of energy and energy vampires, and let's face it: psychic readings are all about energy.

Maybe the goth psychic readers are a strain of the highly intelligent, individualistic indigo upgrade to our human species. The indigo children, who began arriving in the 1970s, are highly sensitive and psychic, can sense dishonesty, and are often misunderstood.

In any case, my new goth psychic acquaintance reached for a boxed set on the bookshelf. It was a set consisting of tarot cards and an instruction manual. After looking at the box for a few moments, he sighed before placing it back on the shelf and said, "It would be awesome if there was a Marilyn Manson tarot deck. Maybe someday, someone will make one." As he walked away, with the book on psychic attack that I wanted, I though for a moment and wondered if he was a true goth or a *spooky kid*. You see, a spooky kid is a "Mansonite" who is into the goth scene in order to find an identity. Whether this guy was a goth or a spooky kid, he was interesting.

This new wave of psychic readers is edgy and different from the psychic readers who precede them. The goth psychics will telepathically feel your thoughts and pick up psychically what will happen for you. Yes, they are dark, but the intensity of their psychic reading style is more in line with what the new generation of psychic seekers is looking for, since our next big commodity will be energy, *psychic energy*. As we develop as a species we will be able eventually to not have to carry a piece of red jasper for protection; we will merely have to think about it and create the energy of protection. We will not have to speak our minds as much because they will be easily read, and secrets once kept in a mental safe might be stolen and sold on the psychic black market.

This is the new era of psychic energy. I guess it's safe to assume that psychic self-defense will someday replace karate as a form of protection.

The Psychic SWAT Team

The psychic SWAT team consists of one human psychic and a posse of spirit guides. SWAT-team psychics don't really need to use tarot cards or other psychic reading tools, because they have mastered the mindful skill of meditation, which allows them to be in contact with their spirit guides. The human anchor of this psychically skilled team acts as the orator for the spirit guides, who are transmitting their messages for the querent. A British psychic I know named Michael Tottey gives psychic readings that include the aid of his guides.

My first psychic-reading experience with Michael occurred over the phone on a three-way call with Michael, my aunt Rose, and myself. Aunt Rose was in the hospital at the time and very concerned about her condition. Michael said, "Settle down, luvie, me guides just informed me that you don't have cancer, just a *bugger* of a gallstone." Michael and his guides were absolutely right; Aunt Rose later found out through tests that her problem was a gallstone.

Michael told us that he has a few spirit guides, including a Native American who is extremely tall, a warrior, and serves as his protector. Michael is skilled at going on ghost hunts, especially in York, England, and this Native American guide always has his back. Michael and his SWAT team of spirit guides act as ghost busters, and some of his stories would scare you, as he would say, "right out of your shorts."

Whether you are a *believer* or a *hater* of the psychic world, you can't escape the fact that we all have spirit guides. Who are these guides, and how the hell did we get them? When we come into this world, this incarnation on earth, we are assigned a guardian angel and connect with our spirit guides. Some of these spirit guides have been with us for many lifetimes, while others may be new hires.

Spirit guides are souls that have learned their lessons on earth and are now able to vibrate in a higher energy octave; they are not spirits that must return to earth to learn more lessons. Spirit guides are not ghosts. A ghost is an energy imprint of someone who doesn't realize they have died. Some ghosts throw things and cause havoc, because they are mad about not being acknowledged by the people that they leave behind. We can't hear or see them but we can feel them, usually in the form of a severe drop in temperature in certain areas of a room. Ghosts have to move on into the light, while spirit guides are *from* the light.

Another guide we all have is our special guardian angel. Guardian angels are the top realm of spirit guides. Guardian angels are very protective of the souls they watch over, whereas the spirit guides are the helpers. Spirit guides will assist you in your efforts, but you must call on them because they are not allowed to interfere with your free will. Your guardian angel is always with you, even if you don't specifically call on him or her.

Many people have experienced being in some kind of trouble, only to have a stranger suddenly appear and help them out. One time, before GPS devices were available to the public, I became severely lost on my way to a function. I was almost out of gas and it was getting dark. I pulled over to the side of the road in a deso-late area; I had no idea where I was. Suddenly, a man wearing a light tan uniform came out of nowhere, approached my car, and asked me if I needed help. I didn't have any feelings of fear about this older man, just a sense of relief.

I told him where I wanted to go, and he instructed me on how to get there. When I went to thank him, he was gone. I thought that he might have fallen under my car since I couldn't see him. I looked in my rear-view mirror to see if he was behind me, but he had simply vanished. There were no houses around, so I couldn't imagine where he went. I somehow managed to drive an addi-tional eight miles with my gas gauge on *E*, eventually reaching my destination. The eight-mile drive seemed to take only moments. Something happened to *time*. Time is an illusion, but I somehow transcended it and arrived at my destination at warp speed. To this day, I believe that I met an angel assigned to protect me.

Spirit guides, unlike angels, need to be called in for assis-tance. There are guides that help you at doing almost anything. I know a woman who is psychic and also a healer. She often calls in her spirit guides who are familiar with health and medicine whenever she has a client. The spirit guides connect with her en-ergy to bring about the desired healing results.

There are spirit guides that help out with writing, art, music, math, carpentry, law, medicine, and just about anything you can think of. You just have to meditate and allow yourself to be open enough to make the connection. Try being of the mindset of a child and remember how to believe, visualize, and trust in the magick of the universe where all things are possible.

I actually called in a spirit guide I have that likes to shop and is a fashionista. I was at the mall one day and needed an outfit for an event I was going to. What I wanted existed in my mind, but I couldn't find it in any of the stores that I went into. Exas-perated, I leaned up against the mall directory sign and called in my *power-shopping* spirit guide. I meditated for a moment, and suddenly something told me to go into Saks. I walked toward a clothing rack as if I were on automatic pilot, and I couldn't believe my eyes! There right in front of me was the top that I had been envisioning throughout my shopping trip. I should have also called in my *banker guide* since the top cost more than I wanted to spend, but I took the plunge and bought it anyway.

Many psychic readers I know work strongly with their spirit guides. The psychic readers who have a good, strong connection with their spirit guides find them to be very helpful during psychic-reading sessions with their clients. The spirit guides are able to go into the Akashic records, where knowledge of the past, present, and future is recorded. The spirit guides will allow the psychic reader to channel the information and provide the client with necessary information. Spirit guides are not meant to give out lottery numbers or lucky days unless the client desperately needs a financial lifeline. Spirit guides may shut off if they feel that the information being requested will interfere instead of help with the client's life lessons.

Who can you go to when you want to have your spirit guides identified? Past-life psychic readers can successfully tell you about your guides. I have been told that I have a short, Asian doctor as one of my guides, and I also have a fourteenth-century monk along with a medieval mystic who primarily assist me with my psychic readings.

Spirit guides want you to acknowledge them for the help that they give to you, so it is important to keep that in mind when working with your spirit guides. Psychics who work strongly with their spirit guides have a certain technique when doing readings. I had a psychic reading with a woman who ran everything past her guides. The psychic-reading session started with her taking a few deep breaths, and a moment of silence was observed before the session began. She didn't ask me any questions, but she went right into the information given to her by her guides. I was amazed. Everything that came through in the psychic reading was accurate and not at all vague. Every sentence of information that came through the psychic reader began with the words, "My guides are telling me . . . " At one point during the reading she heard me sigh when she delivered some information that really wasn't too favorable for me, and she sweetly said, "Hey, hon, don't blame me. Blame my guides, because they are the ones telling me to relay this info to you." (I should try that with my clients when I have to deliver some negative news. I usually tell them that I don't write the news, I only read it.)

Psychics who work with spirit guides are not to be confused with mediums who attempt to connect with deceased loved ones. Some psychic readers can do both types of outer-limit connections, but there are psychics who strictly deal with only spirit-guide connections and don't do readings of the departed.

The spirit-guide SWAT team is the equivalent of simultaneously texting, e-mailing, and instant messaging the other side.

The Dr. Dolittle Pet Psychic

Do you ever wonder what goes on inside the head of your little pet? How do you know what your pet is feeling? Well, there is a special practice of psychics who do readings that deal with the energy of animals. The Dr. Dolittles of the psychic field seem to prefer working with pets as opposed to people. Maybe because pets won't ask the psychic reader that one last question that goes on for hours. It is no secret that racehorse owners have brought in pet psychics to find out if the horse feels up to running in a race, and many a pet psychic has been called in to find out why a pooch trashes a house while the dog's owner is at work.

Since almost everyone I know has a psychic, I figured that my three cats should have one, too. A long-standing acquaintance of mine, Shelley Hofberg, who lives in California, is a pet psychic. At various times she has correctly diagnosed ailments that have affected one or more of my three cats. There was an instance when one of my Siamese cats, Caesar, suddenly became ill. Caesar had been playing and running around per usual, and then without warning he stood still and froze like a statue. When I touched him he fell over and was unresponsive. I called the vet to tell him that I was on my way over. My second call was to Shelley to find out what I should be looking for. Shelley assured me that Caesar would be fine, and that he was just having a reaction to something he had eaten, possibly a little house spider. Sure enough, the vet confirmed that Caesar was fine and that he had most likely eaten a bug.

Shelley has also told me things about my other Siamese cat, Wasabi, and my big black witch cat, Magic. She has successfully diagnosed different emotional and physical conditions with both cats. I asked Shelley why Wasabi, my little Siamese, gallops from one end of the house to the other for no reason. I already know that Wasabi has kitty ADD (attention deficit disorder) because he was overbred, but the intermittent galloping is crazy. Shelley told me that he most likely sees a spirit, since cats are very psychic themselves. As a matter of fact, animals have shown unique displays of ESP and are very sensitive to changes in the energy field around their owners.

I have also heard of a Dr. Dolittle type of pet psychic who will bond with pets before doing a reading for them. She will roll on the floor and bark with a dog, or meow and blink her eyes at a cat so as not to get into an aggressive staring match. This pet psychic begins her sessions by emotionally vibing to the pet's energy field. I would love to see her fly like a bird before hatching a psychic reading for a parakeet.

Pets do not have a logical mind, but they do have an emotional, instinctive mind. Pets respond to the energy of emotions, and skilled pet psychics know how to hone in and get a read on a pet's condition. The pet psychic can assess your pet's aura and notice if there are any weak spots. The pet psychic can also communicate with your pet using psychic vibration, which is achieved through touch and the energy vibration of the psychic's voice.

Pets communicate in a very pure form. There is no ego or logic to cloud their decisions. Everything is instinct. Pet intuition is uncanny, especially when coming to the aid of a master in dire need. There are pets that can smell certain illnesses like cancer, and pets have been known to forewarn their keepers of impending trouble.

The psychic school of choice believes that pets can be energy guides for humans, or there is a possibility that they are companions from a past incarnation. Pets have been known to absorb negative vibes directed at their owners, and some pets have gotten ill and have taken the energy *hit* before it gets to their keeper.

Most people call pet psychics when their pet has a behavioral problem, health issue, or aging problem. They also call for help in understanding how their pet feels about changes in the home, such as a move or a new addition to the family. Since pets can't talk, they express their emotions through their behavior. Your cat may suddenly pee on your rug in an effort to convey to you that she is sick or hates your new boyfriend. These types of issues call for the expertise of a pet psychic.

Pet psychics can also administer a Reiki treatment to your pet as a way of rebalancing your pet's energy. I asked Shelley if it was easier to read some pets as opposed to others. I wanted to know who the difficult pet clients are. Shelley told me that pets are easy to read, especially horses, cats, dogs, and other warm-blooded animals. Shelley told me that reptiles, which are cold-blooded and less emotional than warm-blooded animals, may be a tad more difficult to read, but you can still get into a psychic energy connection with them. They still have energy auras that can be psychically read, making communication with cold-blooded animals also possible.

I have to admit that I find my cats to be very in tune with my emotions, and there have been times when I am doing a psychic reading for a client that my cat, Caesar, has been known to pull a tarot card or two from my deck. I always read the cards he pulls out, and to be honest with you the cards are always significant for my client.

So the next time your dog chews on your new Jimmy Choo shoes or your cat uses your laundry pile as a litter box, don't hide the pet treats for a week or give your pet a time-out session in your back room. Instead, call a pet psychic and get a read on what is going on inside that little furry head.

The Psychic General Practitioner

The psychic general practitioner is skilled at almost all types of psychic readings. The psychic GP can handle all kinds of life issues and is proficient in most areas of psychic reading skills. They make up the bulk of psychic readers. The psychic GP's reading isn't limited to just one method. Going to a psychic GP can mean that your psychic session may consist of a brief past-life assessment, sort of like a spiritual medical history, followed by a combo tarot/astrology checkup, ending with a Reiki treatment and a prescription to go home and meditate, burn some white sage, and do grounding exercises. If the psychic GP feels that you need further assistance in delving into what is psychically ailing you, you may be referred to a peer who specializes in an area of psychic readings. If I feel that my client's current confusion isn't really originating from any astrological problematic transits or from a temporary slump in a relationship, I usually recommend going and getting bodywork from a psychic who specializes in energy rebalancing.

Psychic GPs whose clients have hit the skids with a love interest and are also experiencing financial difficulties pose the same problem as a compound fracture would to a medical doctor. Both areas need to be healed before you are wholly fixed. Psychic GPs are the psychic readers that you go to for everything from asking one question to receiving a full-blown psychic reading. They are like your psychic *family doctor*.

What if you only need a quick question answered? Calling a psychic GP is like calling into your regular doctor's office and inquiring about an ache or pain you may be having. If the psychic GP feels that your concern can be solved by answering just one question, then he or she will do so, but if one question leads into another question, which it usually does, then it is best to make an appointment and get a full psychic reading.

The psychic-reader GPs are easy to find, because most psychic-reader phone lines hire psychics with multiple skills. Some will advertise in the local paper, or you can try to find a psychic fair that is being held in your area. Psychic fairs are like a mini trade show for psychics, who rent tables or booths and tout their psychic skills to the curious public. These fairs host psychics with a multitude of psychic talents, and anyone seeking a psychic reading is sure to find some interesting *vibe vendors*. Psychic fairs are held throughout the year but seem to be most prevalent around Halloween, *"witch"* is the season when psychics and readings increase in popularity.

I personally think that all visitors to a psychic fair should be handed a grounding stone instead of getting their hand stamped at the admissions booth. Psychic fairs are notorious for being places of *psychic energy swells*. The massive amounts of psychic-reader energy mixed in with the energy of the visitors at the fair can be as intense as a psychic-energy atomic bomb.

It isn't uncommon for psychic readers to project some heavy vibes toward a competitor's booth, especially if the competitor is extremely popular with clients. Psychics can get jealous of other psychics, just as any other workers can get jealous of co-workers. I've known a few psychic readers who refused to do psychic fairs, because they experienced headaches and psychic attacks from the other psychics at the fair.

Sometimes the psychics at these fairs are so busy with readings that there is hardly enough time for them to clear out the energy residue left over from one client to the next. If you look around, the psychics doing readings at psychic fairs at times look like tired pony-ride ponies at the circus. Giving one psychic reading after another is draining, and it's rare that psychic readers take the proper amount of time they need to rebalance after each reading. You have to be careful not to go to a poorly balanced psychic, because if you are too open energetically there is a chance that you may catch some wacky leftover psychic germs. Energy is transferable, and if your psychic reader of choice looks tired, acts miserable, or seems like he or she hit the wall, then get up and move on. Being read by a psychic who is burned out may transfer some erratic energy into your own aura or energy field if you are not properly protected by grounding yourself first.

Psychic-reader GPs are often your friend's grandmother or mother who reads tarot cards or even a regular deck of playing cards. Sometimes the least conspicuous psychic readers are by far the best. I remember a woman who lived in a tiny apartment in a middle-class neighborhood. Her apartment was modestly decorated with old but well-kept furniture. She never advertised her psychic skills except by word of mouth, and she was truly amazing. She did card readings so she could make money to go play bingo and poker at the local senior center. She did readings by using a regular deck of playing cards. I often wondered if this obscure, modest, and gifted granny could sit in on a game of poker and read the cards as well as play them. I decided to ask her that question one time when I went for a card reading. She laughed and said, "Funny that you ask. I have tried looking at the different cards dealt to me during a game of poker or gin. The cards mostly imply that I should get the hell out of there and save my money." Regardless of her gambling skills, this unpretentious grandmother was truly a gifted card reader.

Another psychic-reader GP who comes to mind is a woman I knew who gave readings at a small occult shop. She was very much like Aunt Clara on *Bewitched*, in that she always seemed confused. This psychic GP not only provided psychic readings, but she was also knowledgeable about candle magick and essential oils. The only problem is that she was somewhat dyslexic, which means that she often got things backward. Everyone who was familiar with her knew that she was a good psychic reader, but sometimes you had to hold your reading notes up to a mirror in order to get the reversed meaning of what she told you.

The psychic GPs handle all types of problems, from relationships to pet issues. Unlike a psychic reader who is strictly a pet psychic, past-life specialist, or medical intuitive, psychic GPs dabble in most forms of psychic-reading services.

The Twilight Master

The *twilight masters* are some of the most mesmerizing psychic readers around, but also the most dangerous. As a seeker of a psychic reading you may think you're dealing with a New Age maharishi well versed in all things metaphysical, when in reality you are dealing with a psychic reader who is more on the dark side. Twilight masters appear to be one thing, but they are actually another. They project a powerful persona, presenting themselves as someone totally connected with the cosmos. The twilight master attempts to seduce an unknowing soul with recaps of futuristic information given to him by spirit guides. Twilight masters are the more polished, high-end version of the stereotypical gypsy.

Twilight masters are usually well educated, well dressed, and boast a degree or two. Their tactic is to give the seeker unsolicited messages from their guides, and then once they win over the seeker's confidence, they begin to manipulate her into not making a move without first consulting them. They are like gurus with a heavy price tag. Some twilight masters are real slick and try the ploy of befriending the client in order to blur the professional boundary line. Twilight masters know that some people feel special having a psychic as a friend, and they use that scheme to extract large amounts of money from their clients.

Psychic readers who work on the dark side are not beyond "working" on their clients by doing a form of psychic dark magick. The twilight master is well skilled in manipulating energy and giving energetic transfusions that are infused with the desires and wants of the twilight master. Skilled twilight masters, even though they are psychic readers, will misuse their sixth sense and totally prostitute themselves to get what they want from their clients. I have heard of clients buying cars, vacations, and all sorts of big-ticket items for twilight masters.

The thing with twilight masters is that you believe they have your best interest in mind, but that's not the case. Twilight masters only care about themselves. They have been known to cast spells upon their clients to keep them emotionally crippled. Trying to free yourself from the grips of a twilight master is even more frightening, because once the twilight master realizes that you are trying to break free from his influence you may find yourself under a psychic attack.

A *psychic attack* occurs when someone sends dark vibes, entities, or dark spirit guides to penetrate another person's energetic body. These dark energies create havoc in the victim's life and cause not only mental but also physical symptoms of discomfort. It is not unusual for someone under psychic attack to be mistaken for having a mental illness. Outbursts of anger and feelings of being hot and cold are also symptomatic of psychic attack. (Sounds a lot like menopause!)

The twilight master who orchestrates the psychic attack uses the power of his mind and psychic skills to control and conquer the victim. I knew of a woman who was a twilight master. Her appearance was nothing out of the ordinary, and her psychic gifts were very well developed. This woman would entangle herself in the private lives of her clients until she got a strong hold; then she would work them psychically in order to get what she wanted. When the clients would try to cut back from her infiltration into their lives, suddenly there would be a catastrophe, sickness, or some other problem that they believed needed the expertise of the twilight master. Little did they know that she was the one working with their energy on the dark side as a way of ensuring her place as the number one *New Age know-it-all* in their lives.

The only way you can free yourself from the grips of a twilight master is to go to someone proficient in energy clearing and basically learn how to use your own psychic shield to ward them off. You have to be street smart and educated about what type of psychic reader you are dealing with. Whenever someone has access to your psyche, there is the potential of falling victim to some unscrupulous mind games.

Whenever you let any psychic reader have access to your energy field, you are walking a fine line between entertainment and danger. You need to know who you are letting into to your psychic space.

Angel Readers

Angel readers are mostly soft-spoken, very calm channelers of angelic messages. They do best with clients who are transitioning into the world of psychic readings and awareness, because the psychic angel reader gives an appearance of being a pseudoreligious messenger, and therefore clients don't think that they are delving into the occult world of psychic readings. Angel readers are like Mickey Finns to clients who are still on the fence concerning metaphysical subjects; they don't even realize they have been slipped a psychic reading. Some people still have to get over the inaccurate belief that psychics are not of the light. As a matter of fact, most psychics are lightworkers, with the word *light* having the same meaning as the phrase *positive energy*. Light is a form of energy.

The word *angel* actually comes from the Greek word for "messenger," and angel readers channel information given to them from these beings who are from the light. Some angel readers make contact with the archangels, at the top of the hierarchy of the angelic realm. Psychic angel readers have reached a higher level of the ascension process and are more spiritually fit to make contact with the angelic forces. As we evolve on a soul level, we reach a higher vibration that becomes closer and more in harmony with that of the angels. In other words, angel readers can raise their energetic vibration to a higher, lighter frequency so as to be in synch with the vibration of the angels.

An angel reader will channel divine, inspirational messages that will serve as guidance for your life choices. You usually don't go to an angel reader to find out if the guy you like is going to call you within the next day or two, but rather to find out if the guy you like is supposed to be on your path with you. Psychic angel readers focus more on angelic messages for you that are meant to help you evolve spiritually and reach a higher vibration.

Angel readers have to know how to attract angelic energy in order to channel messages from these beings. The tools used by the angel reader are usually a deck of angel cards, rose quartz stones, and angelic music to raise the sound, scent, and color vibration. Since angels are of a higher vibration, they are not weighed down by physical form, so they sometimes make their presence known by scent or by signs such as the sudden appearance of a butterfly. Psychic angel readers use certain fragrant incense to change the surrounding vibration in order to make it on the same frequency of the angels. The scents of jasmine and rose are known to be associated with angels, and some who channel angels have noticed those scents in the air while in meditation to connect with the angelic realm. I remember years ago a woman who did angel readings told me that she used different scents in order to attract certain angels. She would use the scent of pine to attract angels associated with healing, the scent of honeysuckle to attract messenger angels, and sandalwood to bring in the angels who worked with creativity.

Angel readers also work with elemental thoughtforms, such as elves, gnomes, fairies, sylphs, undines, mermaids, and salamanders. These elemental thoughtforms work with the different elements: earth, air, water, and fire. Their job is to bridge the vibration between the humans and the angels and help you evolve and become of a higher and lighter vibration. You have to be conscious of what you think, because the thoughtforms will oblige your wishes; any negative thought vibrations will cause a disturbance in the elements around you, such as a flood, electrical malfunction, or, in a collective consciousness situation, severe weather, earthquakes, and natural disasters, which are reflections of how people think as a whole. Negative thoughtforms will bring you what you create by way of your thinking, and you are supposed to learn by your mistakes to make the soul correction for yourself and be more in the frequency of the light. Some of these negative thoughtforms are not elementals, but rather a multidimensional being created out of the clay of continuous negative thinking and negative actions.

The elves and gnomes are of the earth element and aid you in the material world. They will help bring you the opportunities you need to create your physical comforts. Remember that it was the elves who helped Santa build all of the toys and material gifts for the children at Christmas.

The fairies and sylphs are of the air element and will assist you with your creative and communication endeavors. The next time you are stuck on a creative project, try connecting with a fairy. Fairies will assist with style and color and are the interior decorators of the elemental world. The fairies and sylphs will inspire you to create positive things in your life so the earth elementals can help materialize them for you.

The undines and mermaids are of the water element and will help you with your emotions. Call on these elementals when you need to control and communicate how you feel about something. They are also called in for healing and purification. The water elementals are known to make beautiful sounds that can be heard when you listen closely to a waterfall, babbling brook, or the siren song of the ocean.

The salamander is of the fire element and not the same kind of salamander that resembles a lizard. Fire can create or destroy, and it is also purifying. The salamander represents strong transformation energy and is called on when there is a need to make a new, fresh start.

Angel readers want us to realize that we can live in a beautiful, magickal world if we are willing to put more emphasis on what is in our hearts instead of what is in our pockets. Years ago I went to an angel reader who was very much into her profession of communicating with the angels. Her home was like a whimsical cottage, decorated with hanging fairy mobiles, angel statues, angel pillows, and angel lamps. Her cat was even named Angel. This woman also had an enchanted garden that she had accessorized with statues of garden gnomes and garden-gazing balls, which are known to attract elementals. She was a small woman in her sixties with very blond, frizzy hair, and her voice was soft and angelic.

My angel reading with this woman started out with her burning incense to attract my angels. She took some angelica root mixed with frankincense and burned the angelic cocktail upon a charcoal that was placed inside a brass urn. Next, she put on angelic music and tapped on her hanging wind chimes to fill the air with magick. I was instructed to sit comfortably on a chair next to a small, round table that was covered with angel pictures, angel statues, and a plate of dried rose petals. The angel reader asked me to close my eyes and meditate while she called in my assigned angels.

After I sat there for about ten minutes with my eyes closed, the angel reader finally told me to open my eyes. The angel reader was now sitting in the chair on the other side of the small table. In the ten minutes my eyes were closed, she had costumed herself in a white, graduation-style robe and she had put a hair band adorned with stars on her head. The two large stars on her headgear were attached to bouncy springs, and I wondered for a moment if they were some sort of angelic antenna in order to tune in to the angels. To be very honest, at one point I thought that the angel reader was a little kooky when she sprinkled some *glitter angel dust* around the table. She was so totally into the character of being an angel reader that for a moment I actually thought I saw wings.

The angel reader truly amazed me from the start of my reading session, and I was formally introduced to my guardian angel and my helping angels. I felt a rush go through my body as the angel reader began to deliver to me channeled messages from my angelic posse that were all pertinent to my then-current life situation. One message warned me to check the tires on my car because something was wrong. I thought that was a strange message since my car was fairly new and the tires seemed fine. But about two weeks after my angel reading I had the tire pressure checked on my tires just for the heck of it, and the gas station attendant noticed that one of my tires had a slow leak due to a big nail that was in it.

My angel-reading session also gave me messages of guidance, and one thing that I will always remember is the part of the message that told me to do everything with gratitude, including the things that I wish I didn't have to do. That one message has made the biggest difference in my life and has also brought me the most rewards. I found out that my desired outcomes are so much better when I have an attitude of gratitude. The session ended with the angel reader chanting some positive affirmations, and she handed me a little card with an angel picture on it as a reminder that we are never really alone.

As I left her home I heard her holler, "Hey, Leonard! You can come out of the bedroom now." I guess my angel reader had hidden her husband away while she entertained me and my angels. As I pulled out of her driveway, my last glimpse of her reminded me of a fairy godmother who looked like she had just fallen out of a fractured fairy tale. All in all, she was so very sweet and astonishingly gifted.

Other Types of Psychic Readers

There are literally hundreds of ways a person can give a psychic reading. I have only touched on a few of the most popular methods used by psychic readers and sought after by psychic seekers. Other types of psychic readings include *palm reading* (when the lines of the hand are read), *psychometry* (which is the holding of an object belonging to someone in order to extract an energy imprint), *numerology* (the use of numbers to foretell one's destiny), *candle-wax reading* (used to determine the results of a desired intention), *black-mirror scrying* (looking into a mirror and seeing visions as a means of divination), *crystal scrying* (which is similar to black-mirror scrying, but the crystals may amplify and tune in to the future in a different way), *remote viewing* (the ability to see things at a distance and mostly used by the CIA, governments, and police), *animal omens* (the activity and appearance of animals used as warnings or for good fortune), *smoke reading* (the practice of watching the shapes formed by smoke to see the outcome of an event), and the *I Ching* (a Chinese method of divination that involves reading hexagrams).

If you come across someone who is psychic, he or she can even read the vibration in your voice. A true psychic reader doesn't really need props. Psychics are able to look at you and link into your energy field and read you as if you were a blueprint. Clients like to see props, which serve as a buffer between the psychic and the client. If the client doesn't like what is revealed, then the cards, chart, crystal ball, tea leaves, or whatever else can be blamed for the information being presented. Psychic readers have a moral and spiritual obligation to reveal the truth, so anything goes as far as revealing what comes up in a psychic reading.

Keep this saying in mind when getting a psychic reading: "Don't shoot the messenger!"

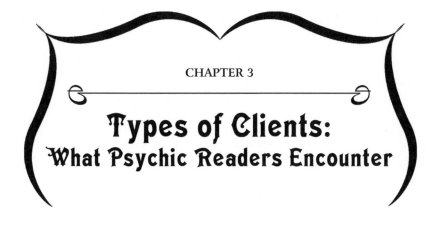

CHAPTER 3

Types of Clients:
What Psychic Readers Encounter

In the previous chapters I offered a brief history of psychic reading and covered the various types of psychic readers. Now, we get into the types of clients. Yes, there are types. *Many* types.

Have you ever wondered what it's like to be on the other side of the tarot cards, astrological chart, teacup, or whatever type of divination method is being used? I'm not only a psychic reader myself; I'm also guilty of being a psychic junkie. I have experienced the role of both psychic and anxious client.

We will take a look at some of the different personality types of clients, and the interesting and often humorous scenarios the psychic reader experiences while trying to break through the often crazy web of frenzied client energy. Just as certain animals possess certain temperaments, the clients who book appointments with psychic readers also have various types of temperaments. These can be as cute as a kitten's or as fierce as a lion's. Some clients are a real handful. It can be like dealing with a hyper kid. The psychic reader doesn't know whether to hand the client the tarot cards to shuffle or a helmet to wear.

I have talked with numerous psychic readers and we all have, at one time or another, dealt with certain client types. Imagine a roundtable discussion consisting of a group of psychics. The discussion group could be called *The Remote View,* where a panel of psychic readers has the opportunity to discuss what it's like to be on the other side of the reading.

Keep in mind that the majority of clients are amazing, and I have grown and learned some valuable life lessons because of my clients. The cumulative life experiences of all of my clients have helped me by giving me the knowledge to help others.

Over the years I have honed my own psychic skills because of the feedback from my *training-wheel clients.* I have also learned to recognize certain client types, and just as a doctor notices a certain symptom in a patient or a psychiatrist is familiar with certain behavioral types that come into the office, as a psychic reader I have noticed that there are some very common types among clients that need to be understood so the psychic reader can better handle the reading. Are some clients difficult? Yes, just as some psychics can be difficult and real ego-trippers.

As a client, I used to wonder what psychic readers thought about me after I left a reading session with them. Did they think that I was making a big deal out of something? Did they think I was desperate and impressionable? When my reading session was over, did they wipe their brow and think that I had asked too many questions? Maybe they thought I was bored and not making any connection with them at all because of my lack of response. I know that I pissed off a lot of tarot readers that I went to because of my habit of *co-reading* the cards with them. Just what do psychic readers go through during their workday?

As you read about the different client personality types that the psychic reader sometimes encounters, keep in mind that my descriptions are meant to be informative in a *street-smart style,* and believe me that the personality types of some psychic readers can be just as quirky. The client stereotypes are not meant to offend anyone, but rather to show you how not to behave during a psychic-reading session if you want to get the most out of it.

I must admit that at one time or another I have been some of the client types that you are about to become acquainted with. By recognizing certain traits in others, I am more able to expose a client type because I know it through owning such behavior myself. Ouch!

And remember, as Confucius said, "No matter where you go, there you are."

The New Client: Mindful or Minefield?

All psychic readers ask themselves this question. The new client who comes for a reading is uncharted territory for the psychic, and as professionals we need to take a quick scan of the new client's auric field to get the right energy feel before we proceed with the reading. The energy of the client coming to get a reading in person is just as intense as the energy picked up over the phone. Sometimes the psychic will pick up the nervousness of the new client, and that type of energy creates a low level of disturbance. Remember, psychics work with energy. Whether they use cards or tea leaves, psychics use those materials as tools to transmit the overall energy of the reading.

New clients are most likely getting a reading because a life situation has presented itself. Clients who get readings at psychic fairs or house parties are more inclined to do it out of curiosity, but the client booking a private session usually has a true need to get some psychic guidance. I can usually tell what type of client I will be dealing with by the sound of the person's voice or even a vibe that I get from their name. Psychic readers sense who is mindful and we also sense who is a *minefield*, booby-trapped with all kinds of issues and problems.

Psychics view new clients as challenging, because we don't know if we are going to make a strong connection psychically with them or not. It is extremely important that clients realize that the first session with a new psychic either makes it or breaks it. Psychics are feeling the pressure more than you may realize. We know that in order to have a satisfied client there can be little room for error. I have talked with many of my peers, and they all seem to agree that the anticipation of the reading has just as much of an effect on them as it does on the client.

A mindful client most likely knows how to conduct themselves during a psychic reading because they have had readings before. They understand that flowing with the energy of the reading will bring about a smooth landing. The minefield client usually has a preconceived notion that no matter what her problem is, the psychic will somehow wave a magick wand and remove the obstacle. The minefield doesn't want to take responsibility for the problem, just a quick fix or a binding guarantee that the reading will somehow dissolve any and all troubles and worries.

A minefield is usually trying to shift blame onto someone else and wants the psychic to validate that notion. The minefield is the type of client who resists advice and usually continues to do what she wants to do regardless of what the psychic says. She usually has at least three or more major issues going on at the same time and comes loaded with problems and complications. Psychic readers experiencing this type of client for the first time find it equivalent to working in a hospital's triage unit.

Here's an example of a minefield. I was dealing with a woman in her early forties who had recently gone through a terrible divorce. For all intents and purposes, she seemed to be doing just fine financially and emotionally. She booked an appointment with me for a tarot reading. Her reason for booking a reading session was that she had recently met a married man and wanted to know if the new guy had any intention of leaving his wife. She spent the first fifteen minutes of her reading trying to convince me that the new man really loved her and that he hated his wife and wanted only her.

I sensed something more from this woman who spoke with such conviction. The cards were shuffled and cut. I began to lay out the tarot, and told her that the new man would be nothing more than a fleeting affair because of some upcoming financial issues. The client, a real minefield, seemed confused. She made it a point to tell me that she had plenty of money, so it must be the new guy's wife spending all of his money, of course! I told her that I picked up a Virgo man and embezzled money. She brushed it off and turned the reading back to her love life.

I gave the woman a few more readings over the course of a few months, and each time the Virgo man and the embezzled money came up, and each time she ignored it. I felt bad. Was I losing my skills as a psychic? The woman certainly contributed to my feelings that I wasn't quite linking into her energy field.

One hot summer afternoon, I received a frantic call from the woman. She was hysterical because there was a detective on his way over to ask her about some missing money from the company where she was the bookkeeper. I asked her if she knew when her boss's birthday was and she told me that it was September 5, a Virgo! I couldn't help it. I had to let her know that the Virgo man I picked up in numerous previous readings had finally revealed himself. She said, "I know, I know."

She pleaded with me to pull a few cards and find out what was going to happen. I told her to calm down and be still so I could tap into the cards. The results weren't good. I saw jail for her. She became extremely upset. I quickly reminded the woman, the minefield client complete with self-sabotaging booby traps, that if she had listened to the previous readings instead of pushing away what she knew was there but refused to believe, she may have been able to avoid this complicated and serious end result.

This client was indeed sent to jail and ordered to make restitution. She told me that another psychic reader had also told her to be careful because someone was going to jail. The client obviously ignored the other psychic reader's warnings, too.

Forming a professional rapport with a new client is like going on a blind date. You don't know what you're in for. It is really stressful to pick up on such negative information and even more stressful to watch a minefield client like the woman I mentioned totally disregard the warnings of the reading.

In defense of new clients, most psychic readers find them to be new and fresh and anticipate helping them with intuitive guidance.

The 1-900 Desperado: Dial "D" for Desperate

Psychic readers who have worked on the 1-900 psychic lines will recognize the *1-900 desperado client*. The desperado, armed with a credit card on the verge of being maxed out, will reach for the phone as soon as there is any turbulence in her life. The procedure usually begins with the desperado placing a call to her favorite psychic phone line. One of the worst things that can happen to the desperado is to have her credit card declined. This type of client will usually try to convince the psychic-line customer service rep that the credit card company made a mistake.

After successfully passing through the abyss of the customer service rep, the desperado must listen to a recorded Rolodex of available psychic readers. The desperado has a list of names to choose from, and often wishes that there were a psychic reader available to psychically pick the right psychic reader. There are exotic names like Magickia, Delphia, Angel Wings, or Song. There are traditional names like Kathy, Mrs. B., John, or Davie. When a choice of psychic reader is finally made, the desperado sits jonesing for a hit of psychic Prozac to arrive on the line to make everything better.

The desperado feels a weird kind of rush as the psychic reading begins. Psychic readers can smell the desperado a mile away. The psychic really wishes that the desperado would calm down and stop hyperventilating so a better psychic connection can be made. For a psychic, dealing with a desperado is like being trapped in a Fellini film: a mix of fantasy and weird baroque images, as the desperado comes at the psychic larger than life with anxious inflections in his every word. The desperado makes the psychic reader nervous. Usually at the end of a call with a desperado, it feels to the psychic like being in an airplane that just had a near miss.

I worked on a psychic phone line for a short amount of time, and I remember my first encounter with a 1-900 desperado. I barely said hello when the desperado began firing her problem at me. She began by telling me that she was on her third divorce attorney, and without coming up for air she said, "What is my ex thinking, doing, or going to do?" The turn of the tarot cards suggested that she best look for attorney number four. Before I could finish my sentence, she was desperately begging me for a name or an initial of the new attorney. I revealed to the desperado that I felt that her new attorney would be a woman, someone who would be a mean cat, ready to pounce on her husband.

The desperado remained edgy as I continued on with the tarot reading, hitting on information she found to be quite useful. The call was about to be cut off, and the desperado begged me to be available so that she could call right back and get more information. She did indeed call back, and she told me that the $2.99-per-minute psychic reading sure beat the hell out of the $375 per hour that she was paying for her primped and preened divorce attorney.

The psychic reader recognizes the desperado clients, and we try our best to calm them down. We pray that our readings will act like a stint in rehab and help them keep off the highly addictive psychic phone lines for the night.

The Persistent Client: Ask Me Ten More Times

All psychic readers have experienced the "ask me ten more times!" client. This seemingly unsatisfied client will repeatedly ask the same question until she gets the answer she wants. The "ten more times" client thinks that she is tricking the psychic by carefully rephrasing the question by using synonyms or similar verbiage.

This "OCD" (obsessive-compulsive disorder) client can mess up the flow of the psychic reading, because she does not let the psychic reader continue on with the additional information that is coming up in the reading. Some clients will spend their whole session constantly rephrasing the same question. It is unbelievable!

I once had a client who had a major crush on her doctor. She came to me often in hopes that a psychic reading would produce the answer she wanted to hear. I was considerate of her feelings, and I tried to tell her numerous times that the doctor liked her but wasn't interested in a personal relationship with her. A session always started out with the question, "How does the doctor feel about me?" Next question: "What does the doctor think about me?" And then: "What did the doctor think when he saw my new haircut?" Followed by: "When will the doctor ask me out?" And so on.

One day I told this woman before we started our session that I really didn't want to spend the whole hour answering questions about a doctor who really didn't care about her other than her being his patient. I told her that the purpose of a psychic reading is to enlighten and present other possibilities. I assured her that if any indication of the doctor developing a romantic interest in her turned up, I would definitely let her know. She agreed to give it a try.

Our tarot session began, and I told her that I did see a relationship for her. I felt that it would begin in the month of October. She was thrilled! Her next question was, "Do you think that he is in the medical profession?" I gave up! Some clients can't overcome their desire to persist until they get the answer they want to hear.

It is the responsibility of the psychic reader to recognize this behavior and discourage the client from living in a fantasy world. I often wonder if the tag on ads for psychic phone lines that says "For Entertainment Purposes Only" is meant for the client or the psychic, because in all honesty, some of the "ask me ten more times" clients are pretty entertaining.

The Answer Client: Is the Answer in the Question?

The client who asks you a question and then answers it before you even get a chance to pull a few tarot cards, tap into his energy, or look at his astrological chart is every psychic reader's dream. The *answer client* makes the job of the psychic reader a breeze. The answer client was probably one of those kids you hated in grade school because he would raise his hand for every question even before the teacher could finish talking. This client has the personality of a *Jeopardy* contestant.

The answer client usually books a psychic reading by calling and saying something along the theme of, "Do you think that it is too soon to get another psychic reading? Because I know that I need one right now." The answer client doesn't even realize that he has just answered his own question with regard to getting a psychic reading; this inquisitive type has determined that the time to get a psychic reading is right now.

Psychic readers like to book this type of client at the end of the day when we are tired, drained, and our brains have been picked for hours on end. The answer client doesn't even expect the psychic to respond, because he is already giving the psychic the answer. Take it from an insider: the psychic knows that the answer client is someone who wants to control the whole psychic reading. Psychic readers who recognize this type of client really find it hard to modify the client's answer reflex. Imagine trying to train a Maltese puppy to be an attack dog, or a greyhound to be a lap dog. Same thing goes for the answer client; he is hard-wired to answer his own questions. It is in his blood to control every single word.

I have a few answer clients. One woman in particular is the poster child for clients of this ilk. She will schedule a psychic reading about once a month to tell me what she wants to hear. The session starts out in the usual manner of shuffling some tarot cards and laying out the spread. The answer client will tell me that she wants to know about a man she just met, because she knows that he likes her and wants to ask her out. The answer client just told me what she expects to hear from the psychic reading. If the tarot cards reveal a different outcome, the answer client will quickly do some damage control and immediately answer by saying something to the effect of, "Well, it shows that I won't be going out with him because he's too shy." I don't remember pulling any tarot cards that imply that the man in question is shy, but the answer client has already given me the answer, which in her mind overrides any other explanation that I give to her.

One time I asked the answer client to let me do the psychic reading for her while she just took notes, not responding unless I said she could. She agreed to try it, only because I told her that I was trying a new method of giving psychic readings and that I wanted her to be the first to experience the new "silent session." At the end of the session, the answer client went over her notes and read them back to me. As you can guess, I didn't recognize a single phrase. The answer client had written down only that which she wanted to believe.

Psychic readers often wonder why the answer client even bothers to get psychic readings. Answer clients would get a better reading if they would try to control themselves long enough and let the psychic do the interpretations. After all, isn't that the premise for getting a psychic reading in the first place?

The Psychic Debunker: The Tester

The *psychic debunker client* is boot camp for the psychic reader. This type of client expects the psychic to part the Red Sea like Moses or bend spoons like Uri Geller before he'll give the psychic any credit for being a legitimate psychic reader. As psychic readers, we realize that the debunker client is on a mission to prove us, the psychic, as being wrong.

The debunker client is immediately recognized by the psychic as someone who has trust issues. Why do debunker clients even bother to go to a psychic for a reading, you may ask, especially if they are quasi-nonbelievers to begin with? The truth of the matter is that the debunker client really does want to believe in psychic readings, but because of trust issues he is afraid to let his guard down and really see what a psychic reading is all about. The debunker is busy planning how to give the psychic a trick question, most likely based on false information. The debunker will usually remove his wedding ring or any other signs of personal commitment before showing up for his psychic-reading appointment.

The psychic recognizes this client as a closet psychic junkie, albeit one who has not yet been outed as such. The debunker claims to have gone to dozens of psychics, and in his opinion all of them have been way off target and wrong. In reality, the debunker is getting accurate information from the psychic readings but won't give the psychics any kudos for being accurate. The debunker, prone to insecurity and trust issues, refuses to validate any psychically perceived information. The debunker is really a scared client, afraid to believe. This client's "I'll prove you wrong" attitude is most likely a common theme in other areas of his life, too.

The debunker is like a schoolyard bully who really wants to be your friend, but must set the pecking order straight by trying to win you over through intimidation. We all know that type of behavior doesn't really get you anywhere. The debunker is power tripping, thinking that he can outsmart the psychic but really afraid that the psychic will tell him something that he would rather not hear yet wants to know. The debunker is also afraid that the psychic reader can see what he truly is. Remember that knowledge is the true power, and the debunker fears the power of psychic perception. As you can see, this is a tough client for psychics to handle. The debunker expects the complete dog-and-pony show from the psychic.

I know a few psychic readers, myself included, who have dealt with one particular debunker client, a woman who actually put a psychic on the verge of a nervous breakdown. This client was tough to begin with, very high-strung, rude, and extremely demanding. She would make appointments with psychic readers so she could get her "debunking fix" for the day. The debunker would get her psychic reading, totally disregard all of the information, go out of her way to change things up, self-sabotage herself, and then call up the psychic and scream, "You were wrong! Wrong! Wrong!"

This debunker contacted me for a psychic reading, and after every statement I made she would say, "I don't believe it." I told the debunker during her session that a business proposal that she was working on would go through, but her client might want to change the delivery date of the finished product. The debunker just made her usual huffing and sighing noises over the phone; I was watching the clock, anticipating every minute left so I could wrap up her session. I found out later that the debunker's business plan did go through, and only because she agreed to a different delivery date. The debunker tried to cover up by telling me that it was her idea to change the delivery date, not the client's as I had predicted.

You can't win with an insecure person like the debunker. The debunker will never give you credit for being right but will waste no time in telling you when you are off the mark. Let me pose this example to you: if a doctor tells you to take your medicine so you will recover, but instead you don't take your meds and you stay sick, then who is wrong, you or the doctor? If a psychic reader tells you information, but you purposely don't take the information seriously and you experience a different outcome, then who is wrong, you or the psychic?

All debunker clients, please take note that psychic readers notice the slightly discolored skin and vague indentation on your ring finger more than they would notice your wedding ring if you were still wearing it. So a word of advice: leave your rings on your fingers. Removing them really doesn't influence your psychic reading one way or another.

The Chatterbox: Where's the Off Switch?

The *chatterbox client* really isn't a difficult client, but this client won't get the most out of a psychic reading because she will talk throughout the whole session. A chatterbox is always enthusiastic about getting a psychic reading, and she anticipates her appointment with the excitement of a kid looking forward to a birthday.

The chatterbox will begin the session by telling the psychic reader every detail of her day. This talkative type even has a tendency to talk at the same time the psychic is talking. Chatterbox clients seem a little ADD, but overall they are usually very sweet. Throughout the whole session, the chatterbox is commenting after every word. Psychic readers really wish that they could put the chatterbox on Ritalin so they could calm the client down enough to comprehend what is going on with their psychic-reading session.

The chatterbox experience for the psychic is like going to the movies with someone who talks throughout the whole show. The psychic really doesn't want to be rude to this harmless client, but finds it hard to concentrate and really give a good reading when someone is talking constantly during the session. All chatterbox clients have one thing in common: when their psychic-reading session is over, they always remark that they can't believe that their time is already up! The chatterbox will still have questions to ask the psychic reader, even long after the reading is finished. If the chatterbox would have been quiet, then the psychic reader would have been able to delve deeper into the issues at hand.

Most psychics have at least one chatterbox client. I have a very sweet woman for whom I give readings, and she is a nonstop talker. This woman has left so many messages for me that she's filled my voicemail to capacity. Psychics don't expect their clients to sit through a psychic-reading session in total silence, but at the same time, constant talking doesn't allow the psychic any time to focus. It becomes very distracting.

Psychics want clients to be involved in their sessions, but they feel bad for the chatterbox clients because they do not take advantage of their appointment time. The chatterbox is a "frequent flyer" type of client because it is necessary for her to book numerous appointments for psychic readings just so she can get all of the intended information that she originally kept talking through. The chatterbox should try to control her constant impulse to talk; doing so would greatly cut down on the number of psychic readings required in order to access the desired insights.

The Daily Doppler: Where Is My Psychic Barometer?

The *daily Doppler* client is always looking for a daily *psychic-weather report*. This client type wants continuous updates concerning every little change or nuance for any given situation of the moment. Daily Doppler clients will call their psychic reader once or twice per day to get a personal psychic-weather report.

We all know that the weather outside can change dramatically within a very short period of time. For example, it may rain for twenty minutes or an hour and then become sunny and clear. Likewise, daily Doppler clients will call at the slightest hint of any change in their own personal "atmosphere," and they require quick psychic insight as to what has caused the change. This type of client will want to know if the upcoming forecast promises to clear away any cloudy issues. One might think that daily Doppler clients could just read their horoscope every day, but in all honesty the information is usually too vague. Reading a few sentences about their zodiac sign isn't enough of a psychic-weather report for the Doppler clients.

Daily Doppler clients want their psychic to be a personal thermostat, showing every fluctuation in the temperature of life. Just as barometric pressure measures the weight of the atmosphere, the Doppler clients want tarot cards, a crystal ball, or the hourly changes in the degree of the Moon to provide them with frequent updates about each day. The psychic doing the reading for this type of client is like the Doppler client's special barometer, giving a readout on vibe changes and moods. Psychics can get frustrated with these continuous psychic-weather updates, because these clients tend to focus on the little variations or changes around them and have a tendency to miss out on the overall climate of their life. Daily readings run the risk of being very myopic and limiting by paying too much attention to incidental details. Doppler clients aren't focusing on the end result.

Just as a meteorologist makes daily weather predictions that can easily change due to some temporary disturbance in the atmosphere, the psychic doing frequent psychic-weather readings also picks up temporary fluctuations in the client's day that are subject to frustrating little changes from outside pressure. Psychics really find that doing these types of daily readings lower the overall vibration of the psychic/client relationship, because of the constant ups and downs in the normal rhythm of any given day. Such readings can actually minimize the client's respect for psychic insight.

Daily Doppler clients sometimes go as far as to e-mail, text, or phone in their moment-by-moment life changes. They expect the psychic to respond as if the psychic were on stand-by, a weather satellite just waiting to spit out continuous monitoring for the client's day.

I have had a few Doppler clients, and for me they are like a group of kids on a long drive who keep asking, "Are we there yet?" Doppler clients are always anxious, and they feel the need to know the meaning behind every little thing that happens to them. These clients don't like surprises. Dopplers most likely peek inside birthday-gift boxes, since the idea of not knowing can drive them crazy. There is also a tendency for the Doppler client to be a little control-freakish when it comes to relationships with others.

A particular client comes to mind when I think of daily Dopplers. A few years ago a woman came to me about . . . what else? A dating relationship with a noncommittal guy. The object of her desire had lied to her about the romantic relationships that he was simultaneously having with other women. She wanted all of her readings centered on this man. I told her during one of her first sessions with me that she would date this guy for a while, but eventually she would wind up with someone else. That information didn't even faze her. She would call me on a daily basis to find out what this particular guy was feeling, doing, and thinking about her. A simple thing like getting a text message from him would send this client running for the phone to call me for some psychic insight into his message to her.

Her constant phone calls to me went on for a while, and at times this client would get frustrated and nasty because her disappointments with this guy were many, and she often didn't like her daily psychic-weather forecast.

I am usually patient with my clients, but one thing I will not tolerate are offensive, belligerent attitudes. It screws up my energy flow and has a direct impact on my subsequent readings for clients booked on that day. I told this impatient Doppler client that this guy would blow in and out of her life like the wind, but the bottom line is that there would be someone else for her.

If I mentioned anything other than information about the guy she was interested in during our sessions, she would say, "I don't want to hear about that stuff. Move on and tell me about the guy I like." She was actually missing out on other, more pertinent information by limiting her daily psychic-weather reports to this one particular area of her life and not the overall climate.

I told her that I picked up that this guy would change his mind about going on a vacation with her, and she flipped out. She said that a few weeks previously I had told her that I saw them spending some exclusive time together, which could possibly mean a weekend away somewhere or a mini vacation. She started to get pissed off at me because her personal psychic forecast had changed due to some outside wind blowing in, namely a new woman that the guy she was after had just met.

I finally told this client what I had tried to tell her so many times before in a nice, easy manner: that daily psychic-weather readings can fluctuate like the weather outside. But she wouldn't take the hint. She pushed me to the point of giving her some kick-ass, street-smart psychic advice about getting readings. I said, "What do you want? A psychic reading or a weather report? Things change, and neither you nor I can stop the guy you're interested in from changing his mind, meeting other women, or doing what he wants to do. Psychic readings will not control his life, but they will give you, the client, some valuable insight into this guy's bullshit so you can move on away from him and meet someone more deserving of you."

I also told this client that just because this guy canceled a vacation with her didn't mean that he wouldn't reschedule another weekend away with her. I told her that getting too caught up on one particular little change in the weather does not a whole climate make. I reminded her to look at the final outcome: the promise of meeting someone else better suited for her.

I can tell a client that a road trip will end at a beautiful resort. Does that mean that the trip along the way will not be eventful in any way? Temporary stops, scenery, and traffic are all part of the trip. How long you choose to take a break or stop along the way is up to you. Detours don't necessarily mean you won't get somewhere; it's just that it may take you a little longer to arrive. Focus on the destination, while enjoying and experiencing the journey.

If I find that a client is becoming a daily Doppler, I remind the client of the many changes in daily psychic-weather reports, and I caution them not to get too hung up on the little reports but rather to look at the whole forecast. Occasional psychic-weather report readings are all right, especially if the client has a temporarily big issue going on, but other than that, daily psychic-weather reports can actually make a client become too dependent on psychic readings. Tempting as it may be, psychic readings are really not to be treated like constant security-blanket conferences or client thumb-sucking sessions.

The Midnight Caller: It's Always Time for a Reading!

The *midnight caller* is definitely a client going through meltdown mode. Many a psychic reader has been jolted awake and scared to death by the sudden sound of a ringing telephone. The midnight caller has a problem, which means the psychic reader also has a problem. A majority of midnight-caller problems are relationship related. A midnight caller thinks that psychic readers are always awake and tuck their tarot cards under their pillows just in case the impulsive psychic junkie needs a nightcap.

Some psychic readers have clients located in different time zones. When a client is melting down at midnight in Los Angeles, that can translate into a psychic reader in New York getting a call at three o'clock in the morning. Psychic readers who work the late shift on psychic phone lines welcome the midnight caller. It beats the monotony of playing tarot-card solitaire.

The midnight caller usually starts the conversation with, "Oh, my God! I am so glad you answered. You weren't sleeping, were you?" Even if the psychic is half-asleep and speaking in a groggy voice, the midnight caller will beg for a psychic reading. The midnight caller will plead with the psychic to talk, if only for a few minutes. The problem in question, nine out of ten times, is about a relationship: a boyfriend who didn't call back or an argument with a love interest are the most common reasons for the call, and the midnight caller has to know at this very moment if her love interest is seeing someone else.

Midnight callers have two modes: crying or pissy. Psychic readers handle this client by trying to calm her down and tell her that the problem can be dealt with during the day. A doctor will send a patient who gets sick in the middle of the night to an emergency room. Psychic readers may send their client to a twenty-four-hour psychic-line tarot-card trauma unit so the midnight caller can get some emergency attention.

One time I asked a midnight-caller client if she thought it might be better to call me the next day at a more reasonable hour. She responded by asking, "Can't we do it now? I won't be able to sleep unless I talk to you." I pulled out my tarot cards and laid them out across my pillow, knowing that I also wouldn't be able to sleep unless I talked to her. I wondered for a moment if I was being a psychic-junkie enabler, dealing tarot cards like drugs in order to calm the nerves of a jittery client.

Believe me, from the psychic reader's side of the tarot cards: you will get a much better psychic reading if the psychic is awake.

The Co-Dependent Client: I Can't Do It Alone!

The co-dependent client needs a psychic reading for every single thing she does. This customer will call the psychic reader sometimes more than once a day. She is a serial dialer and keeps the psychic's phone number on speed dial. Co-dependent clients can drive a psychic reader crazy. Psychics are empathetic to begin with, so we try not to hurt anyone's feelings. But in all honesty, co-dependent clients can really drain the life out of a psychic.

Usually, the psychic will hit the psychic trifecta and get a co-dependent client who exhibits anxiety, paranoia, and delusion. This type of client is always jumpy, thinking that her own decisions aren't right. Some co-dependent clients definitely aren't playing with a full tarot deck, and psychic readers really have a responsibility not to exploit this type of client. The psychic reader wants the co-dependent client to realize that looking at her astrological chart or pulling a few tarot cards from a deck will not necessarily take care of every problem.

The co-dependent client wants to become the psychic's best friend, in hopes that constant psychic advice will be part of the friendship package. Some co-dependent clients form a psychic-reader *Fatal Attraction* and will go as far as to track a psychic down if she is not home. The co-dependent client is prone to stopping by the psychic's home or office unannounced, and calling outside of the scheduled appointment time. Psychics want to give psychic guidance, not become the co-dependent client's conscience.

It is often like going through a breakup when the psychic tries to get the co-dependent client to function independently from the psychic. The psychic starts to refuse calls and won't return calls to the co-dependent client. Sometimes, going cold turkey is the only way to get this type of client to get a grip on her overdependence on psychic readings. Psychic readings are meant to be respected, not abused.

The co-dependent client says the same thing at the start of every phone call to a tarot reader: "Will you pull just three cards for me? I want to see what the cards say! Why don't you just flip three cards? Ask the cards." (For some odd reason, co-dependent clients seem to like the number three.)

I've had co-dependent clients call me outside of an appointment and ask me if I would just pull three tarot cards to see if they should go home after work or go out with their friends. I've had co-dependent clients call and ask me to pull a few cards to see if they should get their hair cut in a new style. I've had clients call me from their cell phone while stopped at a traffic light just so they could ask me to pull cards. I even had a co-dependent client call and ask me to pull a few tarot cards to see why her bowel movement was greenish in color. One time, a co-dependent client called me while she was standing in line in a department store and asked me to pull three tarot cards to see if they would tell her to buy the black dress or the silver dress for an upcoming wedding.

Psychic tarot readers know that there is no such thing as just pulling a few tarot cards for a co-dependent client. The co-dependent client tries to manipulate the psychic into a full-blown tarot spread. Co-dependent clients need to realize that the conditions for getting a good reading are not being met if they call a psychic from their cell phone to get daily "drive-by readings" while sitting in traffic. We take our work seriously. If you want a quick answer for every little question, then you should buy a Magic 8-Ball and shake that for guidance. The co-dependent client exhibits all the symptoms of becoming an ultimate psychic junkie, one for whom numerous daily readings from various psychics has become an obsession.

The Viper: Slowly Sucking Energy Levels Dry

The *viper* is an energy vampire, and psychic readers usually drop this type of client after one or two sessions. The viper is a miserable person to begin with, who lives in victim consciousness, and this type of toxic energy exchange between psychic and client can be as detrimental to the psychic as kryptonite is to Superman. A session with a viper client can wipe out the psychic's energy for a few days. This type of client is always angry and ready to blame all personal troubles on someone else, attempting to vent hostility toward the psychic reader. Blame is the opposite of responsibility. The viper takes no responsibility for her actions.

This client approaches a psychic reading with an attitude of entitlement. The viper is an energy vampire because she gets her fuel through overpowering others. A psychic knows how to spot an angry viper client. This client always seems to have an angry inflection in her voice and treats the psychic reading as if it were her personal bitch session. Psychics deal with energy and this type of client is an immediate turn-off. Psychics have no desire to venture into the viper's dirty pool of problems.

The problem with a viper is that the *viper* is the problem. A viper is usually rude to the psychic throughout a session. These viper clients evidently don't realize that they are definitely not going to get a good reading by having a venomous approach toward the psychic. Once any feelings of animosity or anger enter into the session, it is all over, for those feelings are like lead walls that the psychic finds difficult to break through. Psychic readers can identify the root and cause of the anger, and nine out of ten times it lies within the viper.

The viper, because of some hurt either imagined or real, is now on a spree of self-sabotaging behavior. When the psychic attempts to convey the identified problem to the viper, the viper goes into defense mode. Vipers really need an anger-management group or a shrink more than they need a psychic reading.

I know a psychic who lost her patience with a viper during a session and actually threw her deck of tarot cards at her unpleasant client. The viper even called the psychic again to see if she could book another psychic-reading session! The psychic refused. Some vipers get off on getting a reaction and trying to set up situations where others look bad.

I have had a few viper clients. One client in particular was so miserable that I lost my cool and freaked out on her. This woman definitely had a black belt in wicked manners. During the session this client was trying to direct my every move and injecting her negative energy into my personal space. I told this viper what I was picking up in her reading, and she got upset because it wasn't what she wanted to hear. She tried to get me to tell her what she wanted to hear, and when I refused to tell her anything other than what I was picking up, she got nasty and belligerent. I told her that my fee for the psychic reading would automatically be doubled if she expected me to listen to her vicious ranting.

I believe this woman was really into psychic S&M, as she called me again for another reading. I scheduled her for a telephone session against my better judgment, but I psychically felt that I had to deal with her one more time. In either case, it would be me or the viper who needed the lesson. Maybe we both needed the lesson. The viper called ahead of schedule. When I told her she had to call back in five minutes, she got pissed. We were already off to a bad start. It became a psychic power-play session. She called back, and her usual nasty mood was amplified because I made her follow my rules of appointment-keeping.

I started the session by telling her about upcoming trends I saw for her in her astrological chart. The viper wasn't impressed, telling me, "Let's move it along. I don't want to know about that stuff. Just tell me the best astrological time to get the other girl in my office fired." The viper also wanted the reading to assure her that her ex-husband would grow old alone, with no one around to change his diapers. That was it for me. I told the viper to put the phone real close to her ear and listen carefully. What she heard was the sound of me ripping up her astrological chart. I walked into the bathroom, and the next sound the viper heard was the sound of me flushing her ripped-up astrological chart down the toilet.

I told this viper never to call me again, and reminded her of all the negative karma that she was creating for herself by looking for the best time to hurt someone. The viper was shocked. She never saw it coming, because I had been patient with her in previous psychic-reading sessions. The viper tried to smooth things over, but I knew that she wasn't sincere. I told her that I wouldn't read for her anymore.

Most psychic readers will not tolerate any mean people as clients. The vipers are like nomad clients, who must go from one psychic to the next in hopes of finding someone who will tolerate the abuse.

The Crybaby: Take a Deep Breath and Count to Ten

Psychic readers are all very familiar with the *crybaby client*. The appointment starts out with the psychic trying to make out the words of the client who is uncontrollably heaving and crying. Psychic readers get nervous when there are too many tears. The psychic first has to identify why the client is crying. The crybaby client has usually just experienced some bad news and wants a psychic reading for assurance that everything will eventually work out and be fine. Psychics can't wave a magick wand and make the problem disappear, yet the psychic does want the crybaby client to feel assured that a psychic reading will give insight to the problem and, hopefully, a resolution to the crisis of the moment.

The crybaby client would be best served if he regained his composure before calling for a reading. Keep in mind that psychic readers work with energy, and the crying is adding static to what we are trying to pick up psychically for the client. Psychics can be stymied by continuous crying, because it makes us wary of telling an oversensitive client any information that might increase the tears. The psychic realizes that the crying is just a release for another emotion, which is usually fear. Fear and hurt go hand in hand; the crybaby client is afraid of getting hurt.

Once the crybaby client calms down enough to speak between sobs, the psychic can get into the session and begin to pick up on a solution or outcome to the problem. Crybaby clients perceive all problems as larger than life and overwhelming. The key word here is *perceive*. The psychic tries to convey to the crybaby client that the extent of the power of his problem is in his *perception* of the problem. If a problem is perceived as being insurmountable, then it will be insurmountable; if a problem is perceived as having a solution, it will be resolved. The mind is a powerful thing, and what is envisioned can be created.

The psychic doesn't want to hand the client tissues throughout the reading. The psychic wants the client to stop crying, get centered, and start acting on the solution rather than the problem. The problem exists, and that won't change. The psychic wants to focus on the solution because the solution has yet to take place, and therefore the client has a better chance of achieving a desired outcome.

I have dealt with crybaby clients who continue to cry even when I give them good news. I guess it's true that laughing and crying are the same release. For a psychic reader there is nothing quite like the experience of picking up the phone, saying "Hello," and hearing uncontrollable whining on the other end. Psychics do what they can to make the crybaby dry the tears, but the nicer and more sympathetic the psychic is, the more it feeds the crying jag.

I find that the best way to get a crybaby client through a reading is to ask him to get ahold of himself before proceeding with the reading. The magick words to say to the crybaby at the beginning of the psychic reading are, *Stop crying!* These words are like throwing cold water in the face of the crybaby. It shocks the client into gaining composure so the psychic reader can give an accurate reading. And the crybaby client will retain more information from the reading once the crying comes to a halt.

The Scaredy Cat: Don't Tell Me about Death!

Psychic readers love this client. The *scaredy cat* approaches the reading as if she were being led to the gallows. The scaredy cat is curious about her future, but only to the extent of not being told about death or accidents. This client will make an appointment with the same trepidation that Pandora had while opening the mysterious box. The scaredy cat wants to know, but is afraid to know. Psychics will oblige the scaredy cat's wishes of only being told good things, but what if the psychic sees an accident that can be avoided if the scaredy cat is aware of a possible pending occurrence?

The scaredy cat has to realize that by scheduling an appointment for a psychic reading, she is opening the doors to the unknown. The psychic is stumped during a reading if he has to go around certain psychically picked-up information and only deliver news that is cherry picked and sugarcoated. Scaredy cats are always on the edge of their seats during their readings, and they read into every action and nuance of the psychic. If the psychic hesitates too long before speaking, the scaredy cat thinks the psychic is seeing something bad.

Scaredy-cat clients are sometimes afraid of the good news, also. I told a scaredy cat that I saw a job change for her, and right away she wanted to know if that meant she would be fired from her current job. I assured her that the job change was a promotion for her within the same company. The scaredy cat was now afraid that she wouldn't be capable of doing the duties of her new foretold job. She just found another reason to anguish!

Psychic readers realize that the scaredy cat approaches things with fear, so it is wise to be gentle with this client. Scaredy cats are afraid of not being prepared, and that is the main reason they get psychic readings. Scaredy cats keep pushing the bar of the unknown, as long as there is no information about death or accidents in the reading. The scaredy cats seem to get frequent readings, just so they can be certain that there is no impending doom.

The Delusional Damsel: Fantasy-Relationship Groupies

The *delusional damsel* is a common client for the psychic reader. Don't get me wrong: men can be delusional clients, too, but the lion's share seems to consist mostly of delusional women concerned about a personal relationship. The delusional damsel wants a psychic to listen to all of the unrealistic, fantasy details about a "never gonna happen" relationship. This client is prone to becoming an obsessed groupie toward the object of her desire. Delusional damsels believe that every man they meet is their soul mate. It gets to a point where psychics feel like throwing up if they hear the term *soul mate* one more time.

A psychic really has her work cut out with this type of client. The main objective of the psychic reader is to get this client grounded and prepared to recognize the best relationship for her. A reading begins with the delusional damsel seeking psychic information about another person who either has no interest in her or a person who is spouting lies and BS. The delusional damsel will insist that the perceived love interest is sincere and wants a relationship. The psychic knows better than to weave any more thread into this disastrous attraction.

During a psychic reading, the delusional damsel will block out any information other than what she wants to believe about the man in question. The delusional damsel will ask the psychic reader questions like "What is he thinking about me? When will he realize that he loves me? When will he see me exclusively?" The psychic wants the delusional damsel to realize that we are not playing *Fantasy Island*; we are attempting to give an honest psychic reading.

Delusional damsels sometimes get caught up in relationships with cheaters, and they have this whole thing going on in their heads about a future with these people. The delusional damsels want a reading to confirm and validate their unrealistic approach to the relationship in question. These unaware clients are relentless in holding on to their beliefs, and it is almost as if they are trying to get inside the psychic's head and control the reading.

The delusional damsel tries a bevy of manipulative moves in order to influence the reading. The delusional damsels fall into two subtypes. Type one is fixated on a man who doesn't even know that the delusional damsel exists and, therefore, the psychic reader is put into a position to bring the delusional damsel back down to earth. This type of delusional damsel forms a crush on someone, and then blows the whole thing into a fantasy relationship. A type-one delusional damsel probably started out as someone who would imagine a relationship with a movie star or another celebrity, thus cultivating unrealistic expectations in relationships, which carry over into daily adult life.

The second type of delusional damsel is more voracious in getting who they want. This type will call, stalk, and completely pursue a relationship beyond the mode of a crush. This predator of lust wants to capture her prey. This type of delusional damsel is often caught up in a relationship with a cheater, and she expects the psychic to tell her how awful the cheater's wife or girlfriend is, so that the delusional damsel can feel justified in saving this man from such a mean woman.

There are also instances when delusional damsels will get a psychic reading because they're looking for advice on how to resurrect a dead relationship. Psychic readers can't raise the dead, let alone restore a defunct relationship, but they can psychically pick up the best outcome, if only the delusional damsel would listen.

I have dealt with my share of women who sit by the phone waiting for a call that never happens, or anticipate an invitation for a date from a man who doesn't want to be bothered beyond casual conversation. I had a client who was seeing a married man. Numerous readings with me and other psychic readers confirmed for this woman that this man was just looking for a booty call and nothing more. Yet she would twist and turn information given to her from a reading into her own version of what was going on. She expected me to answer questions with tarot cards and astrological charts concerning weird, hypothetical circumstances that were rooted in her head.

My readings for her would always point to a marriage later in life with a man who was a few years younger than her. This psychically picked-up information was totally disregarded, and she would frustrate me by wanting only to get information about a relationship with a certain man that had no credence. She would say, "Pull a few cards and tell me when he'll leave his wife." The answer would be the same: the man and his wife will separate in a few years, but he would wind up with a woman other than my client. The client didn't want to believe that outcome, regardless of how many times I told her.

Delusional-damsel clients can't accept that type of answer. They want a psychic fantasy, not a psychic reading. I was finally blunt with the client, and told her that the man in question didn't love her. As a matter of fact, I picked up that he was going to back away from her. Instead of going with what was being psychically revealed to her, the delusional-damsel client asked me, "How long will the breakup last before we get back together?"

Giving the delusional damsel a reading is like an arm-wrestling match for the psychic reader. The reading becomes a battle of wills, and delusional damsels don't give in easily.

Who knows? Maybe the persistent fantasies of the delusional damsel are merely a dress rehearsal for a real relationship at some point in time.

Albert Einstein said, "Reality is merely an illusion, albeit a very persistent one."

The "Into-It" Client: The Savvy Seeker

The client who is into it really brings the energy of enthusiasm, openness, and interest to her psychic-reading session. This client is extremely savvy about divination and psychics. *"Into-it" clients* are the carnivores of the psychic reading client pool, because they want the real meat of the psychic reading. This type of client sinks her teeth into the energy of the psychic reading and is fully ready to be nourished by all of the insights and information that the psychic has to offer. This client knows the drill and respects all boundaries.

Into-it clients base most of their daily decisions on the signals that they get from their own intuition, and often seek out psychics and psychic readings as a form of second opinion. In the word *intuition*, you have "in-tu-I," or the practice of going into your own self for the cosmically connected answer rather than the logically devised answer to your query. Ideally, if both the intuitive and the logical sides of ourselves worked in harmony, then decisions could be made that pleased both the material world and the spiritual or energetic world. The problem lies in getting the ego, which resides in the logical side of us, to step back and trust that the intuitive side can also handle life's situations and obtain good outcomes.

The into-it client is like a paralegal who knows the law but doesn't practice the law, or a surgical nurse who assists during an operation but doesn't actually perform the surgery. The into-it client is well read, knowledgeable, and educated about divination, psychics, psi energy, and most other metaphysical subject matter. Even though this client type is hooked up to their own intuition, they do not give psychic readings for others. Into-it clients don't consider themselves to be good enough to do psychic readings professionally, because they worry that the bridge between their intuitive self and psychic self isn't developed enough. Their intuitive side allows the into-it clients to peek inside their own energetic field for answers based on the feelings that they get from their specific chakra or energy centers. These clients read the responses of their own particular feelings like a book, and can be quite psychic concerning perception of their personal issues. They are comfortable with their private intuition and rudimentary psi aptitudes, but doubt their capacity to be psychic conduits for other people. Psychic development beyond individual intuition allows for the developed intuitive/psychic's skills to go beyond themselves and tap into someone else's energy zone, thus providing for the ability to psychically scope things out for others.

Into-it clients are still shy about going outside of their safe personal energy sector, and prefer to remain in the subgroup of psychics who limit their practice to self-healing and a few gut feelings about people who are close to them. It is like someone with a good voice who prefers just to sing in the shower. They are basically shy and need to stop letting their ego, the logic-oriented protective force, send them the message that they might make a mistake or be wrong if they attempt to give a psychic reading to someone.

The into-it client comes to a psychic-reading session totally prepared. They are like good students who have completed their homework lessons. This is one client type who knows how to ground out their own energy before attempting to get a psychic reading, and is quite aware of how to make the connecting cord work between the psychic reader and the client. The into-it client has realistic expectations of what a psychic reading is all about, and rarely if ever asks frivolous questions or desires a psychic reading based on hypothetical situations. This is a client who believes in "keepin' it real."

The into-it client who gets a psychic reading from a psychic telephone service is usually on the other end of the line with their feet flat on the floor for grounding purposes, and has also done a preliminary, pre-psychic reading meditation. This client type will have a notepad or tape recorder handy and will be prepared to log information during the course of her psychic reading. Handwritten notes are taken during the reading session in case the tape recorder malfunctions due to the combined intense psychic energy of both the psychic and client that may affect the electrical charge in the air. It can happen. The scribed information will serve as a crib sheet or answer page, which is often kept in a safe place for future reference.

Some into-it clients prefer to get their readings in person. Psychic readers can tell when they have an into-it client sitting across from them. The first giveaway is the fact that into-it clients often smell like a hot, just-out-of-the-oven pork roast, because they have cleared their energy zone by burning white sage and fanning the smoke toward themselves as a clearing essence before leaving the house to go to their psychic-reading appointment. The next clues that tell the psychic the client is an into-it are the hematite, crystal, and other metaphysical adornments, decorating the into-it client and making her look like a psychic-reading prom queen.

Into-it clients know the routine as if they were the understudy for the main part of psychic reader. This client takes the customary three deep breaths before the psychic-reading session begins and is appropriately responsive to the psychic throughout the appointment. This client comes prepared with a list of things to cover during the session and always makes sure that the energy of the psychic session is closed off properly when the reading is over. At the end of the reading, the into-it client will bow her head to show respect for the gift of third-eye seeing, take three deep closing breaths, and fold her arms and cross her ankles as a way to properly shut down her own personal psychic centers. She closes the hatch to her crown chakra—the linking center to the universal, spiritual source residing above her head—as if it were the hatch to the Starship Enterprise. The into-it client always thanks the psychic reader to show gratitude, and promptly pays for the reading so an energy imbalance will not occur. This client is about grounding, gratitude, and balance.

I remember a psychic session that I did for an into-it client. This particular client called me for a reading and asked me a lot of questions to make sure that I was balanced enough to read for her psychically. When this client called for her appointed session, I could hear her selection of New Age music playing in the background and she rang some wind chimes before our session started to calm the energy. I thought to myself, this client is pretty cool. I think that I can really get into reading for her.

I must admit that, even though I consider myself well versed in metaphysical subject matter, there is a time when the student becomes the teacher. My into-it client actually turned me on to the practice of visualizing a violet ray surrounded by white light streaming into my crown chakra before starting a psychic-reading session. It was like being introduced to a new flavor of Häagen-Dazs that you just can't get enough of. The violet-ray practice really enhances the psychic connection between psychic and client. I asked the into-it client if she would be taking notes or taping our session, and the answer I got surprised me. She told me that she would be holding her clear quartz crystal throughout our session, because the crystal would act as a psychic iPod and energetically download the information from the psychic reading into its database. How about that: a quartz crystal iPsi. She told me that she puts the activated crystal into her pillowcase, then she sleeps on her psychic files to fully absorb the contents of her reading. I thought that it was little different, but actually a cool idea.

When our session was over, my into-it client didn't miss a beat. She asked me to psychically disconnect my psychic ethernet wire from her and to stay on the line while she tapped three times on the top of her head to close off her crown chakra.

Hey! It's all in a night's work.

The Sleeper Client: Reading Time Is Nap Time

Sleeper clients are a hybrid of sorts, a combination of lonely hearts and people who call into the 911 emergency lines in anticipation of having some excitement in their lives or maybe even someone to talk to. What exactly are these clients looking for?

Sleeper clients are not Type A personalities; they aren't impatient, time-conscious, highly competitive, ambitious, or aggressive by nature. Instead, sleeper clients expect a psychic reading to make their life more eventful. But psychics can't make things up or create a life for the sleeper, and frequently we have to tell our sleeper clients that there really isn't anything coming through for them in the session. Some people just have ho-hum lives!

I have been faced with the challenge of reading people with a quiet existence who call often with hopes of hearing about something about to happen for them. They start the session by saying, "What can you tell me?" Yet often the only information I can pick up for them psychically is very mundane. Sometimes the reading is so boring that I can actually imagine the Queen of Cups yawning as the card is turned over. Sleeper clients sit through their reading, staring blankly as the psychic tries to find some information or important message for this quiet type of client.

The sleeper client must realize that psychics can't twitch their nose and make something eventful happen. Sleeper clients don't need psychic readings. What they need first is a life, and they aren't going to get one if they just sit around and wait for life to happen. This client type has to get out into the world and participate in life. The sleeper client tends not to be a risk taker, so therefore the extent of their daily happenings is somewhat limited.

I gave a reading to a woman who was basically a shut-in. I felt like I was playing Stump the Psychic. I truly couldn't pick up anything interesting to tell her. I asked this client if there was a particular concern she wanted me to focus on, but she only wanted to know if it was a good time to buy a new television. I put down the tarot cards and grabbed her astrological chart. I was hoping for an upcoming Mercury retrograde so I could at least advise her not to purchase any electrical equipment. Maybe her chart would have a nice active Mars transit about to appear, or maybe a surprise transit from Uranus. I looked hard at her chart, but nothing was happening. The sleeper's chart was devoid of any excitement.

I didn't know where to go with this client's reading. There weren't any hooks in her astrological chart to expand into pertinent information. I said to her, "Wow! You're lucky. You have a nice, quiet life. I'm jealous. My life is too hectic." The sleeper replied, "I know. My life is quiet. When will things start to happen?"

I felt like telling her that things would happen, but she had to get out of the house first. This woman liked to get frequent psychic readings. I think that the only excitement she had were the one-dimensional readings that were a very quiet reflection of her life. I felt as though I was part of the Psychic Readers' Lonely Hearts Club, here to supply lonesome clients with psychic company.

A psychic medium once told a sleeper client that she had a hard time picking up things for her. The medium said that the other side, meaning the spirit world, couldn't think of anything to tell her. Reading for clients who are really low energy can be just as draining as dealing with high-energy clients. Both types of clients wipe out the psychic, because they can compromise the psychic's energy field, and the readings can become fatiguing.

You don't need to have a whirlwind life in order to get a psychic reading, and if your life is a little dull at the moment a reading may alert you to some upcoming excitement. If your existence is more on the quiet side, try to get your energy level up before you get a reading because the moving energy will act as a magnet for some action in your life. Even if you live alone, you can raise your vibration before a psychic session by listening to music, tapping, drumming, and dancing by yourself. Sleeper clients need to have realistic expectations about what a psychic reading is all about, and know that going to a psychic will not in itself bring things about if they refuse to get into the game of life.

The Friendship-Club Freebie Seeker: The Psychic's BFF

The *friendship-club freebie seeker* (FCFS) client believes that after getting a few psychic readings, an automatic bond of friendship has been established between the client and the psychic. The FCFS wants to be the psychic's new BFF (best friend forever) because then she can call and engage the psychic reader in conversations that turn out to be pseudo-psychic readings. The friendship gig is a slick move on the FCFS's part. But psychic readers have been there and done that, and it doesn't benefit either the psychic or the seeker. Professional boundaries are required in order to maintain a good balance between psychic and client. Psychics work with energy, and if a FCFS postures herself as a friend in order to get free psychic readings, then an energy imbalance will occur. The psychic should not be expected to give out free psychic information if the psychic feels that he or she is being played.

Psychics are very sensitive to energy, and can sense when a client wants to cross the boundaries of business and try to have a friendship. It is so easy to want to be friends with a psychic. Psychics know their client's secrets, hopes, fears, and everything in between. Who wouldn't want a friend who can psychically pick up information for you? A FCFS has to remember that psychic readers can also pick up why such clients want to establish a relationship: the perk of free, twenty-four-hour psychic advice.

I do not like to do psychic readings for close friends or family members, because my own personal feelings make it hard for me to be totally objective. Doing readings for friends and family can cause problems for a psychic, especially if the information being communicated from a reading isn't what the friend or family member really cares to hear. Not all news is good news.

The most widely used modus operandi of the FCFS is to invite the psychic reader to do things with her socially, or call on the telephone to just "chit chat." These overly friendly clients call outside of their appointments and don't realize that they are interrupting the psychic's personal time. This behavior puts the psychic into an awkward situation. Psychics realize that a lot of their business is based on good client PR, so the psychic has to try and be nice when asking a client not to place social calls. Calls outside of an appointment just to try and foist a friendship with the psychic are not a good idea. Psychics deal with a number of clients, and it isn't that we aren't interested in the client's life; we are interested, but only in the context of a psychic reading.

When the reading is over, the psychic has to clear out the last client's energy and prepare for the next client. If psychic readers don't shake off client energy, it can affect the psychic in an adverse way. The psychic's own energy can become discombobulated; headaches are often a symptom of energy leaks and psychic burnout. Look at it this way: people don't like to take work home from the office with them, just as psychic readers don't want to have a daily dose of their clients' lives outside of a psychic-reading session.

One way to break a FCFS's habit of placing personal calls to the psychic is to charge her for any type of consultation outside of an appointment, the same way that lawyers charge their clients a fee for every call made to them. I have dealt with overly friendly clients who call and don't seem to realize they are interrupting my personal time. Some clients are unaware of the fact that psychic readers have a life, too.

I used to deal with one FCFS who started out with making small talk while she was booking a psychic-reading session. She would try and get into my personal life by asking what seemed at first to be simple questions about my family and my life in general. She was always trying to engage me in friendly conversation.

I knew where this was going, and at the risk of being rude I politely cut her calls short if she wasn't booking time for a reading with me. This woman would call just to say hello, and see what I was doing. She would then try to lead into questions about things that were happening in her own life. She would ask me what I thought her boyfriend was thinking about her, inquire about her job, and seek advice on astrological dates that were favorable for her. And she expected this all for free.

This woman thought that we were now good girlfriends, sorority sisters to the end. I would avoid picking up the telephone if I saw her name come up on my caller ID, but there were times that she would call from different numbers or block her number. This FCFS tried different tactics to get me on the telephone. When the telephone rings, I am like Pavlov's dog; I am conditioned to pick up, especially since my psychic readings are done via the telephone 99 percent of the time.

One day, the FCFS called and asked me what I was doing. I told her that I was making my dinner and asked her if she needed to make an appointment. She said, "No, I just wanted to touch base with you. And I want to tell you the latest about my boyfriend's ex-wife. Can I get your opinion on how I should handle meeting her for the first time?" (Opinions are usually free psychic insights.) It is a good thing that the FCFS wasn't also psychic, because if she could tap into my mind, then she would have known what I was thinking: "I don't want to hear about her boyfriend, his ex, and all these other people she talks about." I don't even really know this woman outside of the readings I give her. I wondered if this client also called other professionals that she deals with in an attempt to get free services, such as her mechanic, doctor, lawyer, hairdresser, or accountant. Chances are, she doesn't.

Psychics are dealing with an intangible. The psychic readings have an intrinsic value. The service is unique to the client seeking a psychic reading, and there should be an equal exchange of energy between the psychic and the client. Psychics have to be compensated for their time, or else the freebie seeker's calls become fatiguing. The FCFS client has to understand that psychics don't mind a little pro bono work, but they do not like it when the client assumes that all readings are gratis.

Psychic-Reading Virgins: Read for the Very First Time

Your first experience with getting a psychic reading can be very nerve-wracking. Psychics who deal with *psychic-reading virgins* feel the pressure to make sure that the first experience leaves a good impression. Did anyone ever mention *safe psychic-reading rules* to you or talk to you about *the stars and the tarot cards* (the psychic realm's version of the birds and the bees)?

The psychic-reading virgin feels the nervousness and anticipation of the reading, and hopes that all the articles and books that she has read about psychic readings come in handy during her first experience with a psychic. Once the appointment is made, the psychic-reading virgin may begin to sweat out what the experience will be like. There are the usual rumors about the psychic who predicted someone's death or other bad news, and then again there are the stories of how a psychic predicted who would be someone's future husband.

Sometimes the decision to get your first psychic reading is spontaneous, and a glass of wine to calm the nerves may precede the whole metaphysical experience. The anticipation of what the future may hold can be a scary feeling coated with a dash of excitement. You can't help but wonder if the psychic will notice that you are a psychic-reading virgin. The psychic reader will most likely know that it is your first time, but beyond that a psychic can usually tell by the way that the psychic-reading virgin fumbles with the tarot cards. You never flip the tarot cards like you are dealing a hand of poker, but rather you should gently shuffle the cards hand over hand, hand over hand. That is the technique.

The next big question psychic-reading virgins have is, should they keep their mouth shut or is it okay to talk? Responsiveness and communication are necessary if you want your first reading to be a good experience, but too much talking may be distracting and annoying. It is best to follow the tempo of the psychic as if you were dancing.

The psychic-reading virgin has no idea what will happen once she gets inside the room with the psychic, and often wonders if it is okay to bring a friend along to sit through the reading with her. "No threesomes please" is the most likely request of the psychic, because the first reading experience has to be all about the client; the possibility of someone else's energy coming into the psychic-reading mix may interfere with the psychic doing the energy connection. The first reading is best kept as a solo flight.

Some psychic-reading virgins ease their way into their first experience by opting for a phone psychic session. It is like having phone sex. If the psychic-reading virgin gets too nervous, scared, or freaked out, he can just hang up. When a psychic-reading virgin visits with a psychic reader for the first time in person, any sudden feelings of trepidation leave him no option other than to run like hell out of the room.

Psychic-reading virgins sometimes get an impression of what a reading is going to be like by watching psychic television shows or lingering in the New Age section of a bookstore to check out books about psychics and divination. Some virgins have even scoped out Internet psychic-reading sites and chat rooms as a way of getting a feel for the type of psychic and method of reading to which they wish to lose their psychic-reading virginity.

Up until this point the closest that the psychic-reading virgin has come to getting his fortune told was to read the vague fortune inside of a fortune cookie, or his daily horoscope, or maybe to venture into the self-administered, interactive tarot-reading sites on the Internet to satisfy his curiosity about psychic readings and to get a dose of psychic vibration. So far the psychic-reading virgin has only experienced some *heavy psychic-reading petting* and not the full mind-blowing experience of a good psychic reading.

The psychic who gives the psychic-reading virgin her first real experience with divination has to be prepared to be patient. The virgin may not be as responsive or relaxed as a well-seasoned client. Psychic readers also have to be conscious that if the method of psychic reading chosen for the maiden occasion happens to be tarot cards, the very sight of the Death card may totally make the psychic-reading virgin *trip*.

I remember hearing a story when I was a teenager about a friend of a friend who passed out in a gypsy fortunetelling parlor during the first time that she ever had a card reading. A group of three girls went to a local fortune parlor to get psychic readings. Two of the girls had experience with getting palm readings and tarot card readings, but the friend who they brought along with them to the fortuneteller was a psychic-reading virgin. The gypsy fortuneteller put the psychic-reading virgin at ease by first holding her hand and gently reading her palm. After the foreplay of the palm reading session ended, the reading progressed to a more in-depth tarot-card session.

The gypsy chose the Celtic Cross spread, which is the tarot-card spread equivalent of the missionary position. As the gypsy laid the psychic-reading virgin's tarot cards for the first time, the much-feared Death card flipped over. The gypsy fortuneteller apparently hesitated too long when responding to the card, leaving the girl to believe that her death was imminent. Can you imagine what the gypsy thought as the girl slumped off of the chair? I'm sure that she must have looked at the Death card and figured, "Look at that! *Shit!* I hope that I don't get blamed for death by a *deadly tarot card*." The girl came to and denied that the tarot card had made her faint; she told everyone that the smell of the burning incense in the small fortunetelling room made her sick, and the sight of the candles, crystals, and other adornments for atmosphere were a little much. She said that she was overwhelmed. Sure! Right!

Psychic-reading virgins have to practice safe psychic-reading protection. Grounding is necessary in order to get a good reading, but most novices don't know about such things unless they have read or heard about taking protective measures. The psychic reader may have to ask the first-timer to relax, because getting into the psychic-reading virgin's energy zone may take longer if the client is too uptight. Once a comfortable connection is made, then the natural rhythm of the reading can progress. Most of my first-time clients always say the same thing: "Wow! I can't believe my session is over already. When can I come again?" I am happy when my psychic-reading virgins leave with a smile on their face, totally satisfied that their multiple questions were all answered.

Psychic-reading virgins usually opt for a quick session the first time, and if the session goes well, then they will most likely go the distance the next time that they get a psychic reading. After their first reading experience, virgins have to make sure that they don't go overboard and become *psychic-reading maniacs*.

Once you have lost your psychic-reading virginity, it is acceptable to experiment with other methods of divination and see different psychic readers until you find a psychic to whom you vibe, so you can develop a nice seeker-to-psychic relationship.

The Psychic Client: Peer to Peer

Psychically reading for another psychic reader is a real trip. Imagine doing a tarot-card reading for someone who is micro-managing the whole session. People may wonder if psychics can do readings for themselves. Some believe that it's not a good idea to read for yourself because you can't be clear concerning your own matters. Psychics do respond to psychic hits that they randomly get for themselves, such as a feeling about someone or something or a psychic premonition. I don't like to psychically read myself, because I am not being objective and I have a ten-

dency to get over-emotional with my life situations that call for a
psychic reading. I'll admit to pulling a few tarot cards or looking
at my astrological chart, but I always reach for the phone and call
another psychic to get a second opinion.

Dealing with the metaphysical world for a living gives me and
other psychic readers the predisposition to also become psychic
groupies or junkies. Psychic-peer clients look for well-referenced
psychics to do psychic readings for them. Imagine a want ad in
the classified section of the newspaper that reads: *Psychic reader seeks
psychic readings. Has to be accurate. Precise timing a must. Props not necessary, but
tarot cards welcome. Prefers full names of predicted persons and places but first and
last initials will do. Willing to barter, or courtesy fee acceptable. Over 20 years experience a requirement, but may consider less if you can also levitate while doing
readings.*

Psychic peers are tough clients. If we are good at what we do,
then we expect the same plus more from our counterparts. Peer
clients embody most of the bad behavior of the previously mentioned client types. They are a minefield, because psychics have
to tread cautiously or risk setting them off. They are the "ask me
ten more times" client. The psychic-peer client will ask a question once, and if the answer isn't what she cares to hear, then a
debate begins. Some peer clients sit down for their reading and
begin to direct the psychic who is conducting the session. The
psycho psychic client is even known to answer her own questions by
phrasing the desired answer into the query.

Psychic-peer clients often try and elbow more out of a reading
for themselves by assuming that there should be a professional
courtesy among psychic readers, which translates into freebie
readings. As soon as someone tells me that she is also a psychic
reader, I know that somewhere along the line she may try and
impress me with her knowledge, her accomplishments, and the
names of her *star clients* in an attempt to get more out of me. The
peer client expects the psychic to be her own personal Oracle of

Delphi. A good psychic should not expect referrals from the peer client, as competition among psychics is notorious. The peer client doesn't want her patrons to find out about another talented psychic. Some psychic-peer clients feel that because they share the same profession with the psychic reader, calls outside of an appointment or midnight calls are fine and can be treated like after-work happy hours, where relaxing conversation turns into shop talk and ultimately free psychic advice.

Some peer clients are energy vampires who try to refuel themselves by picking the brains of other psychics. I have been faced with psycho psychic-peer clients who want me to give them a tarot reading or astrology reading concerning issues about their own clients. Some peer clients think nothing of using another psychic as a personal cheat sheet. It is like copying test answers from a friend in school or reading psychic-reader Cliffs Notes.

The psychic-peer client can be lethal if she doesn't clear out her clients' energies before seeking a psychic reading. Remember, we are dealing with energy, and erratic residue energy often clings to a psychic-peer client. For the psychic reader attempting to give a reading to a peer client who hasn't cleared out her own clients' energy, the meeting of the clients' energies and the psychic reader's energy is like an atomic explosion.

One woman I read for was a psychic peer. This woman was madly in love with a guy who was really not good for her. He made his living as an Elvis impersonator, and when he wasn't singing "Hound Dog," he was acting like a hound dog. This woman met him while she was working at a psychic fair. The Elvis impersonator went to her booth and wanted a reading. The psychic-peer client allowed this man to cross over the professional boundary and he soon became her lover. He moved in with her, borrowed thousands of dollars, and was draining her energy. The woman became so drained from this relationship that her own psychic business started to suffer.

The distraught psychic called me for a tarot-card reading. I told her that Mr. Elvis would soon be taking up with another woman, and to drop him now before he hurt her any further. She felt uneasy about the relationship with this man and just wanted confirmation. This psychic peer went from one psychic reader to another, like a bee traveling from flower to flower. To make a long story short, the psychic client didn't pay attention to the warning in her tarot readings, and eventually she was dropped by the Elvis impersonator, who left her for another woman who also just so happened to be a psychic reader. Seems that Elvis was a psychic junkie, and he liked to date psychics.

Psychic peers are sometimes the worst at paying attention to psychic advice. These psychic clients can have the same problems as their regular clients. Often, the psychic peer's problems are amplified because she did not use protection from wild flying energy given off from her clients. Some psychic peers believe that all of their issues can be solved by seeking out metaphysical remedies like crystal healings, past-life regressions, astrological charting, and tarot spreads. True, these things do work, but you also have to recognize your own boundaries and protect your psychic space. Psychic-peer clients are sometimes too open, and their boundary lines disappear, leaving a big gap in their own auric field. Psychics who do psychic readings for psychic peers have to be very careful not to get caught up in this psychic energy web.

It is often amusing to read psychically for another psychic. Before you even tell them what you see in their cards, they are telling you what they see. I have even had psychic-peer clients make comments after a session by saying something to the effect of "I knew you were going to tell me that. I psychically picked it up before our appointment."

With the energy of two psychics coming to the table at the same time, it is not uncommon to blow a few psychic fuses during the reading session. The performing psychic sometimes feels as though she is taking her psychic SATs (satisfying another telepathic).

The Ultimate Psychic Junkie: Hooked on Psychic Readings

The most extreme psychic-reading seeker is the *ultimate psychic junkie* (UPJ). The ultimate psychic junkie gets up first thing in the morning, and even before brushing her teeth, grabs the morning paper to read her horoscope for the day. Next, the ultimate psychic junkie will turn on her computer and get her daily fix of e-mailed horoscopes (usually there are at least five or six daily horoscopes to open). The UPJ may feel some confusion if the horoscopes are not all in synch; her need for live psychic-reader confirmation is overwhelming. The UPJ has to score a psychic reading, pronto! The junkie reaches for the telephone and dials up her favorite psychic readers.

Psychic readers know who their UPJ clients are, because they speak to them sometimes as often as six or seven times a day. The ultimate psychic junkie's favorite daily psychic cocktail is three shots of daily horoscope, two to three jiggers of live psychic readings, with a dash of computer-generated tarot readings. The ultimate psychic junkie calls a psychic for every real decision and imagined outcome.

I had one client who would call me every morning to ask me to look at her chart and pull a few tarot cards to see how her day would go. She would place additional calls throughout the day to me and other psychic readers, and ask us to psychically tap into every daily occurrence. Her evening sedative would be to finish off her night with a few psychic readings to get a brief outlook for the following day. This lady was hooked on psychic readings.

I asked this client what initially turned her on to psychics. She told me that when she was nineteen years old, a fortuneteller laid her whole life out in front of her and that the predictions all came true. She was so amazed by the accuracy of the psychic reading that she developed an addiction to psychics. Throughout her college years, this psychic junkie would hunt down local psychic readers. She had even tried to self-administer psychic medicine by attempting to read her own tarot cards. After her first marriage failed (as foretold by a few psychics), she sought psychic advice and found the psychics to be more helpful than her therapist.

This UPJ client would initially call me for second opinions about other psychic readings that she was getting. Eventually, she began calling me throughout the day for *everything*. I told her that in order to get a good psychic reading, there were certain preparations that both the client and the seeker need to do. Both the psychic and the client have to approach each other with respect for the gift of psychic seeing and not abuse the professional relationship. Her addiction to psychic readings was in place long before she met me, and her compulsion to call psychics was part of her nature.

This client reluctantly cut back her daily dose of psychic readings for about one week, but she quickly reverted back to her old habit of getting numerous readings throughout the day. I did not need another co-dependent client, and I suggested that she seek out other psychics. I did not expect her withdrawal from psychic readings with me to be easy, but I did not want her crazy, obsessive energy mixing into my own energy field every day. She would call and beg me for tarot readings and leave countless messages on my voicemail. She also sent flowers and other nice gifts to my home. I couldn't do it.

Doing psychic readings for this woman was now impossible for me. I developed a guarded feeling toward her constant crossing of my boundaries, and became aware of her failure to respect my rules about not calling without an appointment. This woman was different from other types of psychic junkies that I had dealt with, because she completely ignored my requests to stop calling and would leave pathetic and disturbing messages on my voicemail. This client finally moved on to Internet psychic sites until she found a new psychic reader.

For the ultimate psychic junkie, online psychic sites are like the red-light district of Amsterdam. The ultimate psychic junkie can find any type of psychic reader at any time. Instead of cruising the streets looking for neon palms in the window, on the Internet the UPJ can find anything from computer-generated readings to the "hard stuff" of a live psychic consultation. Many a credit card has been maxed out in search of the most gifted psychic around. Some psychic junkies think nothing of plopping down hundreds of dollars for a reading.

Ultimate psychic junkies are not just everyday people with a need to know their future. Some ultimate psychic junkies are prominent people who keep their addiction to psychic readings well hidden. I personally have done readings for well-known people who require that I keep their psychic-reading habit very confidential. I even have clients who sneak out of the house to place a call to me on their cell phones, because they don't want their families to know that they are getting psychic readings.

What starts out as an infatuation with psychic readings can easily turn into an obsession and eventually a dependence. The ultimate psychic junkie is a risky client for the psychic, because this is someone who is not respecting the correct procedure of a psychic reading. When a dependency overrides a true need for a reading, an abusive situation can develop. There are psychics who are not scrupulous and exploit the addiction of the ultimate psychic junkie the same way that other professionals who are not aboveboard take advantage of their clients.

Psychic readings are to be respected the same way that medicine is to be respected. The addiction of the ultimate psychic junkie can cause havoc in the lives of the psychic reader, who has to deal with the unbridled, erratic, and often confusing energy field of this unstable personality. Psychic readers do not want to get personally caught up in their clients' lives. Psychics work in another dimension and tap into the quantum universe to show the psychic seeker the detours and best route to their essential destination. UPJs are scary for psychic readers to deal with, because they are psychic-reading users who turn into abusers. There should be a PJA (Psychic Junkies Anonymous) or ultimate psychic junkie rehab, where junkies could go to dry out from their extreme addiction to psychics.

For the ultimate psychic junkie, something as innocent as opening a fortune cookie in a Chinese restaurant can spin out of control, and eventually land the junkie in the throes of endless calls to psychic hotlines.

Every psychic reader I know has had an experience with an ultimate psychic junkie. What will it take to calm the ultimate psychic junkie down and relieve her of the addiction to psychic readings? Will it be one bad psychic reading where the predictions don't come true, or will it be massive credit-card debt from repeated calls into psychic phone lines?

The ultimate psychic junkie is the advanced stage of the co-dependent client. The UPJ usually deals with various psychics instead of working with one favorite psychic reader. Dealing with different psychics throughout the day adds confusion to the experience, because there are bound to be contradictions from the many psychic readings. The contradictions in the readings cause additional problems for the ultimate psychic junkie, who now must figure out which psychic reading is the most accurate. A psychic-reading cycle develops, and the life of the ultimate psychic junkie becomes a maze with no easy way out.

The ultimate psychic junkie is often someone who suffers from other mental conditions, such as manic depression, obsessive-compulsive disorder, acute anxiety, bipolar disorder, or even schizophrenia. UPJs distort their problems and often OD (over-dramatize) their life because of their psychic addiction. Sometimes psychic junkies will try to get a handle on their psychic-reading addiction and try to limit themselves only to reading their horoscope each day instead of getting live psychic readings. This is the psychic junkie's version of going sober, but rarely does it work for too long, because everywhere you look psychics are advertised, talked about, and are easily available, especially on the Internet—although the drug of choice for most UPJs is still the phone reading.

CHAPTER 4

How Much Should You Pay for a Psychic Reading?

Why Do You Charge If You Are Spiritual?

The cost for a psychic reading seems to be a big issue for some reason. There is a general consensus that if someone is psychically gifted, then he or she should share the gift willingly for free. Psychic junkies can rack up big tabs for psychic readings and then try to dispute the cost of the psychic services. The information given in the psychic reading has value, but once the knowledge is delivered to the client from the psychic there seems to be *psychic-reading sticker shock*.

Clients get impatient and expect all of the information from a psychic reading to happen in a New York minute, and some clients only want to pay after a predicted event happens. I had a client years ago who was always looking to discount her fee for my services. I told her during the course of a reading that she would be moving within two years. This client didn't want to believe the prediction of another move, because she had just recently moved into a new home. She acted like a disgruntled diner at a fine restaurant who, after eating the full meal, decides that she didn't like what she ate. This client paid for her psychic reading, but she let me know how she totally disagreed with what I told her. She insisted that she loved her new home and the thought of moving again was out of the question. I told her to keep her money. I didn't want anything from her, because the feeling of dissatisfaction was too attached to the payment for my services. The energy exchange would be like inviting an imbalance into my body.

The client called me a few years later and told me that what I told her about another move did, indeed, come true, and she wanted me to give her a psychic reading concerning her new surroundings. I really didn't want to read for this former client again. I reminded her that our last session a few years ago ended badly, and even though she was now ready to acknowledge that her past psychic reading did indeed come to pass, I got a gut feeling that she still seemed a little discontent. I definitely got the impression that she did not like to pay for psychic readings, especially when she mentioned that she thought psychics should help people for free. This client would dispute the information in her psychic readings with me before she even gave it a chance to happen as a way to justify not paying for my services.

What this client really thought was that psychics should share their gift with people and not charge for psychic readings. But psychics have to make a living, too!

My experience with this client was a lesson for me, because I had done plenty of pro bono readings in the past for different people, and my services, even though they were appreciated, also allowed for some clients to abuse my time. I had to learn to put up protective boundaries.

I referred the client in the above-mentioned case to a peer of mine who I thought would be a better personality mix for her. They were both very businesslike women, and I felt that they would be on the same vibe. As it turned out, the former client called me once again but this time to tell me how much she appreciated my past services to her because she felt that the psychic

I had sent her to was a very good psychic but "way too money-minded"! I told her that when it comes to energy, like attracts like and maybe we all had a lesson to learn about fees and services. As the saying goes: no enemies, only teachers.

It's not uncommon to pay $100 for a hairstyle that may only last six weeks, and there's no guarantee that you will be able to style your hair the way the stylist did at the salon. Or just try calling a lawyer for advice. The minute an attorney picks up the phone, you are on the clock and there's no guarantee that the lawyer will win your case. A doctor will treat a patient and hide the charges under the cloak of medical insurance, which costs a small fortune. There is no assurance that the doctor's treatment will be successful, and it may even complicate other medical conditions.

Why is it acceptable for a psychiatrist to charge high fees and prescribe Prozac or some other drug so the patient can cope with reality? Psychic readers do not graduate from an Ivy League college with a degree in tarot and a minor in palm reading, but nonetheless we have spent years honing our psychic gifts with what really counts, and that is hands-on experience. Like doctors, psychics recognize particular symptoms in their clients, and through experience the psychic reader knows just where to go with certain life situations. Psychics are not missionaries or spiritual volunteers, and payment for psychic services is a required part of doing business with a psychic. The Oracle of Delphi was paid for giving psychic readings, and the Oracle was not expected to predict events until sufficient sacrifices, gifts, and a fee were presented.

Psychic readers deal with energy, and any energetic imbalance will cause a shift in the unseen current and bring about undesired events for both the seeker and the psychic. How can anyone expect a psychic to sit and do readings and not be compensated in some way? Some clients believe that the psychic reader's compensation should be the good feeling that goes along with helping someone. Knowing that you helped someone is rewarding, but *honey*, it don't pay the bills!

There are actually clients who try to set the psychic reader's fee by offering an amount that they feel is fair. Imagine going into a store and paying what you felt was reasonable for an item. You wouldn't get very far with the store manager.

Many psychics do their fair share of pro bono psychic readings, especially if there is a client in true financial crisis mode. Psychics know that extending services to someone in need will reap a bountiful karmic payback. There are not too many professionals who will offer their services for free the way that psychics are at times expected to do. Psychic readers are not going to feel sorry for the client who drives a fully loaded car, vacations often, buys nice things for herself, and also expects a discount price for a psychic reading. I did readings for a woman who was between jobs, and her money situation was very precarious. I told her that I would give her a reading to see when she would get back on her feet and straighten out her monetary affairs.

The one reading turned into a few readings, and through a series of psychic readings and astrological timing, this client landed the perfect job and was now making more money than ever. This client would call and ask for psychic readings and preface the request with a promise not to forget my kindness to her. She managed to pay off her debts to everyone but me. For some reason, she viewed my psychic services as gifts for herself. The information that I gave this client predicted the right job for her, and the astrological timing helped her avoid making agreements when the Moon was not favorable for starting new ventures. This client no longer had an income problem thanks to getting the psychic readings, which also acted as a spiritual sedative to keep her calm.

One day this client called me and wanted a psychic reading right away, because she was going on a vacation and needed some insight concerning a relationship. My first thought was that if she had money for a vacation, then she could surely afford to pay for a reading. I told the client that I was glad that she was now in a position to meet the expense of a vacation, and that compensation for my services was now expected. The client seemed insulted, and she told me that she would send me a payment for the session as soon as she returned from her trip. I told her that it would be a bad idea for me to give her a psychic reading, because it would cause an energy imbalance for both of us.

I was psychically picking up on her energy the whole time, and I could feel that she was mistaking my kindness for weakness. I didn't feel comfortable with the arrangement of waiting to be paid for my services. I felt that if this client valued psychic insights, then she would pay for my time. Why would this client think that I would be okay with letting her go on and on about her trip and new relationship and not feel that I wanted to be compensated for my time? I was feeling a little *dissed* by the client. Because of the lopsided energy situation, my professional relationship with this woman was difficult to continue. Instead of being thankful and appreciative, this woman acted with a sense of entitlement. She forgot her recent neediness and how compassionate I was toward her. I was hoping that she would get a life lesson from her experience of joblessness. My own lesson was that once you do something for free, the next time you charge a fee the client feels ripped off.

Whenever you are providing an intangible service, there is a tendency to think that if you can't see it then you don't have to pay for it. Wrong! Once an imbalance has occurred, something has to be done to sway the balance. If you want to get a good psychic reading, you have to approach it the same way that you approach any professional service. You have to compensate the psychic reader. Money is energy.

Feeling Ripped Off by a Psychic Reader

How do you handle a situation in which you feel like you just paid a psychic reader for absolutely nothing? It can happen.

Maybe you dealt with a psychic reader who was burned out, tired, or off his or her game for the day. You have to be street smart when getting a psychic reading, and you have to know who you are dealing with. Whether you know it or not, you are having a very intimate energy exchange with someone who is entering your auric field.

If a psychic reader you have been going to for years, who has previously been accurate, totally misses the mark with you, then you can assume there was a glitch in the energy connection. If you go to a new psychic and you leave wondering, "What the hell was that all about?" you can either choose not to go back or give the psychic reading some time to come about. Remember that the future has not yet been experienced by you, even though it already exists.

You have to be savvy when dealing with a psychic, and not get pulled in to any situations in which you are required to pay large sums of money and allow your problems to be exploited by the psychic reader. Some psychic seekers are so anxious to have their life turn around in a different direction that they sometimes get involved with unscrupulous psychics.

I called a psychic phone line one time and requested one of my favorite psychics. The woman whom I usually requested was no longer working for the company, and the customer service rep kept pushing me to try this other psychic. Now, being a psychic reader myself and having briefly worked on a psychic phone line years ago, I should have known that when a customer service rep adamantly pushes a certain psychic, it can mean one of two things. Either the psychic is new and the rep is trying to help the psychic build up a client base, or the psychic isn't that good and doesn't get many callbacks or requests. The psychics who aren't that good eventually leave the phone line or are let go because of too many client charge-backs.

I took the customer service rep's advice and booked a reading with this highly touted psychic. I figured, *What the hell, I might be turned on to a really gifted psychic.* Wrong! The psychic reader who gave me my reading was way off. We didn't connect energetically. It was like a bad blind date where you have nothing in common. She thought that I was a singer who longed to sing on cruise ships and travel the world. She also thought that I didn't have children (I have three).

At one point during the reading I stopped her and told her that we weren't making a connection, and I didn't want to upset her because I know what it feels like to have an off day. I asked her if I could just have her answer a few questions instead of her trying to figure out where to go with me. The psychic reader didn't like the fact that I was pulling her off of the reading, and she got tough with me and started to lecture me about readings. That was it. I hung up, called customer service, and asked for a refund of my money. I told them that I was sure that the woman who attempted to give me a reading had psychic ability, but she wasn't the right fit for me.

Maybe astrologically we weren't a good mix for psychic communication, but for whatever reason the psychic and I couldn't connect. It happens sometimes that when a psychic attempts to get a reading from another psychic, the psychic energy from both parties gets canceled out. Too much intense and most likely ungrounded energy is the reason for some psychic-reading stall-outs.

The customer service rep's solution was to let me pick another psychic reader from their vault of oracles, which I did reluctantly because my desire for a reading had passed and my energy felt too low. The rep seemed almost desperate to pimp out one of his psychic readers to me in an effort not to lose a sale. I decided to pick another psychic reader and give it one more try.

The next one I had was pretty good. She asked me if I had recently been disappointed in a business transaction. Good call. She later went on to tell me about a situation that I had wanted to know about in the first place. By the time the reading was over, I felt I had really gotten a lot out of the reading, and to top it off the psychic was very good. In this case I had satisfaction.

We have all heard about people who have given psychic readers large sums of money in hopes of being reunited with an old lover or maybe to ensure some other type of desired ending. When the promised results don't come to pass, the person requesting the psychic's services is usually told by the *psychic scammer* to pay more money for more psychic work, or the psychic will try to push the blame onto the client for not following some type of weird ritual. At this point the client should start to feel ripped off and assume that they just had an encounter with a negative energy manipulator.

Here is where you must become street smart, meaning that you have to be wise to the *stuff* that some negative psychic readers pull. No matter how accurate they may seem, psychic readers who want you to ante up large sums of money to bring about a certain result are most likely scammers. In these cases you usually have to pay first, with cash, and then the psychic gives you a *ghetto psychic reading*, meaning that the reading is low end, full of empty promises, and mostly bullshit.

You may also feel like you have been gagged by a psychic reader if you pay for a session and it is over in ten minutes. Always clarify with the psychic how long the session will run. Everyone would like to get the biggest bang for their buck, so make sure you know the length of your allotted time slot. Some psychics are *speed readers*, and after a few minutes have passed they start to wrap up the session, leaving the client feeling hungry for more psychic insight. The speed readers may be good psychic readers, but they like to trim out the fluff and get to the point. They can make you feel like a pain in the ass if you ask more than two or three questions. On the street, speed readers are known for the "Chinese food" psychic reading: it leaves the client hungry for another reading an hour later. Ensure that you don't get shortchanged by a psychic reader, and clarify how long your appointment will last before it starts.

Don't let a psychic determine how many or how often you should get a reading. The choice to get a reading is up to the client. You really shouldn't get more than one reading per day, although if you are having a major meltdown you may need a longer psychic session as opposed to multiple psychic readings with different psychics. Too much of a good thing can cause confusion, and you have to allow enough time for the results of the reading to develop. We live in a society where everything is expected to happen in a nanosecond, but some events just take time to unfold. The number of psychic readings and the length of time between them are directly related to the nature and scope of the client's situation.

Psychics can only look into your past, present, and future with your permission and then give guidance. At no time can a psychic reader go into your life or the life of someone you want to know about and change things around. This is where psychics often get confused with being involved with witchcraft and energy manipulation.

Psychics are familiar with the world of cosmic energy, and as they become comfortable with their skills of energy reading, divination tools, and psychic methods, they also must fully learn and be aware of the responsibility that goes along with being evolved and ascended spiritually enough to be able to rightfully use these acquired gifts. The misuse of psychic ability for greed, manipulation, and ego will bring the psychic a boomerang of bad energy. Psychics have to *keep it real.* It is all about intention. Do psychics intend to help someone or control someone? The intention must be clear from the beginning.

Psychic *perception* is insight into a client's life based on an energy scan and some form of divination. Psychic *prediction* is a calculated prophecy made by a psychic reader based on the client's willingness to adjust his thinking and actions or his refusal to make necessary changes to bring about the best possible outcome to a situation.

An example: I can psychically perceive that you will be meeting a new love interest in the spring, because I may be visually getting that image of you as I do a reading concerning your personal life. If you do in fact meet someone in the spring, then I can go a step further and predict that the relationship might result in an engagement or some other necessary life involvement and see why and how this person had to come into your life.

Now if you choose by your own free will to be a shut-in and not go out and try to meet someone, you have directly affected the outcome of your psychic reading by your free-will choice to not take the opportunity to see what is out there. It is like having the GPS in your car tell you what exit to take off the highway to reach your destination, but deciding instead to get off the road sooner and take the long way. The final destination may be the same, but the amount of time and number of experiences along the way will be different. They could be better, or they could be worse. You fine-tune your psychic reading by the choices that you make. Large amounts of money paid to psychic scammers promising great results will not change anything except your bank account.

Some rip-off psychic readers will try to manipulate a client who already has low energy and a thin auric field due to some problems in her life, and convince the client that for a price her life will become much better. It is like going to a plastic surgeon. For a price you can change your outward appearance, but the real person inside is all up to you. You are the one who must change your outlook about a situation; the psychics are just showing you some before and *possible* after pictures of your life. They keep you alerted to the opportunities along the way so you don't miss out on something good.

Psychics also give you warnings about things that aren't so good for you so you can make the necessary adjustment. At no time should you give your power away to psychic readers and let them run your life. You have to live your own life and go through some rough times to build character and learn life lessons—just as the good times are rewards for staying on your life path.

Disappointments in life are sometimes blessings in disguise and knock you back on track. It's like driving a car, when sometimes a wrong turn leads you to a new restaurant or helps you avoid a traffic accident. Enjoy the adventure of life and get psychic checkups, but do not give any psychic large amounts of money to *nip and tuck* your life. The results will be shallow, not authentic, and basically an illusion of your life.

Some clients feel ripped off if a psychic prediction doesn't come to pass. Many things can alter an outcome. When you get a psychic reading, the psychic is dealing directly with you and your energy. The psychic reader can only keep *smacking* you back on track so you don't get your own energy field corrupted by an energy vampire or some other negative person or situation. You have to take into account that when you get a psychic reading, people you deal with on a daily basis can alter your results by their own independent actions toward you. You can only achieve your desired psychic-reading result if you stay focused on the insight given to you during a session and not allow others to distract you from your visualized results because of their energy mixing with your aura. Keep grounded and put a protective bubble around you as a way to be able to interact with others but not get pulled into their riptide of crazy energy.

When you are home alone the energy may be quiet, but if an unexpected visitor should arrive the energy shifts into a different gear. Same goes for psychic readings. The psychic reading for you may be altered by your involvement with someone, and your mix of energies produce a sub-result of your original psychic reading.

Life changes, and when things cease to change then they are dead. Psychic readings are meant to make you aware of changes and how to best handle them to better your life. You have to be realistic about your expectations from a reading and see how your own mindset and actions can alter the results.

A majority of people who get readings are savvy about them and have an idea what to expect, but novices may feel ripped off if they don't fully understand what a psychic reading is all about. Some clients want things to come about immediately, and don't want to take any responsibility for their own actions in any given situation.

Psychic readers who exploit people's problems and keep them purposely off track in order to get more money out of them are as bad as lawyers who intentionally drag out a case, a shrink who wants to keep you needy and sick, or a drug dealer who promises you a great high. In all cases the outcome is not good for the client.

It is hard to tell sometimes if you are getting ripped off by a psychic reader. Maybe you are not allowing enough time for a predicted event to come about. Timing is an illusion, and to call out an exact moment for a result to occur is like predicting the exact time a baby will be born. Some babies come early, some late, but most arrive in nine months and the exact time of birth is a real crapshoot. Same for psychic timing.

You are not getting ripped off by a psychic reader if you *willingly* make repeated appointments and over time see no results from the readings. Ask yourself if you are altering the events or maybe the psychic reader in not connecting properly with your energy. Are both psychic and client grounded? You also want to make sure that you don't go to a low-energy psychic. That is like starting your car on a cold day with an old battery.

Know that you are getting ripped off if the psychic reader promises and guarantees results but demands a big upfront payment from you, and you don't see one damn thing come about.

It's like giving a divorce attorney a big retainer. You may be strung along and hit up for more money until you call the game.

No one forces you to go to psychics for readings, so please be street smart and look into who you are dealing with. Get referrals. Just because someone promotes themselves as being a psychic reader doesn't necessarily mean that they are genuine. A fake Fendi bag is still a bag, but it isn't the real deal.

It is all about the connection that you make with the psychic reader. Sometimes psychics are embarrassed to tell a client that they can't tune in to them and to choose another psychic reader. It's like a radio station that you can't tune in to because you aren't in the right spot. That can happen with psychics also.

If you honestly feel unhappy with a psychic service, then my advice is to not go back to the psychic reader who didn't connect with you. It is hard to put a price tag on events that have not yet come to pass, but if a psychic reader gets known information wrong, then stop the reading and either ask for your money back or find out why you aren't connecting. Sometimes the static interference is coming from the client who isn't grounded, or maybe the psychic is burned out or having a bad day.

As with any service, if you are not happy then discuss the bill and attempt to resolve the problem. Some clients actually think that a psychic reader may *psychically attack* them if they complain about a reading. That is not true, and if psychics use their developed psychic abilities to harm someone then they will reap the karmic retribution for such actions.

Some clients don't like to pay for a reading that doesn't give them the answers that they want to hear. As long as the psychic gives you the honest truth, then you should pay the psychic for his time.

Money in Exchange for Energy

Energy is a source of power, and money is a medium of exchange for that power. Money carries certain energy, and money that is paid out reluctantly will have a different vibration to it than money that is paid out willingly. Psychics deal with energy and are very sensitive to the energy attached to the money they earn for their services. The client seeking a psychic reading is buying the intrinsic value of the reading. The psychic reading is like a piece of original art: no two psychic readings are alike.

Clients who feel that they are paying too much for a reading are unknowingly attaching that sentiment to their payment, which will be passed on to the energy-sensitive psychic reader. As soon as the payment with the attached resistance hits the psychic reader's energy field, an invisible block is formed. To get a good psychic reading the client must willingly give in order to willingly receive. A client who pays for a psychic reading but continues to feel trepidation about the purchase is not in the right mindset to get a good reading. If the psychic doesn't have the client's trust, it may take longer for the psychic reader to make a good psychic connection with the client. Time is money, and the time a psychic reader spends with a client has a monetary value.

Some psychics, I must admit, focus too much on their fees and make clients feel like they are buying a parcel of future earnings on their life's stock. Psychics live in the material world but work above that dimension in the energetic spiritual dimension, and in all honesty it is a real oil-and-water mix.

The soul rewards for being a positive psychic guide for someone are priceless, and I have often seen amazingly good things come about not only for psychic readers but also for nice people in general, as a return on their cosmic investment of positive energy. The universe knows where to throw a lifeline.

There are some psychic readers who find it hard to work with money and to put a price tag on their psychic skills. Psychics are basically putting a price tag on their time, more so than on their abilities. Time spent with a client takes the psychic reader away from his or her own family, and above all it can be energetically draining and leave the psychic wide open to being exposed to wandering negative client energy if proper psychic protection isn't observed. The client is paying for time more so than for predictions. Let's face it: psychics usually aren't paying back large student loans for the degree that they got in divination, but nonetheless psychic readers have to pay bills and raise families while living in the material world, even though they work in the spiritual realms.

Some people choose to view a psychic reading as entertainment, and for some reason discount the true worth. My children have paid upwards of $200 for a seat at an NHL playoff game only to see their team lose. Is that entertainment? What about the concert attendee who will pay hundreds of dollars to watch an hour performance from their favorite artist? When the show is over, the only thing left is the memory of the event. A good psychic reading, however, leaves the consumer with confirmation of her past, acknowledgement of her present, and anticipation of her future. The most important thing is that the client is the *star of the show*.

Many people get teased for seeking psychic readings, especially the psychic junkies. I have heard comments like, "How can you pay for such a silly thing? Don't waste your money on fortunetellers!" Who ultimately decides the value of what is being purchased? The answer is the client.

A decorator can charge a consultation fee to tell you what chair would look good in your home, but psychic readers who charge a fee for their psychic or astrological consultations are viewed as lepers in the business world. Psychics are often depicted as predators, lurking behind a deck of tarot cards just waiting to turn some unsuspecting curiosity seeker into a psychic-reading junkie.

I had a client who liked to call for regular psychic consultations. This woman was pleasant enough, but nonetheless she wanted me to give her a discount for my psychic services. Every time she paid for a psychic reading, she would go on and on about how she really could not afford readings because her car payment was due, she had a dental appointment, and other guilt-trip excuses for not wanting to pay for the reading. Funny, during her sessions this client would ask about buying a new car, the best day to schedule a dental appointment, and other personal information, yet she felt that this information once given to her should be discounted like day-old bread.

This client also called me outside of an appointment to pick my brain for free and try to get psychic insight from me. The weird thing is that every time this woman would pay me for a psychic reading, I would get a severe sinus headache. Being a psychic junkie myself, I asked a medical intuitive I know to diagnose my bad reaction to this woman and her payments to me. A quick energy scan by the medical intuitive pinpointed my problem. The sinus problems that I was experiencing were a direct result of an irritation to a person or a situation. I knew that this client was stealing my time, and because I didn't communicate my feelings to her about how she really didn't like to pay for psychic readings my body took the hit and my sinuses flared up.

The sinus problems I would get after dealing with this client were situated between my eyes in the third-eye area. My third-eye chakra was being blocked because of this client's attempt to steal my energy. A definite energy imbalance caused my physical discomfort. This client did not like paying for psychic readings, and she expected me to understand that she had other, more important bills to pay.

I finally had to tell this woman that her money was making me sick, because of the bad vibes and the resentment she put into the payment. I told her that I would find it difficult to psychically read for her again unless there was an energy correction and a reevaluation of how she felt about compensating me for my time. The client became embarrassed because she knew that I read her intention of something for nothing. I felt better about telling her how I felt about her attitude with me, and she became more respectful toward the readings and of my time. As it turned out, the block that I had about not being compensated was removed and I was able to focus entirely on her. The woman agreed that our energetic connection was more balanced and that her psychic readings with me seemed more energetic and upbeat. Ironically enough, this client told me that sometimes after a psychic reading with me, she would get a splitting headache. It seems that the energy imbalance attacked us both until we corrected the problem.

How do you put a price tag on knowledge? Psychic readers are not running a lonely hearts' club or a friendship circle. Psychics who deal in the spiritual world often find it hard to translate their abilities into the monetary realms of the material world.

The Business of Being Psychic

Next to prostitution, the business of being a psychic reader may be one of the oldest professions in the world. The Bible is filled with stories of revered prophets, and ancient writings confirm that psychics and mystics have left their mark on history. The psychic is selling the ability to sense the unseen. The psychic reader is the oracle who delivers the psychic-reading product.

I believe that we all are born with basic instincts, and the sixth sense is as real and vital as the other five senses. Society dismisses the sixth sense and treats its existence as an abnormality instead of as a gift. There are people who are naturally very sensitive and develop this sixth sense. Other people only know that they possess such a gift when they have a psychic hit of some sort. Surely, almost everyone has had the experience of knowing that someone would call on the telephone even before the telephone rang, or the gut feeling of knowing that someone needs help. This sixth sense comes easily to someone who is more psychically open, and it can be developed and sharpened into a marketable talent.

Talents are gifts, but that doesn't mean that they should be devalued and given away. Musicians, artists, and writers are all talented people, and the talent of being psychic should be respected and recognized also. The intrinsic value of a talent can be translated into dollars and cents and supply and demand. Experience, skill, and uniqueness all play a part in the worth of a talent. In society, money is the primary source of appreciation for talents, goods, and services. In the universe, good karma is the form of appreciation.

People buy all kinds of products and services throughout their life. The ploys of strategic advertising lure people into a consumer wonderland, enticing them to buy anything from a face-lift to a forklift. Late-night infomercials draw in many sleepless consumers who make impulse purchases. People will rarely question your purchase of a kitchen gadget that you will never use, or exercise equipment that can be yours in just ten easy payments, but as soon as you procure a psychic reading someone will make fun of your purchase.

Nine out of ten times, a psychic reading is an impulse purchase triggered by some unexpected event. The business of being a psychic reader depends on psychic seekers responding to the urge to get a reading. The window of opportunity that the psychic has to satisfy the impetus of the client isn't a very long one. Psychic readers who work on psychic phone lines get the lion's share of the impulse psychic-reading purchases, because psychic readers with private practices are sometimes booked weeks in advance and can't readily get to the client. Psychic junkies with problems are in need of an immediate psychic-reading fix, and waiting for an appointment with their favorite psychics can be as awful as having the DTs (*desperation tarot*).

The psychic business is a tough business because there is little room for inaccuracy. Should the psychic reader miss the mark the first time, there may never be a second time. Psychics have to score at least an 80 percent accuracy rate with the client or else they are history. The type of client that the psychic is dealing with will also have a big impact on the tempo of the reading. Clients who are grounded and focused will get a better reading. When clients are open psychically, the psychic has an easier time getting in and the accuracy potential of the reading will be much higher.

The psychic phone lines not only offer a quick psychic reading fix for the psychic junkie, but they also take credit cards, which makes payment for services a lot easier. Private psychic readers don't always take credit cards, and waiting for a check to clear can take days. Private psychic readers who have their own client base are the most vulnerable to client abuse when it comes to collecting payment for readings. Psychics who work on psychic phone lines at least have the buffer of a customer service rep who deals with all of the payment issues, but there are still some clients who dispute the charge on their credit card after they get their readings. Take note that the stereotypical gypsy segments of the psychic-reader business make their clients hand them the money first. The client places the money in the hands of the gypsy while making a wish. They better wish that they don't get ripped off! I personally don't know of any gypsy who has been cheated out of a payment from a client.

Psychic readers can often sense who will write a bad check for payment or pull some nasty maneuver with a credit card. How do you not insult a client when you sense such a possibility with collecting payment for services? Some clients are desperate for a psychic reading, but are short on funds so they will write a bad check and then make up some excuse that the bank screwed up their account.

I know a psychic who had a client ask her if it was all right to pay her only after all of the predictions came true. Considering that one of the predictions for the client was a marriage for her within the next three years, the psychic reader felt that she would have a long wait for payment. Post-prediction payments are not acceptable, because compensation for the real time that the psychic reader is giving to the client has to be satisfied with a fee.

Psychics are viewed by much of the public as either celebrities or welfare mothers working on psychic phone lines, not as businesspeople. Psychics are often viewed as kooky, unusual, and a little different. At times, I have had some wiseass ask me, "When do you intend to get a *real* job?" Being a psychic reader *is* a *real* job. We make real money, and I often think that the regular working guy or gal might be a little bit jealous of people in the psychic profession. We really do have an interesting occupation. Our employer is the universe, and there isn't any chance of the big "U" going out of business anytime soon. Psychic readers are business professionals. Not all psychics have celebrity status, and surely not all psychics on the phone lines are charlatans. Bad press about the psychic business dies hard, yet the unsavory business dealings of big corporations are more easily forgotten.

I will admit that the psychic-reader business is a weird business to be in. Imagine a Psychic Reader Business Club meeting for psychic practitioners. There would be psychics who would refuse to go to the meeting because they didn't like the energy, astrologers would need the right aspects to their chart to make sure that meetings were favored for that day, and most likely everyone there would have on protection oil, along with sage in their pockets and sea salt in their shoes in order to ward off bad vibes. The business peers of the psychic reader are quite a collection of unique, unusual people, too. My business connections run from A to Z; there is a fascinating mix of everything from angel readers to Zen masters.

My children grew up knowing my group of business acquaintances. This very illustrious, eclectic group included a psychic from Los Angeles who claimed to have made contact with aliens and to have worked with the FBI. There was also the high-strung, chatty astrologer who came to all of the kids' birthday parties and graduations. She helped me plan my parties by astrologically picking the best day to entertain. Another frequent houseguest was a dyslexic psychic who gave readings that had to be reversed in order to get the correct information. My psychic network of business friends also included a pet psychic who came in handy when we experienced a problem with one of our cats. My children have even had some childhood aches and pains diagnosed by the medical intuitive whom I know professionally. Reiki is administered more frequently than aspirin in my home, and clearing the house of negative energy by burning sage is as common as spraying disinfectant to kill germs.

My oldest son remembers that I would ask to borrow his Fisher-Price kiddie tape recorder, so my friends and I could tape our sessions with a local psychic who I'd ask to come over to my home once a month to do tarot-card readings. As soon as he would see me drag a small table and two chairs into the back bedroom, my son would know that he was going to have to give up his toy tape recorder for a few hours because Mom's friend, the fortuneteller, was coming over. I'm sure my frequent gatherings with the psychic du jour made his childhood more colorful, and also raised him up a notch over the kids who only had houseware demonstrators coming over to their home.

While most kids wonder how well they did on a school test, my kids would ask me to pull some tarot cards to get an inside look at their anticipated grade. My children also became accustomed to checking my astrological wall calendar to see if the Moon and aspects looked good for them. They learned to brace themselves during Mercury retrograde periods and to be prepared for any type of communication snafu. For my children, having knowledge of tarot, astrology, and other forms of divination was equivalent to picking up a second language. They were definitely exposed to a magickal childhood with appreciation for all *six* senses.

Most psychic-reader businesses are home-based, although there are psychic readers who maintain professional office spaces. To get a good reading, the client has to be conscious of the fact that the psychic's personal time and space are not abused. Business is conducted during the psychic reader's set hours, and psychics need their down time, too. The client who expects to have an on-demand psychic reading may be disappointed to find out that the psychic reader is on recharge mode and not mentally or psychically in the mindset to drop everything and give the client a reading.

When psychics aren't working, the last thing they want to hear is a client begging for an emergency reading. There are *psychic-reader shoplifters* who try to get free, unscheduled, after-hours psychic advice. It's always about a crisis that can't wait, a soul-mate story, or just one quick question. Psychic-reader shoplifters may not realize that they are causing an energy imbalance for themselves by expecting something for nothing. This imbalance may play out in any area of their life because they didn't reciprocate for the time the psychic gave them. Psychics have a responsibility not to let an energy imbalance occur between the client and themselves, and at the risk of insulting a basically good client, the psychic does have to be firm with setting fees and payment arrangements.

Psychics find it hard to turn their back on someone in need, but guess what? If you don't have insurance, a hospital will kick your ass out, and psychics who overextend themselves to clients need to set boundaries so they do not create an ongoing pattern of *freebie* abuse.

Are More Expensive Psychic Readers Better? Not Really!

How does a client know if the quality of a psychic reading will be equivalent to the price paid for the psychic session? Some of the best psychics around are not necessarily the most expensive. Psychic readers who work on psychic phone lines are not making the full amount charged to the client. The companies that sell and market psychic services are the ones making most of the profit. The profit is used to advertise, which in turn will hopefully generate more calls into the psychic phone line.

Psychics on phone lines usually only make 10 percent of the per-minute rate charged to the callers. If a client is charged four dollars per minute for a call to a psychic phone line, the average profit for the psychic is only forty cents per minute. Some psychic lines also pay out bonuses to psychics who have high call averages and frequent requests. The caller into a psychic phone line has to realize that in essence their favorite psychic is being paid about $24 an hour, less any taxes. Clients who schedule psychic readings with psychics who have a private business can pay anywhere from $50 per hour to as high as $400 or more per hour.

Are *designer readings* better than picking from a carousel of psychic readers on a phone line? That all depends on what the psychic seeker is looking for. Most phone lines employ legitimate psychic readers who prefer not to have the hassle of clients calling their home or stopping by to visit. The anonymity of the psychic phone line allows the psychic reader to get on and get off. The psychic on a psychic phone line develops a following of clients who know precisely when to find her. Only prepaid calls are put through, alleviating the problem of collecting payment for services. Some psychic lines are better than others. Those that do not screen and research their employed psychic readers are nothing more than pseudo-psychic cesspools that give honorable psychic phone lines a bad name.

A client who strikes up a psychic bond with a psychic-line reader runs the risk of not knowing where to find the psychic reader if the psychic should decide to quit the phone line. A psychic junkie can go into severe psychic-reader withdrawal if another psychic of equal and similar abilities cannot be found. I have dealt with *psychic-reader orphans*, and it can take some time to establish trust and make the proper psychic connection with the abandoned client. Losing a favorite psychic reader is like experiencing the death of a best friend or losing a cherished pet. I always thought it would be a brilliant idea to put a photo of the missing psychic reader on the side of a milk carton or on a flyer to help the forsaken client to locate their missing mystic.

Some psychic seekers prefer to go to private psychic readers rather than calling a psychic phone line; these clients want to have their readings in person instead of over the phone. Psychic seekers who like live, face-to-face readings feel that they are making a better connection for some reason. That isn't always the case, because clients can sometimes be a distraction to the psychic, especially if the client is nervously fidgeting in the chair or making a lot of facial expressions. Even little things like a client anxiously tapping fingers on a table can inadvertently put static energy into the psychic-reading session.

Lingering-client syndrome is always a fear factor for the in-person psychic reader. Private psychics may appear to be more expensive, but that's because the client is being presented with the full fee all at once and it is not hidden behind a per-minute rate. If you break it down, a psychic reader who charges $160 per hour is really billing the client roughly $2.67 per minute. Most psychic-reader phone lines charge at a higher rate than that. The difference is that the private psychic reader gets the full fee but must take care of all advertising and related operating expenses. The private psychic reader also doesn't have the shield of customer service representatives, who screen clients and arrange payment collection.

When a client's allotted time with a psychic reader on a phone line is up, the call is promptly disconnected—sometimes even in mid-sentence. If a client pays for an hour, then he gets exactly one hour. Some private psychic readers employ a scheduling secretary who also sends and maintains the billing. A client may pay more for a private psychic who has the expense of office help.

It is not unusual to have to wait weeks or sometimes months to get an appointment with a highly requested psychic. A psychic reader who has a long waiting list may require that a deposit for the reading be paid in advance. The deposit is most likely nonrefundable if the scheduled reading is canceled. Psychic junkies will often get interim readings to take the edge off while they are waiting for their appointment with the super psychic. Clients will even resort to psychic-reading placebos by engaging in computer-generated tarot readings.

The reason most clients want a psychic reading is because they have an immediate need for psychic insight and a prediction of a possible outcome for an event or pending decision. A psychic reader who has a long waiting list may lose out on an impulse client, because by the time the scheduled appointment arrives the client's concerns may already have been settled.

What a client is willing to pay for a psychic reading is a very personal choice. What determines the price a client is willing to pay is based primarily on the psychic's abilities and accuracy. The second most important factor is the psychic's availability and client care. A faction of clients feels that the more they pay for a reading, the more accurate the psychic will be. In all honesty, paying more money for a psychic reading is no guarantee of a great reading.

When I was a teenager I frequently went to a local tea room called Polly's. The psychic readers were among the best I ever came upon, and they worked on tips. The median amount for a tip was about five dollars. I clearly recall the demure, older lady with cinnamon-colored hair sitting across the table from me and my girlfriends at the tea room. This very gifted psychic reader would pull out a deck of well-worn playing cards and hand them over to be shuffled by whoever was getting the reading. After the cards were shuffled, this gifted card reader would lay the cards on the table amidst the plates and silverware and give us the most amazingly accurate card reading you could ever imagine. When this woman wasn't reading cards at Polly's, she was living a quiet, normal life in a Philadelphia neighborhood. She was hardly what you would call an expensive psychic, yet the predictions that she made for me and my friends were all very accurate.

I have also been to very expensive psychics for whom I needed to wait two months for an appointment. Since I am impatient to begin with, the wait for the reading seemed annoying to me, plus the anticipation of finally coming face to face with the booked-up super psychic reader began to freak me out. What if she saw something bad for me? Was I prepared to handle it? After all, this psychic reader is booked up months in advance so she must be great.

The day finally came for me to get my long-awaited reading from the super psychic. I had two months to make a list of questions for the psychic, and some of the questions were obsolete by the time my psychic session rolled around. I nervously sat down in the psychic's living room while waiting for her to finally see me. She was a woman in her mid-fifties who wore a lot of clingy bracelets that sounded like wind chimes as she shuffled the tarot cards. She spent most of the reading complaining about the client before me and seemed disinterested in my life. The psychic reading was very mechanical, and the psychic lacked warmth. She threw out a couple of names and a few initials of people whom I would soon be dealing with, but she did not elaborate as to why I would be associating with half of the letters in the alphabet.

The reading was a little on the vague side, and except for a few long-range predictions, I wasn't too impressed. She asked what I did for a living, and when I told her that I too was a psychic reader, the proverbial pissing contest began. I listened as she tried to impress me with all of her client stories and bragged about how someone wanted to do a book about her life. I wondered to myself if the book would be called *Behind the Cards: Psychics, Freaks, and Sideshows.*

The psychic I had waited so long to see and to whom I paid a very high fee was more smoke and mirrors than super psychic. This expensive psychic actually had the nerve to ask me if I psychically picked up any information about her future. I told her yes, lots of information, but she would need to call me and schedule an appointment. I don't think that she was too happy that I refused to oblige her on the spot. She never called me to set up a time for a reading. Maybe she was afraid of what she would hear.

On a scale of 1 to 10, she rated a 5 for accuracy, a 2 for client consideration, and a 10 in narcissism. The psychic reader's fee was on the high side, but the experience of going to her was priceless because it showed me how I didn't want to be perceived by my clients. Being on the other side of the cards as a seeker can be a very humbling experience. You get a better perspective on what psychic readings are really all about and firsthand experience of how it feels to be a client with too much hype and not enough psychic expertise.

Pricing psychic-reading services really depends on the psychic who is delivering the readings. Some psychics only want high-end clients who can afford big fees, while other psychic readers prefer to deal with everyday people who have a need for psychic services. One thing I've found out over the years of doing readings is that wealthy clients as well as everyday clients have similar problems, and for the psychic, putting a price tag on readings can be a pain in the ass. Some psychics work on a sliding scale, where old clients pay one fee and new clients pay at a higher rate. Psychic phone lines usually have one set rate and everyone pays the same freight.

One time I had a woman call who wanted me to answer a few pertinent questions for her before she booked an appointment. I work strictly by referral, so she apparently knew someone else for whom I had done psychic readings. I would not be recommended by someone if they were dissatisfied with my services. This woman wanted a psychic sampler as if she were ordering appetizers at a restaurant. I told her that I don't do on-the-spot free psychic readings because I have a process of using the client's birth information and astrological chart for the first session. This woman wanted me to audition for the part of psychic as if I were trying out for a show. She was reluctant to make an appointment unless she got a free sample. I immediately knew that this client would be difficult.

Her unwillingness to schedule an appointment equates to her not being open enough to getting a good psychic reading, and her reluctance would find its way into payments for services rendered. She was also expecting some freebies. There are clients who think it is okay to run a tab as if they were sitting at a bar ordering martinis. There are clients who call outside of scheduled appointments to ask just *one quick question* and believe that they don't have to pay the psychic for her time. I especially get a kick out of the client who calls to ask for a reading, and then says that she has your payment for the past three readings in her handbag but she doesn't have a stamp. The other big ploy is to call the psychic to ask for the address to which to send payment for a reading, and while the psychic is on the phone the client tries to get a few questions answered for free.

Clients are prone to losing billing addresses, but the psychic reader's telephone number is tattooed onto their brain. Just as with any business, when the tail begins to wag the dog it is a sign to revamp the methods of doing business. I will tell you honestly that I have some clients who pay me on an honor system, and there are very few clients who try to pull a fast one on me. Through years of doing readings I have learned to psychically perceive the *psychic-reading shoplifters*, and clients such as those are quickly reminded of how to pay for my services. Karma is karma, and if you cheat, then you too will be cheated.

What a client is willing to pay for a psychic reading is very much a personal choice. Clients should not expect psychics to give discounts, wait to be paid, forgive bounced checks, or, above all else, do free readings. My advice is to keep the relationship clean, respect boundaries, and avoid energy imbalances by paying promptly.

CHAPTER 5

The Psychic-Reader Care and Use Guide

Operating Instructions

Anyone seeking a psychic reading needs to familiarize themselves with the care and use of a psychic's services. It greatly behooves the client to know what not to do to turn off, disengage, and have a psychic reader shut down. Once a favorite psychic burns out, the chances of restoring his enthusiasm about doing readings for you are very slim. Clients making calls outside of an appointment are the number one reason for psychic-reader malfunction. If the client wants to get a good reading, it is necessary to respect the psychic's boundaries. Some psychic seekers search for years looking for the right psychic, and finding the perfect psychic match can be an extraordinary event.

Psychic readers don't like clients getting too involved in their lives. Clients who get nosy about their psychic's private life may elicit vague responses from the psychic. Psychics know how important it is to keep the energy boundaries in place. Clients are naturally curious about their psychic's life, because they think that the psychic lives in a mystical, enchanted world filled with magick. If the psychic reader wants a client to know some personal information, then the psychic will offer the facts. Sometimes clients think that they are their psychic reader's keeper. I have had clients leave messages on my voicemail that sound like parents trying to track down their stray children.

I returned home one evening, retrieved my voicemail, and heard, "*Beep.* You have seventeen unheard messages." All of the messages were from the same client, who for some reason doesn't believe that psychic readers go out into the real world. The messages ranged from the innocent *Where are you?* to the final, frantic message of *Call me as soon as you get in. I'm worried about you. Where are you? I hope you're not hurt or in the hospital. Please, please call me as soon as you get in. This is urgent!* I didn't feel like calling the client back, because I was too tired to talk on the phone. But I also knew that this kooky client would start calling hospitals and police stations if she didn't hear back from me.

I called the client back, and she picked up after half of a ring. After the initial hello, she started right in with, "Where were you? Are you okay? I called three different psychic phone lines while I was waiting for you to call me back. Do you know how much money I spent on those psychic lines?" I asked her what the urgent problem was that required her to go into *psychic search and rescue mode.* It turned out that the urgent problem was seeing her boyfriend's profile on a dating site while she was surfing the Internet. She was obviously looking for a new boyfriend for herself or she wouldn't have been looking at dating sites in the first place.

In the few hours that this client was left unattended and unable to contact me, she further complicated her life by making up a phony profile and e-mail address. Then she responded to her boyfriend's advertisement on the dating site. The boyfriend didn't respond to her inquiry, which further fueled this woman's hysteria. She thought an emergency psychic reading would tell her why her boyfriend was on the dating site and if he had met and hooked up with another woman. I didn't feel like doing any psychic readings after an evening out, and I told the client to call me the following evening for a tarot reading.

Well, this hysterical client carried on and became insistent about getting a psychic reading that night. I asked her what the other psychics she called on the psychic lines had told her. She said that they didn't like her boyfriend and that she should dump him. My assessment of her current boyfriend problem could wait until the next day, and I told her that I was too tired to do a tarot spread for her.

I politely got off the telephone, only to have her call me right back. This client had turned into a drill sergeant and began demanding that I pull a few cards. Her tone varied from whimpering to guttural moaning sounds mixed among her pleadings. I stood my ground and told her to call the next day.

She called again, but I didn't pick up the telephone and I let her message go to voicemail. The next morning when I played my messages, I had a lengthy one from the client. She was still trying to convince me to give her a tarot reading and was begging me to call her back. I could see why her boyfriend was posting his profile on dating sites.

I gave her a farewell reading and told her that our professional relationship was over because she was too intense and I couldn't deal with her anymore. I felt bad because both her boyfriend and her psychic were dumping her at the same time, but her bad behavior couldn't be condoned any longer. This client was always a little pushy, and over time she had become extremely difficult. I told her that her energy levels were way off, and I wanted her to focus on getting herself grounded before she seeks out any further psychic readings. She was like a live wire with sparks flashing all over the place. I had told her about grounding during previous psychic-reading sessions, and reminded her that she would *short circuit* me if her erratic, impatient behavior didn't stop.

Dealing with her was hazardous to my energetic well-being, because it would take me a good twenty-four hours to clear her energy. This client's energy was also starting to bleed into my personal life because of her constant personal questioning about my whereabouts. She wanted to know if she was my favorite client and would ask me what my other clients were like in comparison to her. She was insecure and very high maintenance.

Clients like this woman have to take responsibility for their own actions in bringing about a situation and realize that a psychic reading is not a quick fix for problem solving. In previous tarot readings, she was given information about pending problems in her relationship brought about by jealousy and mistrust. If she would have worked on herself and grounded her energy, she would have experienced a better outcome concerning her relationship.

The breakup with her boyfriend would have been handled in a more energetically contained way without mega doses of drama if this client would have paid attention to her psychic readings. Energy cannot be created or destroyed, but it can be transformed. This client handled her relationship problems all wrong and basically changed a trash fire into an atomic explosion because of her reactive behavior.

This client not only had *issues* but also a *lifetime subscription* to erratic actions. She never successfully got past her back issues of abandonment and mistrust, and getting psychic readings was nothing more than putting a Band-Aid on a gunshot wound. I psychically felt that this woman needed a past-life regression and definitely some chakra balancing before she continued on with psychic readings.

I heard from this client a few years later, and she actually thanked me because she got turned on to Reiki and had begun to spend an hour or two each week in guided meditations. She resolved many of her outside issues by going within. She was so calm and centered that I could not believe that I was talking to the same person. She asked me to do a psychic reading for her, but I had to be true to myself and admit that I still needed to do some work on myself and get past the memory of how smothering and draining dealing with her used to be. I told her that my mission with her was over, because dealing with me initially had helped her to find herself. I preferred to keep her as an acquaintance.

I did a quick energy scan, and I could see that even though this client had made progress with her life, the mix of her energy and my energy might be too high maintenance for there to be any type of psychic services from me. Not all things work, and psychic readers have to recognize that when dealing with some-one else's energy. One high-wattage client can short circuit the psychic reader for a whole week or more and have a negative ef-fect on the psychic's business.

Psychics have to keep their chakras spinning at the right fre-quency and keep a check on their energy input and output. Just as you wouldn't take a long road trip with a car that needed a tune-up, nor should you journey along with your energetic field out of whack. The results will not be what they should be, and you may break down along the way. I also recommend that clients keep their relationship with their psychic reader from becoming too personal or familiar because it may blur the energy read. Al-ways be considerate of professional boundaries.

Do I Need to Wear My Hematite Body Armor Before Our Session?

Hematite is a dark-colored stone that has great grounding properties. When worn, hematite will draw negativity away from the wearer. Hematite is also a great deflector of negative energy. I firmly be-lieve that OSHA should require all psychic readers to wear hema-tite in some form when doing psychic readings, either as a ring, bracelet, or, better yet, a body suit. It is a fact that a hematite ring will crack and fall off of your finger after it has absorbed all of the negative vibrations flung at you.

Since psychics deal with energy, it is necessary that we protect ourselves while working with clients. A client seeking a reading also brings her auric field into the session. If the client has crazy, erratic energy, the psychic may easily absorb the client's vibration by venturing and tapping into the client's Akashic records. The Akashic records are a compendium of the client's past, present, and future that are encoded into the ether waves.

Psychics who are remiss about energy clearing easily attract like energy into their own vibratory field. I have known psychic readers who experience a type of possession in which the client's problems begin to manifest in the life of the psychic. For example, if a client is having a relationship problem, the psychic reader may attract similar relationship problems into her own life. Psychics are also prone to having glass break after an intense energy contact with a client. Glass breaking is a form of energy clearing.

Psychics will also find that if protection is not used and grounding is omitted as part of the psychic reading preparation, then electrical problems with appliances can also occur for the psychic. To avoid client problems by osmosis, a clearing and grounding ritual for the psychic is a must.

Doing safe psychic readings is like practicing safe sex. Psychic readings are intimate, personal experiences, and any energy foul-ups will result in psychically transmitted disruptions and aborted or unwanted outcomes. Both the client and the psychic should clear before contact with each other. The psychic reader has to dispel any client energy from a previous psychic reading before dealing with the next client. Even clients who call on the phone are leaving an energy imprint that the psychic reader must deal with. The clearing of the psychic reading room by burning sage is a good way to keep the energy clean, and so is washing of the hands with sea salt. Some psychics use a clearing essence spray, especially misting the corners of the room where energy has a tendency to settle. Burning clearing incense like Nag Champa or juniper will also protect the psychic from client-energy upheavals. I also like to put guardian angel oil on my shoulders before attempting to engage in psychic readings with my clients.

Grounding is rule one before getting a reading. Imagine standing in a bathtub filled with water while blow-drying your hair. You would get electrocuted. For the psychic reader, any client contact made without first taking the proper protection methods will result in psychic shock. The difference between getting a good reading and getting a great reading is in the preparedness of both parties involved in the session. A psychic reader who does not clear between clients is as bad as a doctor who doesn't wash his or her hands between patients. I burn incense and sage while doing psychic readings, and I keep sea salt close by to keep my energy clear.

Clients can pick up negative energy from a psychic who isn't grounded. Clients will sometimes have a streak of car problems, computer malfunctions, and a general malaise after having a reading with a *hot-wired* psychic. A client who senses that the psychic reader seems a little hyped up, preoccupied, and impatient is better off not persisting for the psychic to read him. Good psychic readers can't be expected to be constantly on. Some days—and some clients—are more draining for psychics than others.

Clients getting a reading will find that they get better results if they take a few cautionary grounding measures before their appointment. Psychic readings can be for entertainment purposes, but keep in mind that the opening of any psychic doors and crossing the veil between the worlds of past, present, and future is not child's play. Energy is involved, and tapping into this unseen force carries a responsibility for both the psychic reader and the psychic seeker. There are all kinds of low-level and sometimes nasty vibratory entities floating around just waiting for an open door to slide into.

Clients and psychics can experience forms of psychic attack if grounding and clearing are not practiced. A good method of grounding for the client is to make sure that both feet are on the floor during the reading. This acts as a good foundation before a reading because any extra hyper energy will go into the ground instead of flying around and striking like lightning.

Over the years I have had clients who suffered from some form of mental illness, and reading clients who have unbound energy from a mental disorder is very difficult. How do you get these clients grounded enough for a psychic reading? These clients were not dangerous (although sometimes I wonder!), but nonetheless mental illnesses like manic depression and paranoia do make these clients especially challenging to work with.

The energy of someone with mental illness is like an electrical spider web. When these clients take their meds they are fine, but if they decide to go off of their medication, things can get crazy. Curiously, I have found that my clients who have suffered from some type of mental illness are somewhat psychic themselves. Maybe it is because all of their wild energy is flying around, freely uncontained and making random connections with whatever is out there. Don't get me wrong, though. I've never done psychic readings for anyone in a straitjacket, and I have refused to do readings for clients who could not be grounded.

One woman who suffered from manic depression was very sweet, but after a session with her I too would feel manic. One night after doing a psychic reading for this woman, I indulged the feeling of mania that had been transferred to me and I wound up ordering hundreds of dollars worth of clothes from a fashion catalog. I would ground myself before talking with her, but because her energy was over the top even while on meds, my grounding methods only provided some protection. Mental illness is strong energy and not easily deflected. I didn't want to refuse to do psychic readings for her because of her mental condition, since she was basically an entertaining client in a crazy sort of way. She personified the "fun" in the word *dysfunctional*. This client's moods would go from mellow to crazy every few months because she also had SAD, seasonal affective disorder. Living in the northern region of the United States, where there are four seasons, meant that she wigged out to the fourth power. Maybe if she lived in a state where the climate never changed she would have been better off.

If psychics only read for clients who had no mental quirks, then the number of psychic-reading patrons would significantly drop off. But we live in a world of *please pass the Prozac*, so it is necessary for the psychic to be cautious and responsible when gauging the degree of someone's mental condition, and also if the client can be grounded enough to get a psychic reading.

When this woman was in her manic stage, she would want numerous psychic readings from me and other psychics. She would go into psychic-junkie overdrive. When she was depressed and her paranoia would kick in, her energy felt like a thick fog with no way out. I liked this client and felt bad for her, but I could no longer deal with her and provide her with psychic readings. Her varying moods were affecting my energy, which, in turn, affected my business.

The straw that broke the psychic's back was when this client called me on Good Friday, a Christian holy day, insisting that she was Jesus Christ. I told her to take her meds and call her doctor. This woman called me three more times insisting that she was Jesus Christ. I finally lost it and told her to knock it off. Her delusions of being Jesus were something to be handled by a psychiatrist, not a psychic. The woman called me for more tarot readings after this episode, but I could no longer deal with her energy. She wasn't grounded enough to have tarot readings.

I maintained a friendly relationship with her, but a professional relationship was out of the question. The funny thing was that after I told her I would no longer give her readings, this woman had a manic attack and sent me flowers from eleven different florists as a gesture of apology. One floral arrangement was bigger than the delivery person. I laughed like hell as the delivery man struggled up my front steps and into my home with a potted tree surrounded with flowers that was better suited for the foyer of a grand hotel. The next day this former client sent numerous bottles of Chanel perfume to my home. I called her and told her that she is an amazing person, but psychic readings are not for her unless she can get and stay grounded.

Sometimes women with bad PMS or who are menopausal are hard to read for unless their energy can be grounded. The energy from the accompanying depression of those conditions makes the psychic reader feel as though she is doing readings underwater. The emotions of these clients are very strong, and psychics must protect themselves from the energy fallout if the clients do not ground themselves before a reading.

The midlife-crisis clients also need to be reminded to keep their feet on the floor for grounding purposes during a psychic reading. These clients are usually experiencing an astrological condition called the *Uranus half-return*. The planet Uranus is noted for erratic, rebellious, and sudden, unexpected actions. A psychic reading involving a *mid-lifer* as a client requires the psychic to pass on the rules of grounding. The psychic is dealing with a client equivalent to a teenager who must be grounded for unexpected behavior.

Clients should also keep in mind that by crossing their arms or ankles they are unknowingly blocking off the energy connection with the psychic. Feet must be on the floor, and arms and legs should be uncrossed if the client expects to get a good psychic reading. The same goes for the psychic.

As you can see, there are job risks with being a psychic reader, and there are also risks for the client who doesn't know how well the psychic reader practices proper grounding. Clients should seriously check out the psychics they let in to their energy field, or else they run the risk of getting a psychic reader from a *psychic mill*, where grounding and proper clearing of lingering client energy may not be a common practice. Both the client and the psychic need to be careful about who they are dealing with when it comes to readings.

Plugging into Your Psychic Reader

In order to get a good psychic reading, it is necessary for the client to be open. If someone tries to talk you into going to go see a psychic for a reading and you are not into it, then don't go. Just as you would never think of walking into someone's home without first knocking, psychic readers can't get in if your *psychic door* is locked.

Being open to getting a psychic reading means that you are receptive to the fact—and I do stress *fact*—that there are people who have highly developed sixth-sense abilities and can perceive things psychically. Psychics have different techniques for doing psychic readings, and clients have to find the right psychic fit for their needs. A psychic who is amazing for your friend may not be amazing for you. Simply because someone has psychic abilities doesn't guarantee that they can read successfully and accurately for everyone. Just as some doctors, lawyers, mechanics, hairstylists, and brokers are good for some people, they may not deliver the same results for others. Does that mean that they aren't proficient or good at what they do? Not at all, because a lot depends on the energy interaction between the client and the professional, and the same holds true for psychics and their clients.

Making the energetic connection with your psychic reader is important, and if you feel that after the first five or ten minutes the reading isn't going anywhere, ground yourself. Make sure that your feet are on the floor. Make sure that your legs are not crossed at the ankles, and your arms are not folded in front of you. You may be blocking off the connection by crossing your arms and legs because the body mimics the unseen energy. You are unconsciously exhibiting reservations about getting a reading, and it will show in your body language.

When the connection has been made with your psychic reader during a session, confirm that the psychic is on the right track. That gives the psychic permission to go further into what is energetically presenting itself at that time. If a doctor asks you where it hurts, you tell the doctor. The same is true about your psychic reader. If the psychic asks if you recognize or relate to what is coming through in a reading, then make the confirmation. Don't play baby games during a psychic reading by saying to the psychic reader, "You're the psychic. You tell me." Your validation will raise the psychic's vibration and enhance the psychic's abilities.

If the psychic reader's vibration is elevated, then tapping into a like type of higher energy is possible. Playing guessing games with the psychic will lower the psychic's vibration, resulting in a very slow-paced, mundane type of psychic reading. Keep in mind that the psychic can only access that which you are meant to know at any given time. There are some things that you are not meant to know about until other things have unfolded in your life. Some psychics are short-term psychic readers, picking up what will come about for you within the next year or so. Other psychics are more long-term psychic readers, and able to see further into your future.

Timing is one of the most difficult things to pinpoint psychically because there is no time in space. Time is a human-made unit of measurement for giving some semblance of order to our existence. Psychics access the dimension of space where your prior conceived thoughts have taken root, and they give predictions based on what they see manifesting from your own thoughts. Psychic readers have a highly developed sensitivity to energy patterns that they remotely view, hear, or feel. Clients have to take responsibility for what is happening in their life, whether bad or good. The client's thoughts go out into the ether waves, where a direct manifestation of these thoughts occurs.

Psychics are energy guides who help do damage control in case clients' thoughts have led them astray. There are SOUL-utions to your problems and better choices to help you avoid bad outcomes. Psychics connect with the client and act as guides, helping to do past-life karmic corrections and point clients in the right cosmic direction. Psychic readers can't shield you from all of your life lessons, just as a parent can't keep a child from getting hurt at some time. Psychic readers can make you aware of the road signs along the way.

The psychic may not be able to access certain areas of your life if, on an unconscious level, you are locking the psychic out. Keep in mind that psychic readers can't get in without permission, so you must be willing to be energetically open and fully grounded. Some people complain that they never had a good psychic reading nor had any predictions come true. They are ready to blame the negative experience solely on the psychic. A psychic reader reads energy, and if you are not steady then don't expect the best from your psychic reader. Imagine trying to watch a television show if the station is not tuned in. Everything will be fuzzy and only little blips of the program will come through. The same is true when getting a psychic reading.

Keep in mind that when you are connecting with a psychic during a reading, the psychic is connecting with you. Questions about other people can only be answered in relation to you. Don't ask a psychic what someone else is thinking. The psychic does not have permission from that person to read their thoughts. The psychic can get a sense of their energy, but it is not ethical to tap into someone's life without permission. Psychic readings are not all smoke and mirror games as some people like to believe. Imagine holding your hand over a hot oven. You can feel the heat even if you can't see the heat.

Psychic readers bleed into the client's energy field and feel the psychic heat, psychically defining the events that are surrounding the client. Going further out into the client's energetic field, the psychic can see how future events are shaping up. The energy is sight unseen but there nonetheless. When the energy manifests outwardly, sometimes electrical problems will occur. Did you ever try to tape a psychic session and have the tape recorder malfunction? That is caused by not grounding the psychic and the client energy, or by non-cleared residual energy left over from the psychic's previous client. Even though you can't see the uncontained energy, it manifests as electrical problems or even glass breaking.

People who go to psychics for readings have to realize that the skills that the psychic possesses are highly developed sixth-sense faculties. Everyone has psychic skills to some degree and when a client plugs her underdeveloped psychic sense into a psychic reader's more highly developed psychic sense, then a phenomenal psychic reading is the end result.

Take, for example, the task of driving a car. Even though you, the driver, don't consciously realize it, you are using your psychic intuition. On a low level, the driver of one car must intuitively sense the other driver's moves while in traffic. Signals are given as warnings of impending lane or stopping changes, but throughout most of the ride the drivers intuitively sense the unexpected. Accidents happen when warnings aren't heeded or drivers are preoccupied with events other than driving. The feeling you get after a near miss with an accident is always recognized as "someone looking out for you," or in other words, basic intuition. You, in essence, plugged into the energy of driving and the other drivers on the road with you. Plugging into a psychic for a psychic reading should also have your full attention so you are aware of the signals given in the reading, enabling you to reach your destination with as few near misses as possible and hopefully no accidents. Don't be distracted during a psychic session by answering your cell phone, watching television, or playing on your computer. First of all, it is rude behavior toward the psychic who is doing the reading, and the outside impulses from the distracting electrical gadgets definitely cause interference.

One woman I did psychic readings for was guilty of plugging into too many things at once and causing energy malfunctions. This woman loved to play on her computer while getting a reading. During her reading sessions with me, she played video games on her laptop, answered e-mails, and surfed the Internet. Along with the distraction of the computer, she always had the television on or a radio station. While getting a psychic reading from me, she experienced computer freeze-ups quite often. Maybe my thoughts of how pissed off she was making me by not being attentive to her reading were unknowingly attacking her computer. This woman needed to plug into a "psychic-reading surge protector" before plugging into a session.

I found it hard to keep a psychic connection with her because she would not cooperate by grounding and paying attention to the reading. This woman expected psychic information that was right on the money, yet she continued to treat the service of psychics with disinterested nonchalance. I told her numerous times to shut off her electrical distractions during our sessions, but she kept them on.

Another problem I had with this woman is that I found her to be very difficult, and the thought of plugging into her energy was very disturbing. I decided to meditate on her before our sessions and kept feeling that she was repressing something. The distractions she exposed herself to during our sessions were a way of unconsciously shutting me out so I wouldn't sense her real issues, which obviously frightened her. This woman wanted psychic readings, but she would only venture in so far. Imagine trying to plug in an appliance that only had one prong at the end of the electrical cord. You wouldn't be able to make the optimum connection.

As it turned out, this woman had issues with men, and her feelings toward them were very much closed off. She never really had a good relationship with a man, and she kept getting readings from me and other psychics in hopes that we would foretell the right man for her. I finally told her that the energy I kept getting from her is one of anger and distraction. She was also closed off to men, and until she takes responsibility for her own attitude about relationships, there isn't a psychic in the world who could snap his fingers and make her love life better.

The weird thing about this woman is that she went to psychics because she really wanted to find out what people thought about her not ever being in a relationship with a man, yet during her sessions she would cause distractions so she wouldn't have to hear the truth. This woman had sexual-identity issues but didn't want to deal with them. She really wanted to see if the psychics she frequented could pick up on her sexual concerns. Being a psychic reader means that you have to, at times, walk a fine line between psychic and psychiatrist, and at the risk of being rude you also have to be truthful. The bottom line is that if you want a good psychic reading and you don't want to waste your money and time, or the psychic's time, you must be open, honest, and grounded.

Spirit and Spirits Don't Mix: Don't Drink and Dial

One of the most energetically erratic types of people for a psychic reader to deal with is the client who likes to *drink and dial*. When I briefly worked for a psychic-reader phone line, Friday nights after the clubs closed was the prime time for drunks to call a psychic to get a reading, usually concerning someone they had just met or missed out on meeting. Psychic readers will also have clients who have just gone through some personal crisis that the client initially soothed by getting plastered. Drinking a whole bottle of Pinot Grigio or downing a couple of mixed drinks puts some clients in the mood for psychic-reading time.

Whenever substances like drugs or alcohol are put into your system, it can cause holes or weak spots in your auric field. The tears in the auric field allow for energy leaks and also put the client in jeopardy of letting in outside low-level energy thought-forms. It is impossible to ground a client who is drunk, and the psychic reader can't make the proper psychic connection. Clients who call psychics for psychic readings or show up inebriated for an appointment are wasting their time, because most psychics will refuse to read a client who is smashed. There is nothing more energy-zapping than being sober and having to deal with someone who is intoxicated.

I had a client call me one evening, and she was totally blitzed. She was begging for a tarot reading because she had just broken up with her boyfriend and tried to remedy the pain of the breakup by getting drunk. I told her that I didn't want to give her a tarot reading, because she wasn't sober enough to comprehend any information and most of all because she wasn't grounded. The client cried and begged me to pull just the proverbial three cards to see if she would get back with her boyfriend. I didn't want to read her tarot cards because she was too emotional and really not making any sense. She was seeing double, and I felt like I would be reading double for both her and Johnnie Walker.

The client pleaded with me to let her ask just one question. She wanted to know if her boyfriend was going to call her. I pulled three cards against my better judgment, and I gave her the answer to her query: her boyfriend would call her within a two-week period to discuss their relationship. The drunken client didn't respond to me when I gave her the answer. While I was looking at her tarot cards, she managed to do a three-way call and now her boyfriend was also on the line with us. The boyfriend was confused, and the drunken client was crying and picking a fight with him while I was on the other end of their conversation, listening. I guess that this was one of those *for entertainment purposes only*–types of psychic-reader phone calls.

The client wanted me to agree that her boyfriend's zodiac sign was the perfect match for her sign. She became very insistent and belligerent. The client's boyfriend was still on the other telephone line, and he seemed petrified of psychics. The idea that a psychic reader was hooked into this conversation made him quite nervous. He asked me very cautiously if I could read his mind. I did pick up that there was another woman in his life, but I didn't want to say anything because the drunken client was still fumbling around on the phone.

After fifteen minutes of talking to both the client and her boyfriend, my patience wore off. I was ready to issue a CUI (Client Under the Influence) citation. The client was now calling her boyfriend a creep and he was calling her a bitch. Just as I was ready to hang up on both of them, I heard a tumbling sound. The client, in her drunken state, managed to fall down a flight of steps. I screamed into the phone asking her if she was all right. The client's boyfriend tried to cover up his laughing at her fall by fake-coughing into the phone. The client regained herself and the next thing she asked me was, "How come you didn't see in the tarot cards that I was going to fall down a flight of steps?" I just told her, "Honey, just be glad that you didn't get hurt. Get off the phone and get some rest." It seems that this client's version of a twelve-step program is to fall down a flight of twelve steps.

There are people who are so deathly afraid of getting a psychic reading that they drink before their appointment to calm themselves down. Any imbalance in either the client or the psychic will throw off the equilibrium of the reading. Many psychic readers are also empaths. Empaths pick up transferred feelings and emotions from their clients. When a client is drunk or high, it can be empathically transferred to the psychic. There have been times when I felt like I just had one too many *psychic-junkie slammers* after talking with a client who had been drinking. Remember: psychic readers are connecting into the client's energy field and no one wants a reading from a psychic who can't walk a straight line.

Psychics also have to be wary of the client who does drugs. Doing drugs does open up your consciousness, but once again the possibility of lower vibratory energy creeping into the auric field is likely. Clients who are coked up don't shut up long enough to let the psychic get a word in edgewise. The pothead clients are too mellowed out and give off such a low energy level that psychic readers feel sleepy just reading them. A psychic may even get the munchies after doing a reading for someone who is high because of the energy interaction.

Clients who get readings while they are drinking or doing drugs better make sure that the psychic reader to whom they are going is aboveboard and not some charlatan. Clients are very suggestive while drugs are in their system, because the drug use thins out the aura and changes the consistency of the energy field. Information from a psychic reading can assimilate into the client's actions and interrupt the option of free will.

People who have addictive personalities can easily become addicted to psychic readings. A real problem occurs when someone who has overindulged in drugs or alcohol also goes on a psychic-reading binge and gets numerous readings throughout the day. Mixing psychics is like mixing drinks. The result is a psychic-reading hangover. Clients are likely to get different versions and answers to the same questions that can cause massive confusion for the client. The rule of thumb is that you are not supposed to get more than one reading per day and that the same question cannot be asked twice in the same day. Clients who have been overindulging or partying don't follow the rules for getting a good reading, and can wind up creating chaos in their lives.

It is a sad fact to know that there are a lot of lonely, depressed people who try to relieve their pain with drugs and alcohol. Some clients need the courage from an outside substance before placing a call to a psychic for a reading. These people are looking for some promise of a better tomorrow, but a psychic reading will not always predict just good things. When clients are not sober, any negative information that comes through a reading can seem amplified and make the client feel worse.

Psychics also don't run *psychic-seeker halfway houses*. Clients that are drunk or high have no idea how uneasy they make the psychic reader. I had a lady call me for a reading, and she was beyond toasted. She started the session by telling me that everything in her life was going wrong. I told her that the planet Mercury was currently in retrograde motion, which could explain all of her current confusion. This woman's chaos was further enhanced by the six-pack of beer that she slammed down. She replied, "Screw the retrograde. Everybody is an asshole." I could see that I was dealing with a *drink-and-dial client* who thought that calling a psychic for a reading was the *shot* she needed to go with her beers.

She proceeded to tell me, in slurred speech between taking sips of her beer, that she thinks she is also psychic. I let her rant about the universe, the proverbial soul-mate syndromes, and the Mayan calendar. I will admit that she was a little entertaining. I didn't want to connect with her psychically because she was definitely not grounded, and when she asked me to pull out the tarot cards I had to tell her that I was sorry but the psychic-reading bar was closed and she missed the last call. She called me the next day and apologized for being drunk and was very embarrassed about her condition.

Most *100 proof* clients have a penchant for calling in the middle of the night to get a psychic reading. I guess it is safe to say that it must be *happy hour* somewhere in the world. Psychics have a responsibility to flag clients who are way out in left field and are not cognizant of their behavior.

To get a good psychic reading, you have to be lucid. Any imbalance may cause confusion and further complicate existing issues.

Health Readings Are for Specialists; Death Is Everyone's Fate

Most psychic phone lines have a strict rule that all of their psychics must follow: *absolutely no health readings*. You may wonder why the operators of the psychic phone lines are so adamant about not giving health readings. The reason that medical issues are avoided is because of potential lawsuits. Psychic readers are not medical doctors, and are wide open to legal problems if they diagnose a medical condition for their clients.

A wrong diagnosis or fuzzy information about a client's health can cause the client much needless worry. If a psychic reader feels that there is a health problem that hasn't been detected by a doctor, then it is gingerly translated into advising the client to get a medical checkup. There are highly respected medical intuitives who work along with some medical doctors and specialize in psychic medical readings. Medical intuitives usually abide by a more holistic approach to medical conditions, and often they will have some training in nutrition, bodywork, or psychology.

For the most part the average psychic reader who is not recognized primarily as a medical intuitive can get in trouble for doing health assessments. I know of a psychic reader who had a client ask her to give her the best dates, astrologically speaking, to schedule plastic surgery for her face. The psychic obliged and told the woman the best days to get the surgery. As it turned out, the client was not happy with the results of the plastic surgery and blamed it on the psychic astrologer. As a result, the psychic was served legal papers for some type of contributory negligence and practicing medicine without a license.

The woman blamed the psychic astrologer for her bad facelift as much as the surgeon who did the job. According to the psychic astrologer, the woman was not attractive to begin with and there wasn't any amount of surgery that would make her beautiful. The astrologer had to get an attorney to represent her against the woman's accusations. Eventually, the lawsuit was dropped but only after much aggravation and legal expense for the astrologer.

It isn't that psychic readers can't pick up health issues during a reading session, but the subject leaves itself wide open for potential problems. Doctors are not always correct in their diagnoses of medical conditions, and medical mistakes are often made. Doctors are licensed to treat and prescribe medication for medical problems but also have medical malpractice insurance in case they screw up. Psychic readers get admonished by doctors who think, *How dare you diagnose a patient; after all,* I'm *the one still paying off my med-school loans.*

Just try going to a doctor and saying that your psychic thinks that you have diabetes or some other illness. You would be treated like a nutcase. There was a time when in order to be a doctor, you also had to be an astrologer. There is a famous quote attributed to Hippocrates, the father of modern medicine: "A physician without knowledge of astrology has no right to call himself a physician." Another man of medicine who practiced astrology was Nostradamus. Edgar Cayce, the sleeping prophet, was also an amazing medical intuitive, even though he had no formal medical training.

Unfortunately, in this day of big-time pharmaceutical businesses, holistics and intuition are considered to be New Age cures and sometimes are not taken seriously. What people need to know is that in the word disease you can clearly see the *dis-ease.* When there is a problem in the psyche, the energies will manifest as disease. There is a vibration misfire that causes what is in the mind to show itself in the body. Some physical conditions are a direct result of aging, but many illnesses start as a thought vibration. Some psychics attribute illnesses to past-life karma. As an astrologer myself, I can see medical predispositions in the charts of my clients, and I can advise them to seek traditional medical diagnoses, but because we live in a litigious society I would rather not venture into psychic medical readings.

Psychic readers who also do bodywork and energy clearings may prescribe a combo *psychic prediction, psychic prescription* for their clients. If a client is very negative and having a streak of bad luck, a psychic reader will advise an energy clearing and rebalancing of the chakra centers, which are energy centers for the body. Psychics work on an energetic plane, and therefore will be most helpful to a client who needs help beyond the physical realm. Reiki is also a psychic prescription for clients who have energy imbalances. A Reiki practitioner taps into the universal life-force energy and transmits it to the person in need of a Reiki treatment. The Reiki treatment will put energy where it is needed.

When doing a psychic reading for a client, it is inevitable that at one time or another some health question will come up. I can always tell when someone's marriage is on the skids. The spouse getting the psychic reading will ask about the health outlook for his or her partner.

I read for a very sweet woman at her wit's end now that her husband is retired. Her life has been reduced to a tug-of-war for the remote control and constant eavesdropping on her phone conversations. The sudden appearance of two full-time alpha dogs in the same house has given this client a reason to keep getting psychic readings. It is not uncommon for her to ask me during a psychic session the age-old question, "How does my husband's health look?" She will quickly punctuate the question with a follow-up statement alerting me to all of her suspected health conditions for him.

She makes it a point to tell me that he gets short of breath, looks pale, and gets tired easily. Basically, she should be asking me if she should get a divorce instead of when her husband might kick the bucket. Her spouse definitely has a few health conditions that have been medically diagnosed, but this client is looking for some psychic verification that her husband's conditions might take him out. This client even told me that another psychic reader had predicted that her husband would die on a golf course. I asked her if her husband played much golf, and she replied, "No. He's never played in his life." Her next request was to ask the cards if her husband should take up golf. As you can see, psychic readers often find themselves in very sticky situations.

The reasoning behind most clients asking health-related questions is primarily to ensure that there is no impending death in their near future. Believe it or not, there are clients who ask questions like, "How will I die? When will I die? Do you see any death around me?" Can psychic readers pick up death? The answer is yes. The psychic reader who sees death for someone or around someone is walking a fine ethical line of whether or not to reveal that type of information to the client.

If we are meant to pick up some morbid information, then it will be picked up. Psychic readers are only allowed to access what clients are meant to know. Some things are not for clients to find out. I have had clients ask me to look at their astrological chart or their tarot cards and predict how they will die. My reply to these curious clients is, "Don't worry about how you will die, but rather how you choose to live." If they persist on knowing their type of death, I may give a hint as to what I see in their astrological charts, but I will never commit to any information given.

Just as there is a normal chain of command in any organization, psychics need to respect where their psychic gifts come from and not go above the chain of command and decide everyone's ultimate fate, which is death.

Psychic Overtime (That One Last Question)

Psychic readers who do private readings outside of the psychic phone services always have the problem of the *curtain call*. A majority of clients try to linger and squeeze in that *one final question*. Why do clients who pay for an hourlong session think that means ninety minutes?

I know psychic readers who do private sessions and agree that ending the session is like pulling the plug on a life support machine. Most clients expect an encore performance from the psychic. There is always the client who refuses to recognize that time is up and the reading is over. As soon as the psychic reader tells the client that if she wishes to extend the reading and pay for additional time, the client should take the hint and graciously realize that the session is over. Most clients get the clue that their scheduled time is up, but there are some clients who keep talking. Clients have to take into account that there are other clients also waiting for their appointments with the psychic, and any fluctuations in time can throw the psychic's schedule off.

Some psychic readers who do most of their readings as telephone sessions have the same problem with lingering clients. I have had clients who refused to acknowledge that another call had come in and that their *one last question* was going into psychic reading overtime. Some clients don't want the reading session to end. I also have had clients who called a few minutes early for a psychic session in an attempt to squeeze in a couple of extra minutes.

In my experience, I find it easier to end a session over the telephone as opposed to a psychic reading done in person. I do not see clients in my home, because they never want to leave. Clients try to stay and linger long after their session is over. I also don't like strangers in my home since I didn't want my children exposed to people I don't really know.

One time, and one time only, I had a woman come over to my home for a tarot reading. She was a friend of a friend. After reading her cards for an hour and a half, I started to put the tarot deck away in hopes that she would realize that her appointment was over. This lady asked for a glass of water and continued to stay and talk. I didn't want to be rude, but I told her that I had some things to do. To make a long story short, this client stayed while I vacuumed my house, peeled potatoes for dinner, and returned phone calls to other clients.

While my dinner was cooking, this client (who was still talking about her card reading with me) made a comment about how delicious the food smelled and how she was feeling hungry. I immediately took the opportunity to finally get her to the door and point her in the direction of a very good little restaurant.

Psychic readers who do psychic-reading house parties are sometimes held hostage by the group of people attending such an event. Having a real live psychic in your home for an evening of psychic readings definitely trumps home demonstrations for candles and decorating items. A psychic house party usually includes the host and a group of five or six guests. Once the news spreads that someone is having a psychic party, the guest list can double. The psychic reader is given a private area to do readings in the host's home, and the guests normally get a twenty-minute psychic reading. The problem arises when one person's session lasts more than twenty minutes. The crowd can get ugly as the other guests demand equal time.

Many moons ago I did a few psychic house parties where I did tarot card readings. I remember one woman approaching me and she had me *clocked*. I had apparently given another woman a tarot reading that lasted six minutes longer than the complaining lady's tarot reading. To even things out I allowed the *psychically short-changed* woman to pick the proverbial three cards and have another question answered. This time I clocked her. As soon as the six minutes were up, I wished her luck and put my tarot cards back into my silk tarot sack. Once all of the houseguests had received their tarot readings, I was finally released from my closet-sized dungeon and was offered the remnants of what once was a buffet of the standard spinach dip, onion dip, mini quiches, and assorted pastries.

After doing nine tarot readings in a row I was exhausted, hungry, and psychically depleted. I tried to make my way to a spot close to the front door so I could scarf down my cookies, say my farewells, and run like hell to my car before someone with that one last question could capture me. I gestured to the hostess that I was going home and thanked her for the food.

As I left the house I was surrounded by a posse of psychic junkies looking for one last hit from the psychic realms. The *psychic-reader paparazzi* followed me to my car, the whole time firing question after question about their tarot readings. By the time I made it home there were already two messages on my voicemail requesting information about hosting a psychic-reading party and, of course, both callers wanted me to call them back for *just one more question*.

It is not uncommon for clients to call the psychic within hours of getting a reading in order to ask the psychic for some clarity about something. I recommend to my clients that they should tape their session or take notes during the reading so they will remember what is being said. I have had clients call me two weeks after a reading to ask me about something that had turned up in their reading. Lucky for them that my mind is sharp because after doing numerous psychic readings, it is sometimes hard to remember exactly what the client is asking about.

One woman called me at one o'clock in the morning to tell me that she just met the Virgo man I had seen coming into her life a few months before. She wanted to know if I remembered anything else I picked up about him. I realize that she was excited and couldn't wait to tell me about him, but I have been doing this long enough to know that she was fishing for some free psychic insights.

I told her that I was sleeping, but she didn't care. She just continued to ask me if this is the guy for her. I felt like a trance medium.
I was half asleep. I was too tired to even freak out on her for calling
me so late at night. She expected me to put on my *psychic-reader hat*
in the middle of the night to go over a psychic reading that I had
given her two months ago. I told the client that I was sleeping, but
then she asked me what time I thought that I would be getting up
so she could call me back. I thought to myself that I must either be
a really good psychic, or maybe no other psychic would put up with
this client.

Being a psychic reader is sometimes equivalent to being an
on-call physician. The exploitation of the psychic's time goes beyond the *one last question*. I've had clients call me on Christmas and
New Year's Eve to wish me a happy holiday and then try to sneak
in a question. Clients panic around the holidays, and psychics
seem to do a high percentage of their business then. Holidays
are a deeply emotional time, and people begin to have concerns
about being alone on New Year's Eve. The big holiday question
that most psychic readers get hit with is, "Will I be with someone
over the holidays?"

Clients don't seem to want their appointment with a psychic
reader to end. I have even been guilty of that when I get readings. The beginning of the reading is usually surface scaling, the
middle of the reading really gets the energy connection linked
in, and by the end of the appointed time the psychic connection is full blast and suddenly time is up. It's like having a great
conversation that suddenly ends. Even after their appointment is
well over, clients will often call back for that *one last question*.

CHAPTER 6

Psychic-Reader Risks 101

Can I Collect SSI Because My Client's Back Hurts?

Some clients think that being a psychic reader is easy. What the clients don't see is what the psychic readers *feel*. A majority of psychics are very empathic, which means that they can feel what the client is feeling. The pain of the clients can be anything from the emotional pain of a breakup to the actual physical pain of a bad back. Because psychic empaths are connecting into the client's energy, transference of energy can take place to the point that the psychic reader can actually feel the client's pain.

I have done readings when I would ask, for example, if the client's shoulder was bothering her. I have actually had someone's pain manifest in my own body. This is because of the psychic connection. I also know of a psychic reader who could not do readings for anyone on chemotherapy because the chemo would make him feel sick.

My observation is that many of the psychic readers I know of seem to be susceptible to heart problems, breast cancer, or headaches. This could be a result of the body/mind psychic connection. Medical intuitives know that each organ of the body has its own vibration, and any blip or negative input can cause a physical misfire. Heart problems manifest because psychics will at times feel the pain of the client's loss of love or loss of a loved one. Breast cancer can manifest because psychics are too nurturing toward their clients and don't construct protective boundaries or ground themselves completely. Headaches, especially between the eyes and at the top of the head, are a result of overtaxing the third-eye chakra and the crown chakra. Not opening and closing these two chakra centers completely and properly can cause physical problems for the psychic reader.

Proper protection is mandatory for the psychic who is extremely empathic, because the connection of feelings for the client's pain can actually manifest in the psychic's body. The heart is believed by some to be the seat of the soul. When you connect with heart energy during a reading, the feelings of love and compassion are what thread the reading together. Psychic readers can overtax their heart if there is too much emotional strain being placed on them from clients.

Sure, some psychics are indifferent and mechanical in the delivery of their psychic readings and are able to keep a safe distance from the client's energy, but most psychics identify with the client and go hand in hand with the client through his or her troubles. Some psychic readers who are too nurturing may develop breast cancer if proper protection isn't observed. Every thought is connected to a vibration, and a vibration is the root of an actual event. Being a psychic lends itself to being caring, nurturing, and compassionate, but it is very depleting. Keep in mind that psychic readers have their own families and their own problems; taking on the problems of clients is a setup for psychic readers' symptomatic problems.

The biggest complaint I hear from psychics is that they suffer from headaches. Maybe that's because psychics feel as though their brains are always being picked, or it could also be the fact that the brain is where logic lies and logic often fights intuition.

Psychics repress the logical and go with the intuitive energy. Not clearing between clients will certainly cause formidable upsets for psychic readers, ranging from health problems to a run of misfortune. I have had to have an energy worker properly close my crown and third-eye chakras because I overtaxed these two centers by allowing myself to be energetically drained. My personal psychic centers froze in the open position and were susceptible to negative energies that could not be closed out.

Our bodies run on an energetic current, and any misfire in the body-mind connection will show itself as a physical flare-up. Irritation to a person can cause sinus problems, anger is rooted in the liver, hip problems show a refusal to move forward, and knee problems can manifest as a result of not being flexible. These are just a few examples of how our thoughts are projected through our bodies. People in the psychic profession who are constantly working with and being exposed to client energy may run the risk of having empathic reactions that mimic a client's problems.

Getting a psychic reading may seem like frivolous entertainment to some, but it is a dangerous profession. Working with energy can create things, some of which are welcome and some of which are not. Thoughtforms are created by someone with an intense desire for something, whether good or bad. The psychic reader is dealing with clients who have no idea just how powerful their thoughts are. By walking between the worlds of the seen and the unseen, both the psychic reader and the client, if not protected, can be wide open to a form of *psychic attack*. Psychic attacks are the result of psychic bullying either at home, the workplace, or anywhere else. They occur when someone attempts to impose their will upon an unwilling individual, therefore creating a problem resulting in a client's need for a psychic reading to see what is going on.

The client coming for a psychic reading is bringing the thoughtform energy along with them to the visit with the psychic reader. Even giving psychic readings via the telephone opens up the veil between the worlds enough to let outside energy creep in. Grounding and protection is a must if you want to get a good reading. Since most psychic readings are impulse purchases, potential clients don't usually carry around a piece of sage or put sea salt in their pockets. The decision to get a reading should be taken seriously if you really want to get a good one. Just like anything that you prepare for, the result of the experience is much better if you are organized than if you go in blindly.

Psychic readers buy sage by the pound and bathe in sea salt because they need to discharge any negative client energy or else risk psychic-energy fallout. A psychic can occasionally suffer from *psychic burnout*, which is the result of doing too many psychic readings in a short amount of time or doing too many readings for the same person. The psychic who does an overabundance of psychic readings within a short amount of time is doing the equivalent of plugging too many things into one electrical outlet. The result is that the main breaker switch will go off.

A psychic who is dealing with a psychic-junkie client who requests numerous psychic readings on a frequent basis runs the risk of burnout. How much can one client's life change within a twenty-four-hour period? Some clients don't allow enough time for previous psychic predictions to come true. The psychic junkie mixes psychic readings and psychic readers with the end result being a psychic Molotov cocktail. Getting repeated readings concerning the same issue will result in mass confusion. Different psychic readers may give various answers to the same query because each psychic has a unique way of expressing themselves. The client can become confused in wondering which answer is right. The risk of clients going to an unbalanced psychic who does not practice grounding and clearing between clients poses a potential problem if they pick up some vagrant nasty energy that will compound the original dilemma.

I've had my share of *frequent-flyer clients* who call every day for a psychic update. I don't know if these clients are addicted to getting readings or if they are afraid they will lose contact with me. In any case, unless their lives are a whirlwind of eventful changes on a regular basis, there is no need for them to keep getting daily psychic information. I feel bad because I am not providing the daily client with any new information. Some clients will want psychic insight concerning mundane events and keep asking when their life will become exciting. Well, if these clients would spend more time socializing and less time getting psychic readings, then I'm sure their life would change significantly!

I have one client who spends her day just hanging out, waiting to get her daily psychic reading. She starts her session with the same question: "What do you see for me?" I feel like saying, "I see the same things I saw yesterday," but I bite my tongue because she basically is a lonely woman. I've had the psychic-to-client talk several times with her, each time stressing that too many psychic readings aren't recommended. Psychically reading the same client over and over is like watching the same movie over and over. Eventually, the vibration is lowered because of boredom.

This client will ask the same question night after night, not allowing any time for the events to unfold. She will ask me when I see her moving to a new residence. I will tell her in six months she will move. The next night she will ask the same question about moving. The answer is now five months and thirty days. I feel like the countdown before the ball being dropped from Times Square on New Year's Eve every time she asks me about moving.

Doing readings for this woman has caused me to fritz out psychically as a direct result of her energy overload into my sphere. When I first did a reading for her, I remember getting pains in my neck and shoulder. I may have been picking up that this client would literally be a pain in the neck. I found out two or three readings into our psychic/client relationship that this client also suffers from frequent stiff necks, most likely as a result of tucking the phone under her ear so she can get a psychic reading.

I had one gentleman call me concerning a large deposit for a sale he had just made. He wanted to know when he could expect the money to hit his bank account. I told this guy that I saw him receiving his money in twelve days. He called me every day with the same question about his expected deposit, and each day I told him the same expected due date for the cash. He received his deposit just like I said he would, but his lack of trust in the predicted outcome and repeated questioning about the same bank deposit really wore me down psychically. This guy experienced stomach problems as a result of worrying about the money being put into his bank account and I, in turn, experienced a nervous stomach every time I gave a reading for him. Even though I would ground myself before doing a reading for this client, the intensity of his fears and most likely his improper grounding caused a direct manifestation in my own body.

Psychics really have to be careful about the energy they let into their energetic field, because the possibility of catching a psychic disease from an infected client is very real. The same goes for clients. You have to be aware of who is giving you a psychic reading. Don't be afraid to ask a psychic if he has grounded or cleared between clients. Let the psychic reader know that you are psychic-reader street smart, so you won't be subjected to any vagrant, leftover energies.

Psychic Vampires: Chi Juggers

Psychic readers often fall prey to the client who is a psychic vampire. Psychic vampires thrive on stealing energy, and sometimes these vampires aren't even aware that they are doing such a thing. *Chi* is the universal life force, and sometimes people who are unbalanced or drained can't keep their chi flowing, in which case blocks are formed. The need for energy sends the psychic-energy vampire out to siphon energy from another source. The psychic vampire is very attracted to the psychic reader because of the unique connection and abilities that the psychic has for tapping into outside energy. The psychic vampire sees the psychic reader as a never-ending source for the acquisition of energy and knowledge. Psychic readers can feel when a client is a psychic vampire because they leave the reader feeling unusually drained and tired.

Headaches are a common result for the psychic who has just gone a round with a psychic vampire. Being a psychic reader is no joke. Working on both the physical side and the energetic side of the universe requires the psychic to always be conscious of grounding and clearing of energy. A good method of protection from a psychic vampire is to face east, take your index finger, and draw an imaginary circle around you to contain your energy. Psychic readers who don't use grounding or protection will likely become emotional garbage dumps for their clients and can manifest actual discomforts or illnesses because of the energy drain.

Psychic readers who take precautions before doing psychic readings have a higher energy level. The psychic vampires are attracted to them as the moth is to the flame. There is a natural tendency to go toward the light, and psychic vampires feed off the higher vibratory light of the psychic reader. If the psychic has taken measures to protect herself from psychic vampires, the psychic vampire may feel frustrated at not being able to deplete the energy of the protected psychic reader.

Psychic vampires use manipulation and mind games as a way of trying to wear the psychic down. There is a really serious side to venturing into the world of psychics and psychic readings.

The uneducated client is also likely to become the victim of a psychic reader who may be of an unsavory nature and an energy vampire. *Psychic-reader energy vampires* drain their clients, keep them needy, and take their money. Energy is a real commodity. It is the source of power. Some people know how to generate it and others who can't harness their own energy become energy vampires. Imagine if NASDAQ could put psychic energy on the stock exchange. It would be the most sought-after source of energy in the world.

Everyone is considered accessible to the psychic vampire, but psychic readers put themselves in the direct line of fire. Clients coming to get a reading are most likely in need of an energy boost or an energy adjustment. The psychic reader represents a solution to the energy imbalance of the psychic vampire. The psychic is ideally supposed to point an energy vampire toward the best source for an energy recharge, but some clients latch on to the psychic as the solution to all of their problems. The psychic isn't the answer to the client's dilemma, but rather a compass to point the client in the right direction.

Psychic junkies don't realize it, but they are prone to becoming psychic vampires. Psychic junkies get numerous psychic readings in an attempt to solve even life's little annoyances. The ability to take responsibility for their own actions and find solutions to their problems isn't an option for them. Psychic-junkie vampires get back-to-back psychic readings from psychics as an alternative to finding their own inner source of power. Everyone has an inner power source, and a psychic reading should help clients amp up and generate more energy.

Psychics don't want psychic-reader dependency to occur. I am attempting to educate you about how to get a good psychic reading, not one that is a step above a fortune cookie. Just as parents block off electrical outlets so children can't get hurt, caution should be observed by anyone venturing into psychic-energy sources. Getting psychic readings is tapping into the *big guns* of energy, where all thoughts become things. Being careless or ungrounded can lead to problems and confusion. Psychic vampires indiscriminately take any energy they can tap into.

The client has to come to the psychic reading respectful of the service being provided. A client who is low on energy will receive from the psychic reading an energy boost and hopefully some solution to a problem or an answer to a concern. That alone should raise the client's vibration, get her energetically spinning in a higher direction, and enable her to generate more energy. What if the client hears news that isn't so good during a reading? Will that lower the client's vibration of energy and send her on an energy-sucking spree? Not necessarily, because the anxiety of not knowing what is wrong can cause stress and energy leaks. Sometimes finding out where a problem lies will raise a client's energetic vibration because the client at least knows what he or she is dealing with. Psychic readers should help their clients focus more on the solutions and not the problems.

Knowing what you are dealing with will point you toward the resolution to the problem. Who wouldn't rather know the truth? The truth will send you off in the direction where the most good will come about. Clients who refuse to see the big picture and focus on what they want to happen, even if it isn't in the cards for them, are not tapping into the energy of the psychic reading. These types of clients are energy vampires, because they persist until the psychic reader is too drained to even care about what the client does.

Money is energy, and the psychic vampire who calls outside of an appointment looking for some free psychic advice creates an energy imbalance and also messes with the psychic's energy levels. Psychic readers can't always be *on*, as some clients would like to believe, and boundaries are necessary so there is respect for the psychic's time and energy.

I had a client who was a real energy vampire. This client was also a psychic reader and should have known better, but her energy was all over the place and very uncontained. There was always some drama in her life centering on her relationship with a man who was a real cheater. This client had reached some notoriety for her psychic work and she would dangle a carrot in front of me in order to solicit free psychic readings. She was always going to do this or that for me, or give me a nice client hook-up. Never happened! This lady was the ultimate psychic vampire.

I had heard from other psychics I know that this woman had infiltrated their energy zone, picked their brain, and didn't offer an equal exchange of energy. This woman, even though she was a psychic, never offered to reciprocate psychic readings with me or pay for my services. An energy imbalance occurred, which threw off the whole relationship. After just talking to her, I would feel drained. Doing readings for her wiped me out.

My peers had warned me that she was a psychic vampire and implored me to unload her. I soon found myself dodging her calls and making excuses for not being available. One day she came to my home uninvited. When I peeked out the window and saw it was her, I immediately went into a back room and hid. Moments later she was ringing my phone. It was scary! I was being stalked by a psychic vampire. She finally went away, but she left numerous messages on my voicemail. I couldn't believe that another psychic reader would disregard all the rules of grounding, respect, and boundaries, and behave in such an energy-sucking manner.

I was so drained from the months of putting up with this woman that I had to get a complete energy clearing. An energy clearing is like a psychic reader tune-up. I got Reiki treatments, wore protection oils, and burned sage along with clearing incense on a daily basis. I built my energy vibration back up by listening to music and keeping white light around me.

The psychic vampire continued to try to get in touch with me, but I was able to avoid her successfully. You have no idea what it feels like to be drained by an energy vampire unless you experience it firsthand. The psychic vampire tried one last-ditch effort to contact me by sending me a letter. I ripped up the correspondence she sent to me and burned it in a dish of smoldering sage to clear out the energy. I felt the way Dorothy from *The Wizard of Oz* must have felt as the bad witch was melting: finally free.

You must protect yourself at all times whether you are a psychic reader or a client. People can fall prey to psychic vampires at work, or their other daily routines can leave them wide open for energy zappers like the psychic vampire. An imposing neighbor or a constantly complaining co-worker may not realize it, but they are psychic vampires because they drain you of your life-force energy, also known as chi.

Timing and the Responsibility of Being Accurate

One of the first things that potential clients ask about a psychic reader is what the psychic's accuracy rate is. That is a tough call because a psychic reader interacts differently with each client. Some clients who are more open will get a better reading than the clients who put up blocks. Being uncomfortable with a client can hinder a psychic reading's accuracy because a good psychic connection can't be maintained. Psychic readers all have their own methods of doing readings, and some psychics are very particular about when and where they do their sessions. I prefer to do my psychic readings in the evening because that is when I am the most relaxed and in the mindset to pull out my tarot cards or look at someone's astrological chart. I feel that my accuracy rate is better at night, and I think that it is especially high on rainy or damp days. The rain seems to act as a conductor of electricity for me; it makes tapping into the universal energy source much easier.

Just how accurate does a client expect a psychic reader to be? Predictions are not prophecies. A prediction is an unborn event that can still be influenced by the free will of the seeker. A prophecy is a more fated event and is relatively karmic. Karma is the payback for what you did in past lives and also in this life. The karma can be good or bad, depending on how you treated others. It is a cosmic class that you can't skip if you want to move on to the next level of the ascension process.

I remember calling a psychic phone line for a reading, and being connected to a woman who was very clairvoyant. Many things she told me did come about in a very similar way as she predicted. After she gave me the answer to one of my questions, I asked her if she felt that the outcome to my query would come about. She answered by saying, "That is already written." What she meant was that some things are recorded in the Akashic records, the place where all universal happenings are already written. Some events, no matter what, are meant to take place in one's life. Psychic readers can help their clients through their life experiences by showing them the light at the end of the tunnel, or showing the client that things do happen for a reason. Psychic insight is helpful in navigating through the ins and outs of life.

There are clients who handicap psychic readers the way a bookie will handicap a race horse. Is it the psychic's maiden run? Is the universal track fast or slow, and how did the psychic finish in the last two psychic readings? Is the psychic reader a *mudder*, which means that the psychic is better on rainy days? Who was the trainer and are they the favorite to win? A race horse's success depends a lot on the jockey who is riding the horse in the race. The same is true of the psychic reader. Accuracy, precision, and smooth handling depend a lot on the client. A client who works with the psychic by coming to a session grounded and with an open mind will do much better with a reading than someone who is closed off or just all over the place.

Psychics can read for a group of clients, and maybe there will be one or two who aren't getting the connection. The other possibility that may cause a client to question a psychic reader's accuracy occurs when the client doesn't know how to assimilate the information. Some information may come through cryptically or symbolically, and at other times come through as clear as day. Pressing for more than what is coming through during a psychic reading may throw the psychic off, and there's a chance that what the psychic is attempting to connect into gets disconnected because of a client's impatience for an answer.

I love it when I tell clients something and they get cocky and say, "That will never happen!" Does that mean that they don't want it to happen, they won't let it happen, or are they fishing for more reassurance that it will happen? I had a client who was always very negative about what was being told to her. She disagreed with everything in every psychic reading that she got. I couldn't figure out why she kept getting readings from me if she constantly disputed everything I told her.

When things did come about for this client, she wouldn't even acknowledge it. I wanted to accurately predict, or should I say prophesy, that I wasn't going to do readings for her anymore. Because of the way this client behaved, I couldn't help but feel reluctant to give her information. I was doing a typical *psychic-reader withhold*. Our combined energies were very aggravating, and therefore all of her readings had that aggravation as part of the recipe. I found it so hard to give her an uplifting psychic reading because she personified negativity.

Remember that the horse responds to the jockey and the jockey responds to the horse. The psychic reader responds to the client and the client responds to the psychic reader. I obviously was the wrong energy amp for her psychic circuits, and I feel that she would have done much better with a psychic reader who was more in synch with her type of energy field. There is a lid for every pot. If there are any negative feelings between the psychic and the client, then the proper energy connection can't be made. Psychics are human, too, and if there is a clash of personalities between the client and the reader, then the psychic reader should refer the client to someone else. You never should feed any negative vibes, because both the psychic reader and the client will somewhere along the line feel the residual effects of a psychic connection that isn't quite right.

I used to read for a very sweet woman who would reply to everything I told her by saying, "No way. I don't believe it." This woman wasn't being difficult; it was just her manner of speaking. I wasn't offended by her replies because I energetically knew that her responses were mostly habitual and not meant in a derogatory manner. One day I explained to her that since sound has a vibration, what you say is as potent as what you think because you are basically *putting it out there*. I told her that she may unknowingly be interrupting, delaying, or negating a psychically perceived outcome by responding in a word vibration that has negative tones. She seemed surprised but was willing to adjust her response-mechanism reflex during our reading sessions. Amazingly enough, after a short while this woman told me that she noticed her life going more smoothly due to adjusting her response to things and attempting to isolate negative words from her common verbiage. She made it a point to change her remarks during conversations to more positive sayings like "That's great! How wonderful!"

Of course you would not respond positively to bad news but in general even the things we say have a direct effect on the energy we attract to ourselves. Our thoughts travel faster than the speed of light, and what we think is also a major player in what we create down the road. We must learn to live consciously in a constant state of awareness and gratitude if we want to create a beautiful life for ourselves.

Timing is the one thing that clients want their psychic readers to be accurate with. If I told you to sit for thirty minutes without looking at a clock, it would be difficult for you to determine exactly what time it was. You might be a little off in your experience of time. Sitting without a clock in the room is equivalent to how a psychic reader perceives time. Spirit doesn't recognize time. Tarot cards can give a sense of days, weeks, or months based on the cards pulled, and the astrological birth chart can time important planetary occurrences, but timing is a real hit-or-miss. Some people think that waiting five minutes feels like forty minutes, while other people experience the same five minutes as a two-minute wait. We all experience time differently and if there weren't any clocks on the wall, people would vibe to the rhythms of their own biological clocks.

I believe that when the seeker is ready, the information will present itself. A woman I did a reading for a few years ago felt that her fiancé was cheating on her. The psychic readings confirmed what she felt. She would repeatedly ask when she would catch him in the act. I always got a feeling for a Tuesday, but which Tuesday? During a session I picked up that she would catch him with the other woman but it would involve her keys. Pretty cryptic information! Where do you go with insight like that?

Well, as it came to pass, a few months down the road at a time when she thought that he was being faithful, she caught him cheating. It was a Tuesday, and she had forgotten to bring the keys to the office with her when she left for work. The client went home to look for her keys and, sure enough, there was her fiancé with another woman. Did knowing through a psychic reading actually, on some level, tip this client off to forget something at home on a Tuesday?

What if she had forgotten her keys on a Wednesday? Maybe nothing would have come about for her. They say there are no accidents in the universe. The timing for this event to occur was already set in motion from the first time she thought that her fiancé was cheating. The thought seed was planted, and the manifestation of her own thoughts linked in with the probable thoughts of her fiancé getting caught. When the intersection of the two thoughts met, the event occurred.

The universe is a hologram where the past, present, and future are taking place simultaneously. A psychic reader can tune in to the frequency of the universe and see the shape of things to come. The accuracy of the psychic may depend on many things; the client posing the questions, the general condition of the psychic, the surrounding area, and any outside interference may hinder the psychic reader's ability to tune in clearly. Tarot cards, tea leaves, or whatever tools that psychics use to stimulate their consciousness are only aids in delving into the psychic reading. People with psychic talents really don't need props, but the tools used during a psychic session somehow subconsciously trigger or spark the psychic reader's ability to tap into the unknown. A radio station doesn't always come in clear if there is interference in the transmission, and the same is true for psychic readers. Some psychics like to keep a quartz crystal near them when they read for clients. The quartz acts as a receptor to the cosmic waves being conveyed. Many psychic readers believe that the quartz crystal will improve their ability to be accurate. Just like crystal radios of days past, psychics need good grounding so their psychic antennas can pick up the psychic-reading vibes.

How do you gauge the accuracy of the psychic reading? The client may figure that the psychic is good if an event from the past is precisely described or if something currently going on in the client's life is brought up. Imagine that someone is looking through your personal junk drawer. What do you want them to find? What are you looking for? When a psychic reader sits with a client for a session, the psychic is tapping into the client's life.

Your life has many years and aspects, and there are things in your life about which you may not yet be aware. The psychic has limited time with the client and must start somewhere. Psychic readers do not want to do scavenger hunts through someone's life. They want to get to what is important. A client may think, for example, that her date for Friday night is important, but a psychic reader may be tapping into what is presenting itself as important at the time of the psychic session. Does that mean that the psychic isn't any good because he didn't know about that Friday-night date, or does that mean that in the scheme of things there is something more important for the client to be looking at?

It is ever so important to know what you want from the psychic reader. People don't go to a doctor unless they have a certain condition or maybe just want a general checkup. No one sits in a doctor's office just for the hell of it. You tell a doctor what ails you so the doctor can focus on the problem and recommend a cure. The same is true about dealing with a psychic reader.

If you want a general reading from the psychic reader, then open up to what is being presented and listen. Don't just hear the words but really *listen* to the information given to you. If you go to the psychic for a psychic reading because you are dealing with a particular problem, tell the psychic reader to concentrate and focus on whatever area you need a psychic consultation for. The psychic doesn't want you to lead the reading, but offering an aspect that you want to know about will let the psychic be more accurately tuned in to that sphere of your life.

Psychic readers feel a responsibility toward the clients coming to them, and of course good referrals make for good business. Baseball players don't always hit home runs, but they still tag some of the bases. Let the psychic know when they are hitting on something, because it will help them tune in and get more insight for you. Psychic readers don't want the client to play guessing games and psychic Texas Hold 'em with the tarot cards, but your validation of recognized information will raise the psychic's vibration and enhance the psychic's frequency. The results will be a good reading.

Psychics: The Everyday Shrink

There are times when the psychic reader feels more like a client's psychiatrist. A bond is formed once you confide your deepest secrets to someone. Trust me. Your psychic knows for sure. It isn't unusual for the client to have a tendency to become a little dependent. Psychiatrists want their patients to be able to respond rationally to a crisis. Calling a psychic is usually the client's first choice of a rational response to a crisis. A psychic reader can communicate information to clients (patients) and also foresee where the client is headed. A psychiatrist can give prescriptions and a psychic can give predictions. A shrink usually thinks that a problem is rooted in a past mommy or daddy issue that is being played out as dissociative behavior or some other psychoanalytical type of disorder. A psychic believes that problems are more likely a result of a past-life karmic issue, triggered by some temporary planetary transit or some rudimentary energy that is blocked.

I have had clients call me right after they leave their appointment with their shrink to book a psychic reading. Some people more than others need constant reassurance and guidance that everything will work out for them. One time I was on the phone with a woman who had a call from her psychiatrist come in on her other line. She told him that she would call back because she was having a session with her psychic. Where a psychiatrist has to decide between prescribing Prozac, Xanax, or Ativan to relieve a patient's anxiety, a psychic reader has to decide between tarot-card spreads, astrological counseling, or trance mediumship to best treat their client's angst.

The psychic reader is like a marriage counselor, occupational counselor, matchmaker, best friend, and travel agent. Yes, travel agent. You have no idea how many clients want some psychic input on when and where to go for a vacation. I wonder if *out-of-body* trips count?

The psychic reader may take a client's *mystical history* instead of his medical history. The psychic may ask the client if he has had a psychic reading before, if he is currently under the care of another psychic, or what zodiac sign he was born under. The psychic likes to know why the client is seeking a psychic reading. Clients who keep hitting the wall in relationships, jobs, or finances need psychic input and guidance in order to unravel the unseen energy snag that is holding them back. A lot of recurring themes in a client's life most likely have a strong past-life origin. Psychics have their own school of thought on why clients have certain problems, and many times an energy adjustment and some psychic insight will start the client on the road to recovery.

Astrological psychics will pull in the planetary energies along with their psychic intuition to get a full read on a client's current set of circumstances. Astrologers relate the temperaments of their clients to the planets. Just as you would never expect a poodle to have the disposition of a pit bull, the same is true of the temperaments of clients. A mixed-breed dog will display the temperaments of both types of dogs that make up its bloodline. In astrology, the Sun sign will be influenced by the rising sign or ascendant along with the Moon and the other planets. The astrological mutt is much different from a pure-breed Sun-Moon ascendant of just one sign. Don't expect a Leo to handle a problem the same way a Pisces would. Astrologers have a different way of classifying their clients and their expected behaviors. As an astrologer, I will treat the brokenhearted Capricorn differently from the brokenhearted Gemini. Knowing what mystic medicine is right for your clients is very helpful for them. The clients of psychic readers really do treat their psychics like *psychic-iatrists.*

I had a client who wanted to draw more abundance into her life. She felt that by writing out fake checks for thousands of dollars and posting the checks on her mirrors and walls, she would attract money into her life. She got very caught up in this exercise and overconfidently spent her money like water in the belief that just by writing abundance checks to herself, her financial problem would be solved.

Well, she called me one day crying because she was broke and wanted me to help her figure out what to do. She needed a psychic banking bailout! The whole conversation was more like a spiritual counseling session about the energy of money instead of a psychic reading. We talked about money, the karma of prosperity, and the built-in Jupiter aspects in her chart that predispose her to be a little manic with cash. Together we figured out how to get a grip on her finances and straighten out her pocketbook. She thanked me profusely for making her feel better. The initial project of leaving prosperity reminders around her house was a good idea, but she was not grounded with her energy so it just dissipated her money—which is a form of energy in itself. Grounding is the secret to anything you attempt to create in your life.

A majority of the shrink-type psychic sessions involve relationship problems. Clients go to psychic readers to find out what makes their partners tick. They also want psychic guidance concerning problems that crop up in their relationships. I have had clients come to me who are in destructive relationships and want to find out why they keep choosing the same type of mate. Insecurity in relationships is an epidemic, especially since the Internet has opened up a whole new world of available potential partners to choose from.

Internet dating sites are the new bar scenes. Clients have sent me pictures of prospective dating prospects and want me to help them choose who will be best for them in a relationship. It is like operating a *psychic mail-order bride service* instead of a psychic-reading service.

A client of mine decided to follow her cheating boyfriend. She wanted to wear a disguise so he wouldn't notice her. The client asked me to give her a psychic reading to see if she should camouflage herself by putting on a long blond wig or if she should dress up to look like a man. She evidently thought that I was *Austin Psychic Powers*, and together we could crack the case of her cheating boyfriend.

This client was very uptight about things, and she would check her boyfriend's cell phone, car mileage, and credit card statements in hopes of catching him in a lie. I would constantly talk to her about how this relationship really was doomed because there wasn't any trust and she was just looking for an excuse to get out of the relationship or else she wouldn't be snooping around. "Why not just walk away from this guy?" I would ask her.

She wanted me to tap into things psychically to find out why she sabotaged relationships, why she didn't trust anyone, and how long it would take before she would be all better. I sent her to a past-life regressionist, where the root problems of her behavior were acknowledged so she could move forward. After this client cleared out her base past-life issues, she was able to get psychically fit and more in control of manifesting the type of relationship that she wanted. Sometimes cosmic medicine is the best medicine for the soul.

Some clients love to relate all the details of the very personal sexual side of their relationships. Over the years I have heard some pretty racy things. These psychic-reading sessions are like an episode of *Psychic Sex and the City*. Some clients think their psychic reader is also their sex therapist. I have heard questions like, "Pull some cards and find out how I rate compared to his other partners." Women ask these questions: "What did he think about having sex with me? I know that I blew his mind!" "Is he thinking about me? Why hasn't he called me back in the past two weeks? Is he sleeping with other women?" The psychic reading becomes a combo tarot–sex therapist session, and sometimes there is too much sharing. Forget television. I haven't watched it in years because my clients are more interesting. Truth is stranger than fiction.

There is always a time when a psychic reader is also a major player in crisis intervention. I have had people call me for a reading who were feeling so low that they just wanted to end it all. These clients really needed someone to make them see the positive side of what is happening to them instead of just their problems. Psychic readers are sought out to identify the problem, energetically moving the blocks out of the way and advising of the advantages of making certain choices. It feels so good to hear a client say, "Thank you. You made me feel so much better."

Being a psychic shrink also puts you in the line of fire to have clients misdirect their anger and look for someone to blame for their problems. Sometimes I will hear a client say, "Hey, how come you didn't tell me that the job I took would make me miserable?" Well, the answer is simple. Maybe you were supposed to experience the rotten job so you could make certain contacts that would lead you to a better position elsewhere. Clients don't always realize that walking through the fire is necessary to get where they ultimately have to go. When things are too easy it isn't good, because there are no challenges along the way to help build character.

I had an astrologer friend tell me that astrological charts have a whole psyche unique to them. The energies of the planets are sometimes in a high-tension aspect and at other times in very easy aspects to each other. Too many easy aspects can also make it easy for problems to occur and not just necessarily let it be a breeze for nice things to happen. The same goes for the hard aspects in a birth chart. When things are difficult, it gives you a chance to test your own emotional endurance and see how clever you are at figuring a way out. Hard aspects don't always have to be about restrictions, but rather they serve as an opportunity to slow things down until a better plan arrives. Psychic readers can give insight as to what energies are presenting themselves at that time, whether it is because of the planets acting up or maybe it is just some pain-in-the-ass causing an energy block in your life. A psychic reading will help you identify and move past the problem.

I will tell you firsthand, and I am sure that most psychic readers will agree: the Full Moon definitely brings out all the nuts. Since our bodies are mostly water, the gravitational pull of the Moon affects us the same way it affects the tides. The energy is different, and clients have told me on more than one occasion that the Full Moon is wigging them out. The Full Moon has a tendency to bring things to a head, and psychic readers are usually busy during this phase of the Moon when the subconscious mind is being illuminated.

Emotions run high at the time of the Full Moon, and psychic readers roll out the celestial couch for all of their clients in need of a *psychic-iatrist*. I find that at the time of the Full Moon, more so than at other times, clients use their psychic readings as a form of therapy instead of just for insight.

Psychics are sometimes like a cosmic combo marriage counselor/divorce attorney/psychic private investigator when going through a divorce with a client. One woman going through a terrible divorce found that getting readings not only helped her get a peek at the behind-the-scenes dealings of her husband, but it was also very therapeutic in helping her heal while going through this rough phase of her life. She would get psychic readings, especially wanting to look into why her husband was so uncooperative and arrogant. I could see through the tarot cards that living with this guy was bad but trying to divorce him was hell. The only thing this woman wanted to be assured of was that she would be able to get rid of this creepy husband and move on with her life.

The tarot sessions were a remedy to all of the emotional strain that her sneaky, lying husband was putting her through. I felt like telling her that she didn't need a divorce; she needed an exorcism to get rid of this jerk. The psychic readings helped her discover some hidden assets and also foretold of her future successes. The psychic readings that she got from her *psychic-reader dream team* actually provided her with information that her own attorney couldn't get. Vacations to exotic islands, hidden businesses, and some other tidbits of her husband's doings were psychically uncovered for this woman. She had a successful resolution to her divorce and she managed to come out of it with minimal emotional damage because of the healings provided by the psychic readings.

Psychic readers are oracles providing knowledge, wisdom, and predictions, and they must also be prepared to wear many hats to best serve their clients. The new phrase of the upcoming years will most likely be "Are you Freudian, Jungian, or Occultarian?"

The Psychic's Side of the Psychic Profession

I wonder if there is any other profession in the world that gets as many laughs as when someone blurts out that he or she is a psychic reader. Most of the laughter is nervous, I'm sure, because everyone knows that a psychic can read your mind or tell you something embarrassing about yourself, right?

Let's put everyone's mind at ease. Psychic readers can tune in only if invited by the seeker. We can't just walk into your mind— the same way we wouldn't just walk into your house without knocking first. When I tell people that I do psychic readings, the usual response is for someone to make a twirling motion with their finger up by the side of their head indicating that I must be a nut. The next biggest response is one of trepidation and remarks like "Oh, how nice for you," as they walk backwards away from me.

But I must confess, the all-time winner of a response is for someone to say, "Psychic? There's no such thing as a psychic. If you're really psychic, then tell me something about myself. Make a prediction. Tell me my middle name. If you're really psychic, then tell me what color I'm thinking about."

I think people who respond in such an aggressive manner must not realize just how uneducated they are concerning psychics and the metaphysical world.

If you met a surgeon, would you ask the surgeon to perform an operation to prove it? Does anyone ask an artist to paint a picture to prove that he or she can paint? Telling people that I do psychic readings seems to require proof that I can do such an amazing thing. What lots of people don't realize is that in order to do a psychic reading, certain conditions first need to be met—such as permission from the seeker, grounding, no interference, and the psychic reader has to feel energetically up for doing a reading. Oh, yeah! Let's not forget the psychic reader's fee. Everyone wants a free sample, but why should we have to give our psychic expertise away just to prove that we are really gifted psychic readers?

There is always one person who corners a psychic reader as soon as this person finds out about the psychic's profession. Such a person will attach themselves to the psychic while talking about their own psychic experiences, their weird dream from last night, and how this stuff is so interesting. After the psychic reader has been given enough props, which is a street term for compliments, then the psychic-opinion session starts. The curious captured audience will start with simple questions like, "Do you think I will move soon?" "When do you think I will meet someone?" "Do you have your tarot cards with you?"

I can't tell you how many palms I've had shoved in my face because people tend to think that all psychic readers are also palm readers. Being a palm reader is synonymous with being a psychic reader for some folks. I make sure to clarify that I am not a gypsy, since saying you're a psychic reader gives some people the impression that you're part of a traveling show!

When I tell people that I do psychic readings, everybody wants me to give them winning lottery numbers. I knew a psychic who gave her friend some lucky lottery numbers and the woman won big money. The psychic was pissed off because the woman only tipped her with $100 and a free lunch at a fancy restaurant.

Spirit is funny. Getting and giving lottery numbers isn't what psychic information is to be used for. You can only tap into the cosmic energy and have success with the results if you drop the ego. Psychic information is not to be abused, because the karmic responsibility is the primary concern when giving out psychic information. If someone is meant to win the lottery, then spirit will come through the psychic reader and lucky numbers will be given out during the course of the reading. Being demanding and telling the cosmos what you want, instead of getting what you need, is not the way psychic readings work.

As I've mentioned, psychic readers use different methods to give readings. Some psychics use tarot cards, some use numerology. There are astrologers, tea-leaf readers, and trance mediums, just to name a few. People who expect psychic readers to drop everything and prove that they are psychic by giving on-demand readings are out of touch with what this profession is all about. Not every psychic reader carries around a deck of tarot cards nor any other tools used for tapping into the unknown.

Psychic readers don't like to work with *dirty energy*, which comes from a client who is not grounded. If you saw your hairstylist at a party, would you ask the stylist to trim your hair using whatever tools were available at that moment, or would you wait until the stylist was in the right environment to cut your hair? If you want the best that someone has to offer, then you can't expect that person to go into something as if it were last-minute homework.

It gets a little tricky when the psychic reader has to put down what her occupation is when filling out forms. I know a psychic reader who applied for a car loan, and when she had to list her occupation she wrote *psychic clairvoyant*. The car salesman seemed awkward and nervous with this term, and then he got silly and asked her to predict the score of that night's baseball game.

I always found it challenging to fill in the emergency-contact information forms that my kids would bring home at the beginning of each new school year. Let's see . . . *occupation*. What sounds more legitimate: astrologer, intuitive, or—what the hell—how about just plain old psychic? Employer information is always a fun blank to fill in. Who employs me? I believe that the universe is my employer, although sometimes I get subbed out to a few spirit guides trying to get information through to a client. Length of employment is questionable. Do they want me to include past lives, too? Contact information is usually satisfied by providing a phone number, but in case of emergency just think about me and I will telepathically connect to you through ESP.

Some people have the impression that a psychic reader should look a certain way. I've had people comment to me that I really don't look like a psychic. What does a psychic reader look like? The stereotypical psychic reader is depicted as someone who is a cross between a gypsy and a Halloween witch. People expect a psychic to have dark hair, bohemian attire adorned with chunky jewelry, and to be on the older side.

Also, in the eyes of the client if the psychic reader owns a cat, then that helps to boost up psychic credibility. If you look too normal, clients may have a hard time relating to you as a psychic. Being older gives most psychics an edge because with age comes wisdom, but then again if you are younger and look goth, then you may be given more credence for your abilities as a psychic reader. Look out for the undercover psychic readers posing as soccer moms or everyday office workers. This strain of psychic walks among us and is usually a very talented and gifted group because their egos are intact and they don't need to wear a sign that reads, *Psychic reader, try me!*

One thing that really needs to be cleared up is that psychic readers are not Satanic nor are they devil worshipers. The word *occult* means "hidden" or "secret." And FYI, the Vatican Library in Rome has one of the largest collections of occult books, some of which cover the subject of divination. Divination comes from the *divine* source of the unseen and is to be respected and not abused for self-grandiose purposes. To be truly connected to the psychic source, the ego has to be pushed aside because it is the ego that is very controlling of the environment and wants to conform to reality. Spirit is open to the surprises of the universe and detaches from everyone's perception of what happiness is. Spirit allows the individual to find pleasure in daily existence and be thankful for whatever karmic experience that individual is destined to have. Remember that the journey will bring you to the destination, and life's twists and turns are what make the trip adventurous.

It really isn't necessary to wear a garland of garlic around your neck or throw a handful of salt in front of your door to ward off psychic readers. Most psychics work with the light and refuse to play around with any dark energy that may become an interloper in their own energy field. There are some psychic readers who dabble with the dark side, but a full knowledge of what is written in the ancient texts is necessary before doing any manipulation or magick with energy.

Psychics get lumped into the world of witches because witches were believed to be able to communicate with the spirit world, practice psychic arts, do magick spells, and shapeshift their image. Wicca is nature's magick and not to be confused with demonic practices. Psychics can be of any religious denomination. It is interesting to know that some revered saints were said to possess the gift of seeing or prophecy. One of the more formidably gifted saints was Saint Teresa of Avila, a Spanish Carmelite nun who was also a mystic.

Many times I have heard the saying "You don't want to piss off your psychic." I asked a client exactly what she meant by saying that to me because I have heard it said many times before. Her explanation was simple and to the point. She relayed to me her sentiments that since psychic readers work with energy and can project their thoughts, it really wouldn't be a good idea to have a psychic send any negative thoughts your way. I reminded her that psychics are of the school of thought that what you send out, so you shall receive. I educated this client and assured her that psychics don't keep a cauldron brewing with magickal herbs and an oak box filled with potions and oils. Some modern-day psychics use a microwave instead of a cauldron. (Just kidding!)

There Are Charlatans in All Professions

The profession of psychic reader lends itself to being wide open for charlatans. Just as with any profession dealing with people who have life problems, the opportunity to exploit their plight is very tempting for some. When people are vulnerable it makes it easier to take advantage of them, and the less people know about the profession they're dealing with, the more likely it is that the opportunity for being taken advantage of will arise.

How many billable hours does a lawyer charge to unsuspecting clients who have no idea if the attorney has even looked at their case? How about the unscrupulous doctors who bill insurance companies for thousands of dollars and keep elderly people coming for checkups that they don't really need? How about the pharmaceutical companies that are using our children and senior citizens as pin cushions and guinea pigs for drugs that later prove to be lethal? Mortgage and investment fraud, banking irregularities, phony politicians, pedophile priests, and some home-improvement salespeople are more dangerous, demonic, and treacherous than your typical psychic reader.

The psychic-reader charlatans are identifiable because their shtick usually involves making the client fearful, and the price to quell that fear keeps getting higher and higher. Psychic charlatans who have a constantly rising fee schedule that increases with each reading are a red flag that there might be a scam brewing. Granted, psychic readers are entitled to fee increases, but when a psychic encourages you to get frequent readings with the price going up with each session, you can bet that you are being taken advantage of. But unless the client is really naïve, the charlatan psychic reader doesn't get too far. Clients are not going to keep coming back to a psychic reader who is always shooting blanks.

To some people, the profession of being a psychic reader looks easy. They think that they only have to buy a *How to Read Tarot Cards* book and they can set up shop. The *lemonade-stand charlatan psychic reader* is really just someone who has an interest in psychic readings but has latent or underdeveloped psychic ability. These people aren't charlatans as much as they are just apprentices who are touting themselves as psychics. This profession is not about easy money because if you stink, you're finished. Clients expect information down to the last detail, and bullshit can only get someone so far.

Because I'm a psychic junkie, I recently had some dealings with a charlatan psychic reader. On a Sunday afternoon I saw a house in a nearby suburb with a sign in the window advertising psychic readings. I decided to check it out. The house looked nice on the outside so I got out of my car and walked to the door. An older woman came to the door, dressed in a housecoat, and informed me that she doesn't do readings on Sundays but she would make an exception for me.

The inside of the house was in a disheveled state because according to the woman, she was redecorating. It looked more like she was packing to *get out of Dodge*. She invited me into her reading room, which was the size of a closet and adorned with some Egyptian wall art.

The woman kept staring at my neck, and I finally asked her what she was looking at. She wanted to know why I had on a necklace with an evil-eye charm. I told her that a very good friend of mine, Kat, sent it to me as a gift and that I always wear it. My necklace made this woman very uncomfortable. She asked me to remove my necklace because she didn't like the charm facing her. I told her that the necklace stays on. (I am very superstitious and always think that a strange psychic reader may try to zap me with a psychic attack.)

She wanted to know what I do for a living, and I told her that I do tarot and astrology readings. She looked at me and said, "What is this astrology stuff?" I was stunned. I thought everyone knew their zodiac sign or had some basic idea of newspaper horoscopes. I got the vibe that this wasn't going to be what I thought it would be. The old lady kept looking at me and I psychically picked up that she thought I was a cop. I felt bad for her at one point, because my presence seemed to upset her whole Sunday afternoon.

I assumed that she was just trying to make some extra money, and advertising as a psychic reader appeared to be a good way to make some cash. By putting some exotic Egyptian artifacts here and there, it was a cheap way to convey to unassuming clients that she had it all going on as far as being a psychic goes. This psychic impersonator eventually laid out some tarot cards and said that she saw law enforcement and cops around me. I asked her what that meant. Would I be in some kind of trouble? She didn't really answer my question, although she once again asked me to remove my necklace because it made her nervous. Maybe she thought that I was a member of the *Psychic Reader Task Force*, an elite group of psychics who bust phony psychic readers.

We had a brief conversation about grounding and putting salt around the tarot cards to keep the energy clear, but still after twenty minutes of sitting with her I wasn't getting a psychic reading. The psychic impersonator knew that she was busted and made it a point to tell me that I didn't have to pay for the reading if I didn't like it. It wasn't a matter of liking the psychic reading; it was a matter of not *getting* a psychic reading. I gave her $20 and considered it a tip. After all, she had given me a firsthand experience to write about.

When you call the psychic phone lines, how do you know if the person on the other end of the telephone is a real psychic reader? Well, if the reading is nothing more than a question-and-answer session with the psychic asking all the questions instead of answering them, you'd best hang up. Psychics will ask questions to get confirmation from their clients that they are on the right track, but if the psychic reading turns into an interrogation, then you may be dealing with a fake psychic reader. Use your street smarts. Your gut feeling will never lead you astray.

It is unfortunate that good psychic readers are not always taken seriously because of the stigma that is built into the profession. The charlatan psychic readers who continue to bilk people out of money and masquerade as mystical seers make the sketchy image some skeptics have of us even harder to shake. In this case, don't hate the game, hate the player.

CHAPTER 7

Psychic-Reader Match Dot Com

How to Find a Good Psychic Reader

How do you find a good psychic reader? Wow! This is a trick question. It's like asking, how do you find the right mate?

The relationship between a client and a psychic reader has to click. You can usually tell after the second reading if the relationship is going to continue or not. The relationship between psychic and client is very special. It is built upon trust, truthfulness, and respect. These qualities work both ways and are expected to be abided by.

The real test of the endurance of the relationship between psychic reader and client is accuracy. If the psychic connection is a good one, then the prospects of the psychic reader being precise with predictions for you are much better. A psychic who is a perfect fit for your friend may not be able to read your energy as well. It's hard to find a psychic who can read flawlessly for everybody. If the psychic reader feels any animosity toward the client or if the client isn't open and grounded, then the psychic connection may just be adequate.

Look at it this way: everybody is capable of giving a kiss, but with some people the sparks will fly and the passion is strong.

There's a big difference between a peck on the cheek and a real kiss with instant chemistry. The same is true about psychics from whom you choose to get psychic readings. The chemistry has to be there because it is an intimate energy exchange.

The psychic readers are looking at your naked soul. They see what others don't see, and you are basically letting someone into your very personal space. The energetic space is where you create things, develop the situation, and then drop it down to earth so you can have the experience of what you established in your thoughtforms. The psychic reader is looking at your sometimes primitive, freshly seeded work in progress, and the psychic is the one who is giving advice and guidance so your finished results will be good.

The psychic reader is often the person you go to when you need some advice and damage control should you somehow get off-track in the psychic energy zone. The psychic is the person who knows your secrets, and under no circumstances should psychics breach your confidences by repeating what they know about you to mutual contacts. You have to feel secure in knowing that *what happens in Oz, stays in Oz.*

Some people don't like to ask their friends if they've heard of any good psychic readers, because they don't want anyone to know that they are going to a psychic for advice. Just as some people don't like to tell others that they are going to the doctor for a checkup or a therapist for help, the same feelings are also true about going to a psychic. The Internet provides information on thousands and thousands of psychic readers. The problem is, which one do you choose? Will this or that psychic be a good fit for you?

Just like dating, you have to venture out there and see who you click with psychically. Psychic reading is one service where there absolutely must be chemistry and a real energy connection. The advertisements for psychic readers all sound good: *Gifted, ex-*

perienced psychic reader, clairvoyant. Spirit guide connections and angelic wisdom. Helps in all matters. And then here's the hook: *Relationship specialist re-unites loved ones. Visa/MC/AMEX.*

Psychic readers who advertise as relationship specialists are the top cats of the psychic-reader world. They definitely get a big client draw because most people want to know about their love life (or lack of a love life). The Miss Congeniality contestants in the psychic-reader pageant are the psychics who tout themselves as being able to connect with spirit guides and loved ones who have passed over. The third-place runner-up deals with issues about finances and career, followed closely by pet psychics and generalist psychic readers.

Be street smart when reading a psychic's advertisement. Don't be pulled in by psychics who promise and guarantee to return a lover to you. The outcome of a psychic reading mostly depends on the client's willingness to evolve through life's situations, not on a psychic reader's promise to make it all better. Some ads should more likely be phrased *Palms, Tarot, and Rims,* especially when pertaining to certain charlatan psychic readers just looking to make some money off of a client's desperation for a desired result. Hey, maybe while they're at it, they'll sell you some over-the-top, tacky rims for your car, too.

After a few hits and misses, a client will usually decide which psychic reader feels best. It is like *Psychic-Junkie Goldilocks and the Three Psychic-Reader Bears.* Some psychic readers are too hard on you, some psychic readers are too vague with you, and then there is the psychic reader who is just right for you!

Once the relationship is established with the psychic reader, some clients are excited about sharing their great find with friends, while others keep the psychic/client relationship hidden like a sordid affair. The clients who choose to share their psychic-reader discovery with friends are very particular with who gets the psychic reader's contact information. It's like news of a private trunk-show sale at Barneys.

Clients like to take credit for turning their friends on to a great psychic-reader find. It's as exciting as hitting upon a new band, a great new restaurant, or the perfect vacation spot. If the psychic reader is good at giving names, initials, and dates with a pretty high success rate, then the word is out that this is the *hot new psychic reader* of the moment.

For some clients, the psychic-reader relationship becomes the new hip thing to have. Some people who are very open will boast about having their own psychic reader. After all, in some circles it is considered chic to know a psychic. It provides the client with instant access to the vast picture scope of the universe. Always remember that responsibility is foremost in the relationship, and big egos will get both the client and the psychic in trouble. Respectfully look into the future, but be careful of overstepping ethical boundaries because you may accidentally open a Pandora's box, a vault of restricted knowledge that may lead the seeker into a world of trouble.

Most people recount stories about what their psychic reader has told them, and that is what spurs others to go and book a psychic reading. You will hear people say that the psychic correctly predicted when they would change jobs, predicted a name of someone in their life, and there is sometimes the macabre information about how a psychic reader picked up that someone around them would soon pass away. In any case, clients like details, and the more details that a psychic reader can tap into, the better their chances are of becoming a sought-after psychic.

The way that people are attracted to certain types of partners holds true for the client's allure to a specific type of psychic. Some clients prefer male psychics and others prefer females. If the psychic reader has an accent of some sort, that may also be intriguing for a client. Being a psychic reader myself, I wonder how my strong Philly accent fares against a psychic with a British accent, or maybe even a mysterious Eastern European accent? I guess as long as the psychic information is correct, the clients don't really even care if you talk baby talk.

Michael, a friend of mine who lives in haunted York, England, is also a psychic reader. I had a psychic-reading session with him over the phone, and his British accent gave the reading an old-world feel. I experienced a strong past-life type of connection to England as the session went on. A hooting sound in the background further enhanced the rainy afternoon in Philadelphia on my side of the call. At the end of the reading, I mentioned to Michael that the owl in the background certainly gave me a strong visual connection to my reading. Michael seemed surprised. He said, "Luv, that was no owl that you were hearing. That was a fussy baby howling in the flat next door." Oh, well! The sound transported me into a different realm, and whether it was a baby or an owl howling, Michael's British accent made it all seem more authentic.

Advertisements, the Internet, and word of mouth are all ways that a psychic/client connection is made. I, for one, have never really advertised my services. I view my clients as one large human chain letter, in which somewhere in the client genealogy tree, one client knows someone who knows someone else. My clients all have roughly two degrees of separation. We are like one big Mormon family, somehow all interrelated. My clients live everywhere, and they all seem to like the exclusivity of knowing that they can deal with me directly without going through a scheduler or customer service rep.

The fact that my clients somehow or another may have common friends or acquaintances calls for me to be ultra-confidential, so as not to breach anyone's confidences. Whenever I relay an interesting client situation in the hope that it may help someone else to know that there is someone else out there going through the same type of situation, I have to make sure that all names, places, and occupations are carefully guarded and not revealed.

The biggest fear that some people have about referring their psychic reader to their friends is that the psychic may slip up and repeat some very confidential information to a gossipy client. Relax. Psychics are your personal *CIA agents* (confidential, intuitive advisors).

Once I had a very nosy woman call me who didn't want to make an appointment. She pretended that she was concerned about her friend for whom I do psychic readings. This woman wanted me to divulge the contents of her friend's psychic-reading session to her. I told her that it wasn't any of her business, but she persisted. She kept saying that she had to know if the woman was having an affair or not because she wanted to help her. I told her to stop asking about my client, and if she was curious about what was happening in her friend's life then she should ask her directly.

This woman is the poster girl for gossip. She is a walking, talking *New York Post* Page Six. She took my avoidance of her questioning as an indication that her friend was involved in a relationship outside of her marriage. I told this woman to drop the subject and leave me alone. She kept calling and pleading with me to give her details. This woman even started to e-mail me requests for information about her friend. I told her, "Stop asking me to break the karmic laws of trust." Her insistence that I talk to her was so smothering that I had to dispel all of her negative energy.

After I got off the phone with her, I quickly ran and got my sage out of the cabinet. I was in such a hurry to dispel her negative energy that I placed the giant abalone seashell holder filled with the burning sage too close to a can of hairspray that was on my vanity. As the flames of the sage shot up like a rocket, I managed to quickly grab the can of hairspray before it ignited from the baby bonfire I had burning in my bathroom sink. I fanned the smoke from the burning sage toward me for clearing, then I ran to open a window to let out the negative energy.

In the meantime, the smoke from the burning sage set off my smoke detector. For a minute I thought, "What the hell am I doing? Was this lady's energy so bad that I had to go through all of this aggravation to get rid of the negativity from her?" Guess what? It worked, and the nosy woman never called me again. What a relief.

Once you establish a relationship with a psychic reader who is the right fit for you, it is easy to think that the hard part is over. Just as with any relationship, though, you have to work at keeping it good. Do not become so comfortable with the psychic/client relationship that you start to take it for granted. Dependence is to be avoided at all cost, as is being inconsiderate with the psychic's time. Do not abuse the psychic reader's free time. You have to adhere to an appointment, and don't blur the lines between professionalism and friendship in an effort to get out of paying the requested fee for the psychic readings.

Psychic readers on the other side of the cards have a responsibility to the client not to help create a co-dependent relationship and to be aware that making money isn't the only objective of the psychic profession. A true caring and respect for the client's issues has to be fairly acknowledged. Psychics are supposed to be guides who help us when we venture into our own personal twilight zone, the dimension above our earthly existence.

Psychics Have Off Days, Too

What does it mean if suddenly the psychic reader who has been right on with your readings for the past few years suddenly starts to bomb out? There are a few things that can be wrong, and the first thing you have to do is troubleshoot the problem. Check to see if you owe the psychic money for past readings. Sometimes, the feeling of being taken advantage of will make the psychic temporarily shut down. Don't run a lengthy tab with the psychic because once the feelings of animosity set in, the psychic may not want your energy around if he or she thinks you are conniving.

Another reason for psychics to keep crashing when it comes to predictions is the ever-so-probable bad day of their own. Psychic readers who are also dealing with their own earthly problems sometimes can't detach enough from their worries and stay grounded long enough to work with their clients. Not feeling well and suffering from allergies, headaches, and whatever else is ailing them may be enough to throw the psychic reader off their mark until they recover.

Asking a psychic reader about the same situation over and over again will be a real turn-off and cause *psychic-reader apathy syndrome*. That is a condition in which psychics are so sick of the badgering about the same situation, they really don't care to read around it anymore and their psychic readings become vague because of the client's refusal to keep things moving.

I had a woman who wanted psychic readings about a man who didn't want to move their relationship forward. She had been dating this guy for five years and he was content to keep it that way. From the beginning, I'd told her that he is a past-life connection for her and the relationship is comfortable, but because of a bad first marriage this fellow is never going to ask her to get married. I told her that if she was looking for marriage and children, then this was not the man for her. I assured her that the universe has a way of filling a space that it is empty, and if she wanted a marriage and children, then she would most likely meet someone else.

She didn't care, she wanted this guy. After five years of telling her basically the same thing, I started to get bored with her. I could only read her on days when I had a few exciting clients before her just so my energy would stay up. I needed the intriguing clients to spice things up before I had to deal with her same old story.

One day, after we finished our psychic-reading session, she told me that I hadn't told her anything different in the past few readings. I told her that when I do psychic readings concerning her staid relationship, it feels like an *off day* for me psychically. The first year of readings pretty much gave her all there is to know about her relationship with the man in question. How many different ways can I say, "This guy ain't budging. He doesn't want to get married"?

This client tried every trick in the book to get me to renege on my original insights about her stalled-out relationship. She would tell me that other psychics told her that the guy would ask her to get married and that they would have three children. Interesting! Since the client was already close to fifty years old, she'd better get on with the notion of having three kids. It was pathetic to see her behave like this since she wasn't a stupid woman. She had a very successful career and made good money. After giving her psychic readings, I always had to go lie down because I was drained from boredom.

When a client challenges the psychic reader about things that come up in a session that the client doesn't necessarily want to hear, the client will try to work it until she hears what she sets out to hear. Doing things like this will lower the psychic reader's vibration, and there you have it: the beginning of the psychic reader's off day. So if your psychic reader isn't delivering as well as before, troubleshoot for boredom and make sure that you are not stuck or fixated on one particular outcome to an overworked topic. Some clients never get a chance to peek into their future because they are stuck in their past.

There is a good chance that if you are not grounded before a psychic reading, the psychic may seem a little off, too. Like energy attracts like energy. Psychic readers deal with energy. If you or the psychic reader are dull, the energy around your psychic reading may also be dull. The energy needs to be spinning in order for things to start moving along in a psychic session. You can tell by the psychic's voice if the psychic might be having an off day. If psychics are distracted, preoccupied, or tired, their voice will be a dead giveaway. I know that by the end of the day, my speech is slower and I start to shut down. If after the first few minutes into the reading you notice that things just aren't clicking and resonating, then your psychic reader may be having an off day. It is best to cancel the session and let the psychic re-schedule for another time.

Some clients don't want to believe it when you tell them that you are not up for doing any psychic readings because you feel drained or out of it. They will book an appointment anyway, which makes the psychic feel obligated to put out. The psychic may be psychically out of shape at the moment and not charged up enough to do any psychic work. We hate to disappoint our clients and send them away, but there are days that we need to recover from all of the energy output from our profession.

My aunt Rose is a very talented psychic, and she has had clients who call her and wake her up out of a sound sleep. Even if she says that she is not reading at the moment because she is too tired, the clients keep moving forward with their questions. As a psychic reader, you feel bad that you are basically talking in your sleep, but the clients don't care—they just want their cards read. I guess the clients think that they're getting a trance-channeling session. It's terrible when you can't even remember what you just told them.

Aunt Rose on occasion has told clients that she isn't up for doing psychic readings because she doesn't feel well and she needs her rest. Some psychic junkies don't believe it when you tell them you are sick. Clients have volunteered to bring her soup or medicine, anything so she will get better. You can't have your psychic reader down too long because it would be like walking around with a lobotomy. These women will do anything to get a reading with her, even going so far as to drive her to the doctor to make sure she fully recovers. Aunt Rose's psychic-reader stories are a potential bestseller in themselves.

If a psychic reader is having an off day, it may be attributed to not clearing and grounding her own energy properly. Something as simple as raising her own vibration could get the psychic up and running again. When I feel like I'm having an off day, I resort to lifting my vibration by listening to music. Music is the psychic's shot of vitamin B12. Sound is a vibration, and it resonates throughout the universe. Sound is healing and elevating to the psychic in need of an energy lift. Drumming music definitely gets the vibration moving in an upward direction.

If a psychic reader is not getting any psychic insights for the client during the course of a reading, it could be because the psychic just isn't in the mood that day to perform. Maybe the psychic doesn't feel 100 percent or has a headache. Who wants to have an intimate energy exchange with someone who isn't in the mood and has a headache? Dealing with a psychic reader on an off day mimics the same energy of a relationship that has fizzled out.

If the psychic just can't deliver for you anymore, there's a chance that you have gone as far as you can get with that particular psychic. Maybe it's time to try another psychic reader. I am not suggesting that you go full-blown psychic junkie; I am only recommending that you test the problem to see if the problem is with you or with your psychic reader. By going to an alternate psychic, you will see if that psychic is also vague with you. Maybe this other psychic will amaze you and tap into things that the first psychic wasn't getting for you.

I always suggest that my clients get second opinions because it keeps things fresh. I stay sharp when they tell me that another psychic reader and I both picked up the same information, and it also avoids co-dependency. Checking in with another psychic reader is fine, but checking in with five or six psychic readers is not recommended. There's a difference between having a psychic-reader relationship with a psychic-reader affair on the side, as opposed to a psychic-reader reading orgy. Grounding, intimacy, and trust make for a good psychic-reading experience, as opposed to multiple psychic partners.

As with any profession, there are times when you just get tired of doing the same thing. I am guilty of saying that if I see one more tarot card, I will throw up. Dealing with a difficult client will suddenly put the psychic reader into an off mode.

As long as the majority of the psychic's readings are good and on target, I wouldn't worry too much about an occasional off day. When the psychic is continuously inaccurate with you, then it is time to move on because the client-reader relationship may have just burned out.

This Is Not Ego Based

I'll admit that there are some psychic readers who have huge egos and become really jealous when they hear about another good psychic. Everybody is so afraid of being disposable and replaced by someone better. The competition is high in *psychic-reader land*, and the exposure that the Internet has given to those in the psychic profession makes for a very competitive market.

One tarot-card reader I knew couldn't stand any competition at all. One time I told her that I heard that some woman was a really good psychic reader and she went ballistic. She said, "Dear, you must be kidding me. That woman is no psychic reader. She used to work at a hot-dog concession in a bowling alley and I heard that she keeps a cheat sheet of tarot-card meanings handy when she is doing someone's cards."

So, as you can see, some psychic readers interpret someone complimenting another psychic's abilities the same way someone feels when a partner compliments an old flame. *Ego* stands for *Everybody's Got One*, but keeping the ego in line isn't always a simple task. It is so easy to feel pumped and powerful when a client calls to tell you how right-on you were in making a psychic prediction; but for the most part, people who do psychic work are of the same mindset that giving psychic readings should not be ego-based.

It's amazing to hear clients fluff a psychic reader's ego by saying that they wish that they could develop their psychic sense. Clients think that it's really cool to be able to know hidden things about someone or *psychically spy* on people they are curious about. I don't want to disappoint anyone, but psychic abilities don't always work that way. A psychic reader usually finds it hard to read themselves, if they can do it at all. Because we are acting both psychically and logically with ourselves, our own perception may be off.

Think of it this way: if you are on top of a mountain and look down, then you can see the whole village. If you are standing in the center of the village looking around, then you can only see what is around you. The full view is not possible because you are looking from a different place in space. On occasion, I have been right-on with my own predictions concerning my life, but only after I put myself through the emotional wringer. Plus, I second-guess myself.

There is an old adage that says, "A lawyer who represents himself has a fool for a client." The same can be said about psychic readers who read for themselves, as they then have a *psycho psychic* for a client. I will read my horoscope in every local newspaper, including the daily zodiac websites. Then I will do my planetary transits for my astrological chart, followed by pulling a few tarot cards and finally consulting a pendulum to get a simple answer for a matter of personal concern. Afterward, I feel like, "What the hell, I should have just called a psychic and scheduled a reading!"

Even if my psychic consult tells me the same things that I have picked up about myself, I always feel better if someone else confirms the findings for me. I try not to let my ego out of its cage when I do my psychic work. Everyone has a sixth sense, and it is just a matter of being open to using it. I have met my share of pompous psychic readers who parade around like they are some deity, to be revered for their psychic powers.

Psychics who misuse their gifts in order to bamboozle a client are creating horrible karma for themselves. The people in the psychic profession are a little unusual to begin with and have different views about life, both this life and past lives. Psychic readers with big egos spoil it for the rest of the psychics because they give the impression to the public that we are all top-billed *carny acts*. There are some psychic readers who have big egos and big price tags to match.

I went to a big egotistical psychic once (and *only* once). He dressed all in black (you look more mysterious that way), displayed crystals on his office table, and pretended to be shuffling through some papers stuffed into a Hermès briefcase. It made him appear very important and extremely professional. He started the session by giving me strict rules not to interrupt him or ask any questions during the psychic reading. When the session was over, I asked him a question about something he said that I couldn't quite relate to (which was 90 percent of the reading). He became very agitated and reminded me that my time was up. He never did answer my question because he admonished me for going five minutes past our appointment time, then he showed me the door. He looked like a psychic reader, but what I actually got for my money was a big egotistical display of pure showmanship.

Another type of psychic reader thinks that she is at a Halloween party every day. She will have some kind of pashmina scarf around her shoulders, a large crystal pendant hanging from a chain around her neck, a large ring on one of her index fingers, bright lipstick, and excessive and slightly smeared eye makeup.

This type of psychic reader is always *on* and even goes grocery shopping dressed like a psychic. They love it when someone asks what they do for a living so they can go on and on about how psychic they are. I am not implying that all psychic readers who wear black or don scarves have an extra-large ego; I am just showing how some psychic readers flaunt, brag, and display their profession with stereotypical visuals and, sadly, their abilities become secondary.

At times it is the client's ego that gets in the way of getting a good psychic reading. It's fine to have a healthy ego so people won't use you for a doormat, but where spirit is involved there is no room for the ego. The ego attaches to material things as a way of defining and measuring its existence. The ego is also very cognizant of time because time and timing will assure the ego of a future existence.

No one wants to think that they won't wake up tomorrow. Some clients push a psychic reader to give them timing for a certain event to happen, but time is merely a measurement used to see how fast something will take place. When a client keeps asking, "When, where, who, how?" it is their ego looking for those answers. Spirit already knows that these things will come to pass and doesn't need to be tested by giving an hour or a day. Psychic readers who give timing do so in an effort to shut up some impatient clients.

I love it when the client's ego attempts to tangle with a psychic reader. A client may say something like, "You told me it would happen in two days. Well, it has been three days and nothing has come true yet." The psychic reader already knows how difficult it is to take the "I" out of everything and must make the spiritually underevolved client understand what bliss there is in awareness and not in precise timing.

Instead of looking at a clock, stay in the moment, feel your breath, and enjoy the consciousness of now. There is no better high than to experience every moment with the awareness of being connected not to your ego, but to the moment. Each instant, each breath, is a unique moment that will never happen again.

Psychic Reader vs. Psychic Reader

Some clients who go to multiple psychic readers about the same issue might become confused if they get conflicting answers to the same query. Just because one psychic told you something doesn't necessarily mean that another one will tell you the same thing. This is a fact that people who are psychic junkies have to realize. Clients will go to a psychic to find out about a certain situation, and if the information that the psychic gives them isn't exactly what they were hoping to hear, they will start comparison shopping for the answer that they want. There are even clients who start from the get-go of their psychic reading to convince the psychic about the desired answer to their questions. They preface their reading by recounting all of the details from a previous psychic reading with another psychic. Only insecure psychic readers may take the client's bait, but the experienced psychic readers know better than to be led astray.

Let's take a peek into the *psychic-reader trenches*. First of all, psychic readers have heard everything, and I do mean *everything*. Psychics don't even have to use their psychic talents when it comes to sniffing out the *hear what I want to hear* client. A client who starts out a session by telling the psychic all of the details of their prior psychic readings is sure to begin the session by already *coloring outside of the lines*. Making the psychic reader feel like he is competing with a former psychic reader is like telling your lover about all of your ex-partners. Ouch! Competing and comparing don't mix well with spirit, and it may send the psychic reader down a dead-end road if you cut off the natural flow of the energy exchange between you and the psychic.

It might be a better idea if the psychic seeker gets another reading from a different psychic reader first, then after the reading session assess if the two psychics gave similar information but maybe conveyed it differently. Some psychics read in a more visual style while others are more abstract and cryptic.

After the reading is complete and the client wishes to recount some tidbits of information given by a different psychic, both the client and the psychic can see where the information from both psychic readings intersects and get a complete picture of what is going on. I personally like to see where there are similarities between my psychic insights and another psychic's take on the same client situation. Comparing psychic notes is different from clients downloading information into a psychic reader before the psychic-reading session begins.

A woman who came to me for a reading told me beforehand that an amazing psychic reader told her that her boss would be leaving his wife and that he would develop an interest in her. This woman had a huge crush on her boss and wanted her fantasies about him to materialize. I did a reading for her and was truthful: I told her that her boss did find her attractive, but he would never risk mixing business with pleasure.

She started her mission to convince me by telling me that the other psychic she went to saw them together as a couple, and she told me that at an office event the boss kept staring at her even as other men flirted with her. She thought that the boss was getting jealous. I told her during a tarot reading that she was wasting her time because nothing would come of her desires for her boss. This woman spent every waking hour thinking about this guy. She practically OD'd on psychic readings from numerous psychics. Some said she would wind up with him while other psychics told her to move on.

There really isn't anything that can be done with a client like this. She eventually wore herself out after three years of fantasizing about the boss and quietly moved on to another man, whom she later married. What this woman really needed to do was stop looking at the boss as the desired end result for love in her life. This woman needed to be open to just allowing love to come into her life, and the universe would surely provide the man she is to have in her karmic contract.

Another ploy that clients use when tying to pad the reading is to pretend that they are seeking a psychic reading concerning a friend. If the client thinks that the psychic may be judgmental about the subject matter of the reading, then the client suddenly talks in the third person.

A woman came to me for a reading and started by telling me that her married friend (who was really her) was pregnant, but the baby's father was not this woman's husband. She wanted to know if the tarot cards would tell her what would happen. She wanted to know if her *friend's* husband would ever find out. By conducting the psychic reading in the third person, she was a dead giveaway. I don't see too many people who will really get a reading about a friend. Sure, questions concerning friends do come up during the course of a psychic reading, but rarely does someone pay for a psychic reading to hear all about a buddy.

I asked her why her friend didn't just book her own reading and find out for herself what would be the outcome of the pregnancy. She thought for a moment and said that her friend was afraid of psychics. I looked at the tarot cards, and I really didn't want to embarrass her any further but I did see that there was no pregnancy to be worried about. I asked her if she knew for sure that a pregnancy had been confirmed. By this time, she was more relaxed, especially after hearing there was no pregnancy, and she confessed to me that the psychic reading was concerning her own fears about being pregnant.

She told me that a previous psychic reader saw her getting pregnant by her boyfriend and that her life would be ruined. She said the other psychic was so convincing about a pregnancy that she thought for sure that it was true. I reminded her that just because one psychic told her about something doesn't mean that I would tell her the same thing. I told her to buy a pregnancy kit and check for herself. As it turned out, she just had a pregnancy scare, most likely from the stress of being in an extramarital relationship. Now, if she isn't careful and continues with the affair, then the other psychic's prediction of a pregnancy could come about. Psychics pick up the thoughts you send out into the vast universe, and often psychic readings will be warnings for the seeker to get back on track before they complicate life with undesired events.

When clients get manic and book psychic reading after psychic reading with different psychics, there is going to be confusion. What would happen if you took your car to a different mechanic for the same problem? Too many opinions are bound to create confusion and possibly cause more problems. You don't know who to believe, and the chances of getting good results become extremely diluted.

When I worked on a psychic phone line, I would always get confirmation after the reading that another psychic who worked for the same company as me also picked up similar information. I feel that if more than one psychic reader picks up the same information for the same client, then chances are pretty good that you can count on the information being accurate. But clients have to know when to stop comparing notes. How many times does a problem have to be diagnosed before something is done about it?

Don't play psychic-reading roulette and always expect to land on the same spot. Psychics pick up different things about you at different times. The outcome of a psychic reading is random in the sense that a lot depends on the energetic condition of the client at the time of the reading. If you're going to a psychic to get a reading concerning a job, it's also possible that the psychic will pick up on other things, too: for instance, a relationship. You never know!

Keep in mind that a psychic may tell you the same thing as another psychic reader, but it may come across differently to you. Different psychic readers have unique ways of expressing and communicating the same information. If you ask two different people to describe the same house, you will most likely get alternate descriptions. One person may focus more on the inside while someone else pays more attention to the outside. Still, the same house is described but diverse images are given. The same is true if you go to two different psychic readers. The readings may differ from one another even though you are still the same person with the same concerns. There will be differences along with some similarities.

What happens if one psychic tells you one thing but another psychic reader tells you something totally opposite? This is where you have to be a *psychic forensic client* and piece together all the pertinent information. Only you have control over how the outcome of a situation in your life will be perceived and handled; psychic readers are only the guides along the way, never the last word.

I had a woman come to me who wanted to know if she should stay with her boyfriend or leave him. The relationship had some serious control issues built into it, because both parties involved were very strong willed and independent. My psychic reading and astrological-chart comparison for the woman and her boyfriend indicated that even though the relationship had its problems, they seemed to be put together by the cosmos so that they could both learn the lesson of compromise. She listened for a moment, then she told me that another psychic told her to get rid of her difficult mate and find someone more easygoing. I can see how this woman could be confused by two totally different takes on her relationship with this guy.

Well, if she leaves this boyfriend, chances are that she might attract a similar energy in another mate. Like energy attracts like energy. Even if the new boyfriend seemed more compromising, he might be the other extreme of being passive-aggressive, which is just another form of control. In any case, this client has a soul lesson to learn concerning giving, taking, and compromise. If she doesn't learn it through her boyfriend, should she break up with him there's a possibility that she may get the lesson through her job or her friends.

The soul needs to evolve and learn through life lessons, and just because you skip a class doesn't mean that you don't have to take the final exam. Sometimes when dealing with a relationship, the devil you know is better than the devil you meet, so to speak. Since her relationship with her boyfriend wasn't violent or abusive, I suggested that she work more with the astrological energies of their combined astrology charts and consider it an opportunity to evolve on a soul level and learn how to put the ego aside.

Psychic seekers should also be aware that if they go to different psychic readers for the same concern, one psychic may pick up more on the past and what caused the problem to develop. Another psychic may be someone who is more of a here-and-now type of psychic reader and will look at the current conditions. There are psychic readers who go deep into the future and tell you of the probable outcome because of the seeded past events. Keep in mind I did say *probable outcome*. At any time you, the querent, can change your future by adjusting the way you are thinking momentarily about a certain person or situation.

If you choose to get different opinions about the same life situation, it would be *street smart* to go to different types of psychic readers. Go to a tarot-card reader to tap into the collective consciousness. Try an astrologer to see what planetary trends are aggravating or helping your current dilemma, and seek out an angel reader to get some divine guidance from the other-dimensional beings. There are endless choices for different types of psychic readers and readings.

It is understandable that some clients prefer a certain method for getting readings, but why not give other methods of divination a try so you can become fully acquainted with all that is available to you while you are on your earthly journey and spiritual path?

Psychic/Client Breakups

When the psychic reader and the client go through a breakup, it can be as emotionally devastating as a divorce. Sometimes, the relationship reaches burnout stage, and the psychic reader doesn't really know where else to go with the client. Once the client has successfully resolved the problems that he or she initially needed psychic advice for, the time to move on is apparent. The psychic knows that the cure is sometimes in the poison, so to speak, and guides their clients psychically to see that often right inside of the problem lies the solution.

Psychic readers are like *energy doctors*, and when the patient (or client, in this case) has made a recovery, it becomes necessary to give the client a psychic reader *clean-soul* bill of health and a discharge from psychic care. From time to time, it is acceptable for the former client to seek out *psychic-reading checkups* to ensure that they stay in the light and on the right path.

It's also understandable that some clients will go through psychic-reader withdrawal and will start to call about every little issue in their life. When a client goes through psychic-reading withdrawal, *psychic-junkie rehab* may be necessary. Psychic-junkie rehab is an extreme approach in which the psychic junkie usually finds solace by hanging with Born Agains and Bible thumpers, while going cold turkey with anything psychic. Psychic-junkie rehab condemns daily horoscopes, prays for psychic readers (because they all work for the devil), and strictly prohibits Internet psychic sites. Most psychic junkies relapse and are right back to searching for a psychic in order to *cop* a psychic reading or two. The ones who stay in psychic-reader remission are warned not to have any relationship or communication with anyone who dares to even practice any of the metaphysical arts.

The real meaning behind having a professional relationship with a psychic reader in the first place is to get a grip psychically on your life situations. The client needs to understand that frivolous calls to a psychic reader will cloud the energy. The readings become routine, repetitive, and the lines of psychic communication begin to break down. Once the psychic readings become mundane and boring, the time to move on becomes apparent. The psychic reader and the client become like old bed partners where all the moves are predictable and the only thing remaining is a common comfort zone with each other. The relationship between psychics and their clients has to continue to be electric because energy is the driving force behind getting a good psychic reading. The anticipation of getting a psychic reading coupled with the responsiveness of the psychic reader makes for an amazing psychic-reading connection.

Sometimes it is the client who chooses to end the professional relationship with the psychic. The reasons can be anything from a reading rate increase to not making the right energy connection with the psychic any longer. Once a client starts to shop around for a new psychic reader, the possibility of psychic-reader adultery comes into play.

I have a great client, and when she first came to me for a reading, one of her first questions was, "Do you think that my other psychic will know that I am getting readings from you?" I thought that the question was strange and I wanted to know why it would make a difference either way. The new client explained to me that she had gone to this one particular psychic for years, but she felt that the woman knew her all too well and the readings were more like advice sessions instead of psychic readings. I told her that the psychic was giving her intuitive advice, but this client wanted more. She wanted to know about what was going to come about for her instead of some well-grounded advice on how to handle her life.

Starting a relationship with a new psychic reader is like starting any new relationship. The energy and the chemistry have to be there. You have to like the psychic's style of doing readings and feel comfortable with the psychic. I went to a psychic reader once, and the first reading with her was strange. She had these really long pauses between phrases but when she spoke, the psychic information was detailed. There was a comforting energy emitting from her, and by the end of the reading session I decided that I liked her. I told my friends about her, but they didn't vibe to her energy, so it just goes to show you that there must be a personal connection between the client and the psychic.

The bottom line is that if clients have successfully resolved their issues and no longer need psychic readings, then ending psychic-reading treatments is the obvious next step. Some clients are afraid that if they don't regularly check in with their favorite psychic, they may lose contact, and the psychic could move, change phone numbers, or stop working on the same psychic phone line. Over the years I have gone to psychic readers who were amazing, only to find out one day that the psychic's phone number has been changed or that the psychic no longer gives private readings.

Losing communication with your favorite psychic is like losing your best friend, preferred hairstylist, or in some instances, like losing your partner. Some psychic/client breakups can be disastrous. Clients become sullen and upset because their energetic psychic umbilical cord has been cut. I personally have had clients send me gifts and flowers in an attempt to resurrect our psychic/client relationship. There are even clients who will go so far as to stalk a psychic reader in order to get one last reading.

Some clients will try to swing the psychic/client relationship into a friendship in hopes of never losing contact with their favorite psychic. Can you still be friends after a serious psychic-reader relationship ends? Being friendly with your ex-psychic is fine, but trying to twist the professional relationship into a friendship is crossing boundaries. Friendly is one thing, but full blown friendship is not in the cards. Just as some patients fall in love with their doctors, clients often bond with their psychic readers.

These friendships aren't a good idea because the door is wide open to abuse the friendship and once again try to squeeze out a few free psychic readings. I don't like to read for friends, because it puts the friendship into a precarious position and problems can arise should any information picked up psychically not be very promising or complimentary. Clients will get into transitional psychic-reader relationships after the relationship with their favorite psychic comes to an end. Some of these transitional relationships may evolve into new psychic/client relationships and the psychic junkie may find a new psychic-reader drug of choice. The client's endorphins are on a new high, and the need to get psychic readings can still be satisfied.

Some clients never get over losing a favorite psychic, and the loss can be discombobulating for them. Some clients become too attached to their psychic reader, and that can cause a very unhealthy relationship. The client unknowingly begins to function as a couple with the psychic, and all decisions made need to be run past the psychic for that psychic to tap into the outcome. The clients confide, trust, and totally believe in their psychic reader, and sometimes consider the relationship with their psychic to be of primary importance. The psychic reader realizes that clients come and go, so a rotation of clientele is totally recognizable. A psychic may miss a former client, especially if the client had a really great personality or a very interesting life. However, the psychic reader has other clients, so even if a few clients drop off, there are usually more clients around to serve as ready replacements.

A psychic/client relationship is very special. This is a relationship in which having a very intimate energy connection is a must in order to get a good psychic reading. There is a special bond that develops when you go through life situations with someone and see them through both good times and bad times. Clients feel close to their psychic readers because they are the ones who really know all their secrets. A client can usually tell if a breakup is imminent because the psychic reader will start recommending that the client take a break between readings and let former predictions come about before getting any more psychic readings.

The whole purpose of going to a psychic for a reading is to become aware of and in tune with your own personal energy. There comes a time in the psychic/client relationship when it is healthy to move apart. Occasional spot checks are fine, but frequent psychic readings are no longer necessary. The psychic's clients sometimes frown at redefining their relationships with psychic readers to whom they had become so addicted.

Just as mother birds push their baby birds out of the nest so they can learn to fly on their own, so must psychic readers help their clients learn to trust their own intuition and keep an energetically clean life where grounding is practiced. Psychic readers have done their job in the psychic/client relationship if the clients have learned the importance of grounding, the awareness of now, and the freedom of knowing the truth.

CHAPTER 8

The Client's Side of the Cards

How to Get a Reading Like a Rock Star

In the previous chapters we looked at the history of psychic readers, the types of psychic readers, and methods used to give a reading, along with types of clients and the psychic's side of the reading experience. The importance of grounding your energy, protecting yourself from charlatans, and basic courtesy toward the psychic profession were all touched upon, including the fees that psychics charge for their time.

Now it's time to get into how you can have the *ultimate* psychic-reading experience.

First, you have to establish why you need psychic insight and what you hope to achieve by getting a reading. Hopefully, all of the subject matter covered in this book has made you street smart when it comes to getting a good reading, and also informed enough to know how to make the ultimate cosmic connection. The real challenge for clients, however, is wondering if they will get the information they need to know and, of course, their money's worth. A client doesn't want to pay four dollars per minute to a telephone psychic-line reader only to be asked questions by the psychic and given some vague general information about life. A client wants to get a *rock-star reading*.

What is the ultimate psychic reading? Is it when the psychic reader gives you names and dates? A psychic who tells you about something that happens within days is always a high scorer as far as readings go, but the best reading is the one when the client leaves the reading feeling energetically high and empowered. Clients who educate themselves a little before getting a reading will know that if they ground their energy before a reading session starts, then a better psychic connection can be made. The more you know about how something works, the better experience with it you will have.

Having been on both sides of the cards myself, as a psychic reader and a client, I will give up the Cliffs Notes to the psychic-reading manual so you can fully enjoy your next session with a psychic reader.

A majority of psychic readings are impulse purchases, when the client reaches for the phone as soon as a problem or life crisis arises. It is like calling *Psychic 911,* in case of a cosmic emergency. The first thing anyone should do when they suddenly feel rattled or unnerved is center, calm down, ground, and breathe. Breathing in and out is extremely important before making any decision, because breathing properly will immediately reduce your stress levels and send oxygen to all of your organs. If you call a psychic for a reading with your energy all over the place and spinning out of control, the psychic will find it hard to make a clear and concise connection. By the time a connection has been made, it may not be very strong, not to mention you are paying for time that is spent just trying to stabilize your energy. The impulse client has to at least be able to ground out a little before attempting to get a reading.

Once you have made contact with your psychic, allow the psychic a moment or two to adjust her RPMs to be in synch with the spinning energy of your own chakra centers. If you remember, chakra centers are like your body's energetic spark plugs, and if they are firing off in the right sequence and not shutting down or getting stuck, then you will idle at the right energy levels. The psychic reader will link into your energy and begin to get a read on what is happening to you. Chakras are like computer diagnostic centers for your energy zones.

You can feel when a psychic has successfully made contact, because a different sensation will come over you. It is very calming, and any feelings of anxiety and nervousness seem to pass. Keep your solar-plexus chakra open, because that is where you will get the "gut" feelings telling you if it is still good to go or to shut down. Listen to your body because it is a direct readout of what is happening to your energetic self, where thoughtforms and all of your personal creations are conceptualized and sent out on life's assembly line.

If at any time during the reading you feel as though the psychic reader is getting stuck or blocked, make sure that it is not coming from you. Troubleshoot and see if you accidentally crossed your arms or legs in an unconscious attempt not to be too open and vulnerable. If the problem is not on your end, feel free to communicate with the psychic reader and tell her she is off-track. Most likely, the psychic reader needs some client feedback to assure her that she is, indeed, making a connection. Psychic readings are about communication, and it is beneficial to be part of the reading instead of a bystander. This does not mean that you have to tell the psychic the answers to your questions, but do communicate with the psychic to keep the energy of the reading spinning at a higher rate. The higher the vibration of the psychic reading goes, the better the reading will be. Confirmation and acknowledgement of correct information will bring the energy levels way up, making them spin faster and better able to attach to more information for the client.

Be open to receiving information other than what you initially called the psychic reader for in the first place. You may be so caught up in a distracting situation that you are totally missing out on some very important opportunities. If the psychic gives you an answer other than the one that you think you want to hear, don't try to rephrase the question or confuse the psychic so you get the desired response. Pushing too hard for what you want to hear instead of what you need to know will cause static and possibly get the whole reading off track. Go with the flow of the psychic reading.

It is a good idea to take notes during a reading so you can refer back to what the psychic told you and see how the information played out. I am always amazed when I look over notes from my past readings, because at the time of the psychic reading there was possibly some information given that I couldn't relate to, but down the road I see where things came to pass.

If a psychic reader gets timing for an event to take place, then she will surely give it to you, but if you press for exact timing a psychic may not be able to get that information in clearly. Be accepting that there is no time in space, and understand that psychic readers provide estimated times for events to unfold. A lot of what you do and how you handle things will directly influence how things in your life are timed. Timing is personal, because everyone perceives time differently. If it weren't for clocks, most of us wouldn't know how long we were doing something. Our timing would just be an approximation.

To get a good psychic reading, you have to be honest with the psychic. Often, very personal situations come out during a reading, and if you are cagey and play guessing games with the psychic you will lower the overall vibration of the session and start to stall out the psychic reading. Be truthful and honest, so the psychic can give you the correct advice. Don't forget the old adage that if the person doing the reading is psychic, then that person should know that you are not telling the truth about something. Psychic readers can tell when a client is bullshitting, and have to determine how to handle the situation without insulting the client. Be truthful because truthfulness vibrates higher than lying, and you will benefit more by being honest.

Confidentiality is a rule. Don't ask a psychic reader to tell you what she told your friend. You are free to discuss your psychic reading with anyone you want, but psychics have to protect the identity of their clients. Psychic readers may tell you about someone who had a similar situation to yours, but they are never to divulge who the person was.

Now, what if you are having a meltdown at two in the morning and your psychic swami is most likely asleep? What psychic phone line do you call? Well, to get a good psychic reading, *don't* wake up your favorite psychic, because the psychic will be in no condition or disposition to give you a reading. My advice is to either wait until you can call your psychic or else go to the psychic-reader phone line *first-aid kit*. Most psychic phone lines operate 24/7, but if you are on the East Coast, a psychic on the West Coast may be a better choice because it is three hours earlier there. Some psychics like to work the graveyard shift, so if a line is operating, then give them a call.

Emergency psychic readings are a crapshoot because you don't know who your psychic reader will be, so lessen the chances of being disappointed by grounding, grounding, and more grounding. You will be easier to read if you are steady. If the psychic reader seems to be having a hard time connecting, then you have possibly overgrounded and closed off your chakras. Visualize your chakras slowly opening until your body signals you that the psychic and reading feel right. Whenever you go to a new psychic for a reading, practice safe psychic-reading rules because you have no idea if the psychic who is reading you clears out previous client energy after each session. And you don't want to risk being read by an unbalanced psychic.

A very important thing to keep in mind is not to get a psychic reading when you are drunk or high. When your mind is altered by drugs or alcohol, you can become very suggestive and your free will and actions can possibly be distorted. The energy of a client who is using any sort of substance directly affects the psychic reader's ability to tap into the client. For the psychic reader, giving a reading to a blitzed client is like playing Celine Dion music in a biker bar. It doesn't work!

During the psychic-reading session if you feel that the psychic is trying to hustle you, immediately drop roots into the ground and imagine all of your chakra centers closing off to the psychic's energy. Cross your arms and legs and end the session. There are some psychics who aren't credible and try to exploit your problems and psych you into thinking that they can change your fate for an additional fee.

Once you have successfully connected with a psychic who is accurate and who has really proven helpful to you, then keep the psychic/client relationship clean. Both the client and the psychic will continue to have a good relationship if personal boundaries are kept in check. Feeling friendly toward your psychic is natural because she knows you intimately in a psychic sense, but keep business as business so the lines between psychic and friend don't blur the psychic's ability to be objective with you during a reading. Always compensate the psychic reader for services provided, so you don't create an energy imbalance and run the risk of causing negative feelings to creep into the relationship.

If you are scheduling an appointment with a psychic for a reading and you are not in emergency psychic-help mode, then you will have more time to prepare and you will really get a good reading. Make sure that you schedule enough time with the psychic reader because you don't want to book a thirty-minute session for a complicated situation that will require more time to discuss. Putting a Band-Aid on a cut is a lot less complicated and takes less time than taking care of a bullet wound, so schedule your time accordingly with the psychic. Sometimes a client who is on a budget will try to squeeze a complicated matter into a fifteen-minute scheduled psychic reading. By the time the psychic connects into the client's energy, the meat of the reading is coming in at the tail end of the session and the client will most likely wind up needing an additional appointment to complete the reading. It's much better to schedule a longer appointment so you don't have to interrupt the flow of the reading because of time constraints, and you will most likely leave the session feeling satisfied and not really needing another reading for a while.

What if you only need a quick answer to one particular situation going on in your life? You can get a psychic-reading *quickie*, which is a reading limited to your one big concern of the moment. Realistically, psychic readers need a few moments to connect with you, so if you are calling a psychic for a quick on-the-spot answer to a question, then at least ground your energy before placing the call to the psychic so the psychic can easily get into your energy zone and give you a *short-stop* psychic reading.

It is also beneficial to know what type of psychic reader you need. A tarot-card reader is like a general practitioner and can psychically give you an overall view of what is going on and coming up for you. If you have been in a slump for a while, you may need to schedule with an astrologer to see if you are temporarily caught up in a planetary loop or being hit with some solar or lunar eclipses. The play of the planetary energies can affect your own personal vibration, causing some life issues to come about. If you need to be reconnected with your spirit guides, then a medium or angel/elemental psychic reader may be who you need to speak with to get your energy levels up and running.

If you can adhere to the above-mentioned collection of tips on how to get a good psychic reading, then I am sure that you will have a whole new perspective of just how amazing a well-grounded psychic connection can be with a chosen psychic.

The Ultimate Psychic Reading

In this situation, you are not freaking out because of a life crisis, and therefore you have more time to prepare for your psychic-reading session. The tips I am about to provide you with on how to get a top-shelf psychic spa treatment will allow you to experience the true essence of getting a good psychic reading.

It is truly advisable that everyone take care of their energetic self as well as their physical self. People will spend thousands of dollars on clothes, exercise equipment, cars, and other material things but overlook the part of themselves that truly triggers how happy all of these material things will make them. Your energetic self, or spiritual self, needs regular checkups, clearings, and adjustments so you can continue to create, attract, and enjoy what your personal energy magnet draws to you.

Getting a good psychic reading as a starting point for clearing all the nonsense and clutter out of your life and raising your personal vibration meter up a few amps will not only manifest better things coming into your life, but a good psychic reading and clearing can actually make you look better because it will remove the heaviness of stress that not only pulls down your vibration but also outwardly shows by pulling your face down, too.

A good psychic reading can raise your vibration. I've had clients tell me that they feel lighter after getting a good reading. Sometimes the ethereal lightness is even reflected physically because the energetic body recognizes that heavy burdens have been dealt with, understood, and released through a good psychic reading and the overall feeling of lightness shows through on the physical body as a more youthful appearance or even slight weight loss. We are nothing more than a creation of our own thoughts and a direct reflection of what we put out into the universe. Here is a little psychic physics for you: *Your physical self is equal to your thought-creation vibration, threefold.*

What you think you shall bring about. How and which things manifest is totally influenced by our thought vibrations and our thought interactions with others. Grounding and psychic protection should be a regular practice like brushing your teeth. What we attract back to us and our perception of what is happening around us all starts with the thought vibration. Every organ in our body has its own vibration, and negative thoughts can actually accelerate an illness or cause changes in your cellular structure. The power of positive thinking can help you stay healthy and also help you reach most of your goals. Some issues are karmic, and a psychic reader, especially one well trained in regression and past lives, can help you do a vibration correction so you don't have to keep repeating the same mistakes over and over again.

Our energetic bodies hold all of what we have downloaded into ourselves through thoughts, actions, and reactions. Our physical DNA holds the memory chips from past lives and ancestral lineage. It is amazing to think that somewhere in your DNA is a trait or feature of a long-gone ancestor. Think about it: a component of your DNA may have been around when the pyramids were being built or during the Middle Ages.

Your brain is like a computer firewall that lets your ego step in for physical protection, but there is a part of the brain that can connect into your own personal psychic centers that is activated by directly connecting with a psychic or through your own abilities to activate this area. We all have this ability to be psychic and as we evolve and accelerate spiritually, our vibration will be high enough to access this amazing part of who we are. The brain provides logic, and the brow chakra, or third-eye chakra, which lies between our eyebrows, is where our intuition center is located. Logic, intuition, and our own free will to choose, if used properly, provide us with all of the necessary ingredients to design an amazing existence for ourselves. Ego vs. spirituality: a balance between these two centers is optimal for earthly survival because the ego wants to protect and adorn the physical body, while the intuitive center wants to protect and enrich the energetic body. The challenge is learning how to blend the two centers so our physical incarnation doesn't dismiss who we are eternally, which is spirit.

Our perception of how successful we are as a person is often measured by where we live, what we drive, and what we look like, rather than who we truly are. Are we the sum of our bank accounts or the sum of our life experiences? Spirit is free and unlimited, so don't restrict the definition of yourself with the weight of material things. Get acquainted with who you really are on an energetic spiritual level before getting your next psychic reading. The goal is to integrate successfully the logical part of our body with the intuitive part of our soul so we can spiritually and energetically function in a material world.

Getting well prepared for a serious reading from a psychic with whom you are comfortable and who can connect with you psychically will be off the charts if you really set some time aside and prepare for the psychic session the way you would prepare for a special occasion. You will be blown away by the result you get from the psychic-reading experience.

The first thing to do is set aside an hour for meditation and concentrate on what it is that you need guidance and answers for. If you have some white sage, burn a little to clear your space before getting a reading. You can also burn some clearing incense, or spray some clearing essence in the room where you will be receiving the reading—even if you are getting a phone reading. If you really want the reading equivalent to a super spa treatment, set out a bowl of spring water as an electrical conductor. If you have a clear quartz crystal, cleanse it in salt water, then place it near you while you get your reading. About thirty minutes before your psychic-reading session begins, play some music to raise your vibration. Drumming is good if you are feeling low on energy, but any type of sound that resonates with your mystical mood will be fine.

Most people want to get a psychic reading to give themselves a lift and raise their vibration, but keep in mind that the psychic will be connecting and tapping into your energetic vibration, and if it is too low the psychic may take a while to get you going energetically. The psychic reader can help you lift your energy, but the psychic is not your energy source, only a jump-start. Before the psychic reading begins, take three deep breaths to awaken all of your bodily organs. Keep your feet on the ground and arms and legs uncrossed. You can do most of these preparations before a reading if you are getting a telephone session. If you are getting a psychic reading in person, you can still do some of this prep work before you leave for your appointment. The psychic reader you visit with in person may have psychic tools and crystals around the room, but you can bring your personal crystal with you to amplify your reading. Hold the crystal in your left hand or put it in a pocket on your left side to receive the energy of the reading. When you go home you can hold your downloaded crystal while in meditation to reassess your psychic reading. Consider your personal crystal to be your metaphysical iPod.

Once the psychic-reading session starts, visualize your psychic reader locking into your energy the way the space shuttle docks into a space station. Feel the energetic umbilical cord link into you and keep your feet on the floor, or sit on a wooden floor or chair for basic grounding. The energy may be so intense at times that it is possible that electrical equipment in the room, such as tape recorders, could malfunction—or sometimes light bulbs even blow out. Grounding should alleviate these problems.

Allow the psychic some time to start to get a read on your energy patterns, and the psychic should start to read your energy grid the way a doctor would read a graph of an EEG or EKG. The vibration, intensity, and pattern of what the psychic is picking up will be translated into words, and a visual will be presented of what was seeded in the past and is taking shape for the future. This is your opportunity as the client to be given information about what you have either consciously or unconsciously brought into your life, and to do a quick correction if you don't like the predicted outcome of what is being told to you.

As the client, you must at all times realize that the psychic reader is the connecting link giving a diagnostic readout of what is going on in your life. You are the final word and decision maker concerning all of your life's matters. If you don't like something, then change it. You cannot have a full existence living in victim consciousness and blaming others for your problems. Blame is the opposite of responsibility, and if you push it onto someone else it will somehow make its way back to you, its creator.

Getting a psychic reading covering in-depth relationships in your life can be a little tricky. A psychic is connected into your psychic energy field, not into your partner's. Expectations of being told what someone else is thinking, doing, or planning can only be read as patterns that belong to the energy that has been created between you and that person. Asking a psychic reader to view remotely and link into someone else's energy so you will know what that person is up to can sometimes cause vagueness or shallow responses, because even though it is possible for a highly developed psychic to perceive something about someone you want to link into, it is also somewhat of an invasion of the other person's psychic self. It is like being a psychic voyeur or peeping Tom. The psychic reader should only give you information about someone as it directly relates to you. Remember that the psychic reader is linked into you, not the other person.

If you do want a psychic to give you information about someone you are involved with or a missing person, then you should bring a personal possession of the other person to the psychic-reading session, or hold on to something that belonged to the person in question if you are getting a phone reading. Psychics use *psychometry*, which is a method by which a psychic can feel the vibrations embedded into an item belonging to someone else. Personal items like jewelry and keepsakes can be read as a fingerprint of the person who owned them. Psychometry comes from the Greek words *psyche* (soul) and *metron* (measure), which basically means "soul-measuring." Make sure you come prepared for a reading if you want to get the most out of the experience.

Once the psychic reading is over, respect the time limits and realize that there is a point when you will begin to burn out the psychic reader, not to mention that you might go into information overload and risk crashing. Know when to bow your head and graciously end a psychic-reading session.

How a psychic reading ends is important for a good vibration to carry over, and the psychic reader should ask if there are any final questions or explanations before cutting the linking cord with the client. As a client I always thank the psychic for the reading and immediately compensate the psychic for his or her time. I don't want to create an imbalance, because I don't want that seed sowed anywhere in my energy grid. Also, being a psychic reader, I find that the closing of a reading should be upbeat and leave the client with a higher vibration than what the client came to me with. I want my clients to leave a reading session feeling good about themselves, as they would after going to a spa.

Some psychics are like the Energizer Bunny and can go on and on, while other psychics drain out after a lengthy psychic session, and you will feel when the energy of a psychic session has pretty much thinned out. Just like the doctor who reads your test results or the mechanic who does the diagnostics on your vehicle, the psychic reader can only tell you what the readout is on your psychic reading report. Recommendations on how to do the repairs, where things look weak, and what your best course of action is will be advised during your psychic-reading session. Following up on the treatment, repairs, and maintenance are all up to you. The remedies can only be suggested, and how and if they are carried out is totally up to the client.

By approaching a psychic reading with a sense of respect for the information being tapped into and creating an atmosphere conducive to getting a good reading, I promise you that you will have a much better experience than if you get a quickie psychic reading on your cell phone while you are driving.

I would be remiss not to mention the proper way to close out of the psychic-reading session. After the session has ended, sit quietly for a few moments and visualize your crown chakra slowly closing down a bit. While you were getting your psychic reading you were, I hope, wide open psychically. Proper closing is required so you are not too open after getting a psychic reading, because you can fall prey to an energy vampire or some vagrant negative thoughtform that tries to slip in while you are completely open, similar to someone sneaking into a movie theater without a ticket. The crown chakra is located above the head linking the individual and universal energies. The crown chakra is associated with the pineal gland, brain, and central nervous system. It ensures a connection to universal sources of energy and with the world as a whole. A balanced crown chakra allows for expanded awareness.

The psychic reader must also properly cut the cords and close his or her crown chakra after giving a psychic reading so as not to have any energy leaks or risk carrying some of the client's energy imprints into the psychic's own life. I tap myself on the right shoulder three times and ask Saint Michael the Archangel to take his sword and cut the cords that bind. By doing this, I am releasing the connection to the psychic reading and clearing myself for the next client. I am also ensuring that I don't confuse my own life with client energy.

There is more to getting a good psychic reading than it would appear. Be creative with your psychic readings and experiment with different methods of getting readings. Just don't get addicted.

Staying Psychically Fit

It's very easy to become addicted to psychic readings because they are informative, intriguing, mysterious, and, most importantly, all about you. The anticipation and excitement of a psychic reading is similar to what a child feels while waiting for a birthday and wondering what's underneath the wrapping paper. Your endorphins can go off the charts as you hear the psychic reader tell you some desired predictions. It is a high. Even if you hear things that you don't necessarily like, nonetheless you can't help but want to go back for more about *you*. I guess you could say, *Curiosity killed the cat, but psychic readings brought her back*.

It is easy to cop a psychic reading. You no longer have to wait days to get an appointment with a psychic reader; you just have to go to your computer, punch *psychic readings* into a search engine, and a whole myriad of psychic services will appear before you. The choice is endless; you can even procure a psychic reading from eBay.

Clients who attempt to adhere to a psychic fitness program will find that when they do get a psychic reading, the connection will be much better and they will continue to evolve on an energetic level. Just as an athlete trains for a physical sport or a student studies for a test, so should the psychic seeker stay on top of her energetic psychic-fitness regime. The client has to be psychically tuned up in order to resonate at a better frequency with the psychic giving the reading. The harmony of the universe is accessible to anyone who wants to tune in to it. The universal energy is like one huge symphony, and any out-of-tune thoughts, words, or deeds will at some point be kicked back to the person who needs to learn his or her part over again until he or she gets it right.

How is psychic fitness achieved? First of all, you need to be conscious of your energetic diet. Avoid negative people and situations and if you must indulge, then limit your intake to a mere minimum. Sometimes we fall off the wagon and find that we overdid some shots of negativity, leaving us feeling confused, sporting low energy, depressed, and in a nasty mood. A good psychic clearing can help your negativity hangover, and in severe cases some bodywork like acupressure, massage, and Reiki can help recharge your battery and get your chakras back in tune. Bodywork is necessary to maintain full spiritual balance because the physical body houses our energetic, spiritual self. Keeping a balance between the two entities is necessary because an imbalance on either side will cause problems down the road.

The saying "as above, so below" is very true. We eventually turn into our thoughts, and the intention behind our thoughts is what really shapes the outcome of things. Every thought, word, and deed will imprint an energetic fingerprint onto our physical body, as well as our astral body. The Akashic records hold our spiritual memories while the muscles of our body hold on to physical memories and traumas. When we are stressed, our muscles tense up, causing discomfort and contortions. Look at the face of someone undergoing a tough time. The muscles of the face will be an instant readout that the person has or is currently undergoing a stressful situation. The same goes for someone's posture. Bending forward shows that the muscles are holding the memories of a very stressful situation and the curving over, almost back into a fetal position, is indicative of wanting to regress back into the safety and security of the womb.

When a client goes to a psychic reader, releases the psychic memories of negative situations, and is rerouted back onto a more energetically beneficial path, then amazingly enough the new spiritual levity may result in feeling better physically. As soon as the energetic body has a new outlook, the reflection is apparent on the physical body. For example, a dowdy woman who meets the man of her dreams may suddenly reflect her new enthusiasm by suddenly having a more vibrant physical appearance. The uplifting energy will lift the muscles of her face, and her mouth will be more upturned instead of downturned. Her posture may become more upright as a reflection of feeling pulled upward by the new relationship. An overall beneficial physical effect is connected to the spirit.

Likewise, a bad relationship can take a toll on the energetic body, leaving physical signs of stress, which are translated into tight, aching, twisted muscles. The bottom line is that muscles hold memory, and these memories need to be released along with cutting the psychic cords so we can stay in good shape. A person getting a psychic reading who also maintains her chakra energy zones and releases muscular tension will have a better overall vibration, and the psychic will make a connection based on a higher frequency.

Consider it this way: antenna versus cable, dial-up versus broadband. The reception and variety of information will be given at the higher frequency if you stay completely in tune. The results are also based on how good the psychic provider is. Psychic readers also have to be cognizant of keeping clear, well-maintained body/spirit connections. Sometimes psychic readers neglect themselves, and the result is psychic burnout, which will adversely affect their psychic readings. Both the client and the psychic have to be conscious of doing routine maintenance.

Clients who are not psychically fit also run the risk of becoming psychic junkies and energy vampires. The inability of the client to be able to raise her own vibration and keep energetically up will drive her to get frequent psychic readings as a method to stay psychically high. The psychic readings begin to serve as *psychic drugs* instead of psychic guidance. The psychic readings may get the client's *thought-creation vibration* process moving along, but if the client has not maintained her own chakra energy centers and maintained protection from psychic attacks directed at her, then the results will be temporary. The client needs more and more psychic readings to continue to function, and then psychic-reading dependency develops. The psychic reader who deals with a client out of balance begins to feel as drained as a car battery that has just jumped ten cars on a cold morning. Just as doctors have hypochondriacs and retailers have shopaholics, the psychic reader is prone to attracting psychic junkies.

The cause is in the cure. What the psychic junkie really needs is a complete overhaul on her energetic self, a vibrational reprogramming, a high-endurance chakra spin class, a negativity-free diet, and an energy tune-up. A good psychic reader can recognize when a client is becoming addicted and will help the client identify the energy imbalance and recommend to clients how they can raise their own energy levels and get psychic readings more for maintenance instead of dependence.

Clients going through a tough time may want to get frequent psychic readings until the situation is corrected. Then the frequency of psychic-reading sessions can be toned down to be more for psychic checkups.

Here are a few tips that clients can follow to ensure that their psychic sessions for prediction don't become a psychic-session addiction. Your psychic fitness regime should include limiting the reading of your daily horoscope to no more than three servings per day. Reading twenty different horoscope sites or newspaper columns will cause confusion and the astrological information may be conflicting, leaving you wondering which outlook for the day is the right one. Instead, find an astrology site or column that you really resonate with. Also, find out your rising sign or ascendant so you can read that along with your Sun sign in order to get a quick glance at your day ahead.

Some clients like to get a daily mini psychic reading for an energy read on the day, but it is not a good idea to call ten different psychics during the course of your waking hours for a daily mini reading. If daily psychic readings are part of your personal psychic fitness regime, then limit them to no more than one reading per day with one psychic. Multiple psychic readings may throw your own vibration out of whack. It is like over-exercising: at some point you burn out. Remember to ground yourself first before getting any type of psychic reading so the information given during your session will be more tuned in and satisfying. Psychic readings without grounding are like eating empty calories. You will crave another psychic reading until you feel full.

If you're feeling depressed and can't seem to get your energetic body moving along, try some meditation, even if only for a half hour, because sometimes going inside yourself adjusts how you perceive what is happening outside of yourself. Once you get a view of your vibes toward a certain situation, then go and get a psychic reading and let the reading serve as a method to help you fine-tune your vibes and show you what is ahead for you. If you don't like the outcome, you can change the vibration and experience things differently.

A very important step to staying psychically fit is to always cut the cords of the day. Release all of the things that you do not like. Don't go to bed with attachments to negative situations. Releasing the vibrations that we don't like doesn't mean we are ignoring our problems, as much as we prefer to dwell more on the positive solutions. It is important to cut the cords that bind because carrying around any upset will lower your own vibration, tighten your muscles, cause physical symptoms like aches and pains, and, in really severe cases, allow your physical body to drop its resistance and ability to fight off disease. *DIS-ease* is a vibration imbalance caused by uneasy thoughts and feelings toward someone or something.

Remember that some of life's situations are necessary to help you develop character and evolve on an energetic level. *Aggravation* is like your energetic body's set of weights, and the people in the metaphysical, holistic, psychic profession are your energetic body's personal trainers. Your overall success depends mostly on your own commitment to staying psychically fit.

To stay psychically fit we have to always keep in mind that sometimes we will need to deal with people who aren't too nice and maybe even deal with someone else's illness or problems. Sometimes these other players in our life have a contract with us on a soul level to come back as a nemesis so we learn how to do the soul vibration correction. We learn how to be healed through someone who agreed to come back into our lives as someone sick. We learn about relationships by someone who agreed to come back as our partner, and we learn how to understand these things and look beyond the physical by getting in touch with our own vibrational responses through psychic awareness. There are no enemies, only teachers. Keep that in mind, because your thought vibration travels very fast out into the universe and lays the groundwork for your next set of events.

Your psychic fitness depends on you realizing that who and what is around you is a reflection of your own vibrations. It is like looking in a cosmic mirror, and if you don't like what you see then you have the ability to start to make changes. Always breathe, because doing so will let your vibrational body settle for a moment and you are more apt to be proactive and grounded instead of reactive and out of control.

If you want to get a psychic reading that really "kicks ass," then come prepared to the psychic-reading session. Even if you are not yet in perfect *psychically fit* shape, then be realistic about what a psychic reading can do for you and make the necessary adjustments to your vibration and perception. It's never too late to make positive changes in your vibration. The psychic reading should show you the before and after results of your own energetic body upkeep.

I hope by now you have become aware of what a good psychic reading is all about, how to get a good psychic reading, and how to maintain your energetic, vibrational self.

A good psychic reading will show you the blueprints of the thoughts with which you choose to construct your life, and help you make modifications so you have the best possible outcomes. Every thought was once a *twinkle in your eye*.

If you believe in yourself, then you believe in magick.

CHAPTER 9

Psychic-Reading Outtakes from the Client's Side of the Cards

Throughout this book you have gotten a look at what it's like to be a psychic reader and how the client is viewed from the perspective of the psychic doing the reading. In this chapter I am including a few client outtakes, so that the psychic-reading experience from the seeker's viewpoint can also be seen.

Here are just a few of the many worthy contributions that I have received. With permission from these clients, you can take a peek into their personal lives. The following samples will give you an opportunity to see if you can relate to any of these matters and also take a look at the psychic diagnosis and recommended treatments.

Brokenhearted

(Sent in by R.)

As I sit here wondering which of my experiences in life that I have shared with you (my favorite reader and my dearest friend) might be worthy for your book, the last two and a half years of torture stand out most in my mind after years of readings and blessings of friendship.

Over ten years ago, you were there for me when I called to say that B. and I were getting remarried, and I asked for a date that would mean we would be married to each other forever. Though the first marriage broke up, we found our way back together. I was so sure he was what I wanted.

That first breakup was another one of my tearful adventures you endured with me. I am sure you recall his "alien abduction" in North Carolina. You kept telling me he would come back, and he did. Well, now that I had him I wanted the next relationship to stick. We chose the date that would stick, but also the one where we would always have enough money.

You were there for me when I called in tears. Once again he had called me on the phone, months after he had driven away from our house without a word about leaving me. He told me he wanted a divorce, which has led us down a path I look at as my own personal hell. Two and a half years later I am still married, living without him at the moment, but I am still married. And the money, well . . . he apparently has all the money, too!

In a reading you told me there was a younger woman around him. There is indeed; she is thirty-four compared to his almost fifty. Not sure what we should say about H. B., my husband's friend and sneaky, conniving business associate who is definitely behind the *divide and conquer* scenario currently going on in my life. Perhaps he ate my husband? That might be the interference you have seen in my marriage. Do you suppose H. B. washed his hands before he sat down to eat?

You also asked me if he had a cat, and several weeks later I intercepted mail from the vet. His cat's name is Jimmy. And of course, I see that he has flown the cat from New York to California. Yeah, he has a cat . . .

In a reading you asked about Hawaii. I later found out that he was there partying with our money. I also intercepted a piece of mail that is a check from our company for over 75 K. Yeah, he has the money all right . . .

You also told me about a business venture that he was involved in that was far removed from his usual line of work. Well, we found it!

When I attempted to move back home, you told me I would find something on a desk or a counter, on a flat surface. I did! There was not only a small animal in the house (the cat named Jimmy) but a woman's purse on the counter! (I never saw the cat or the younger woman while at the house, by the way.)

The woman (with a very young voice) called down to me from upstairs and asked, "Who is it?"

Oh God . . .

You had told me that there was deception all around me. Yeah, she stole my house, my husband, my money . . .

You had told me that I should check the title to my property, and it appears he must have forged my name! What he was attempting to do remains to be seen. He was blocked from taking it completely over, but you have told me that I am protected, and apparently, I am.

I have asked you so many times if I will stay married. We picked a date that was forever. If he returns to me and you are not sure if I will want him back once I see what all he has done, and how would I ever trust him again, I don't know . . .

You have asked me if he is drinking and my response is that he never drank, although I have receipts that show he is charging large amounts of money at a liquor store, at bars, and right before he walked out on me he was drinking and told me he drinks. For heaven's sake, I have known him over twenty years, you would think I would know if he drank!

(And of course, the drinking is known now, and we wait to confirm the drug use.)

You tell me he has changed. That is what he told me on the phone, too. I guess he has. I feel like I am in someone else's twilight zone and can't find the portal back out!

You have told me that there is a lot of money there, and of course there is. I married forever, and he married (for money) forever.

If worthy of your book, your readers will have to stay tuned to see your next prediction, and if I decide to take him back this time or move on. And who gets to keep the forever money.

You can sign me brokenhearted.

Psychic diagnosis: In this situation, the client is definitely under a psychic attack by outsiders, which became a hostile takeover of her material life. The client is a loving and giving woman whom I have known for years, and her openness to others was not protected with grounding. The negative vibrations around her are very thick, and her constant and justified worry about how she will survive on a material level is distracting and keeping her preoccupied with negativity.

The negative vibrations have manifested as lawyers (who are crooks), and her dwindling sources of money are a reflection of her dwindling energy. This client has learned about what is going on around her through psychic readings verified by actual events. Psychics alerted this woman to schemes going on around her and told her what to look out for. She is one woman fighting off a troop of energy bandits, and staying positive is hard when you are scared.

The best treatment for her is to stay grounded, meditate clearly on the best outcome for all involved, and realize that she is control of how this experience plays out. The challenge is in not giving any of her power or energy away to the negative circumstances. A disappointment may open the doors to a hidden opportunity on a better life path.

Relationship breakups are hard, but when you get to a certain point, honor what you had and release yourself from a negative situation so the energy will be free and not blocked. The heart muscle holds the memory of love and it is protected by the rib cage. It's not an easy place to reach physically, but *psychically* you can let the love flow past the rib cage and out into the universe instead of holding it inside and hurting.

Even though this client's situation is tragic on a material level, spiritually I can see how she has become more in touch with her own psychic centers and aware of her own power to change the things that she can, and be at peace in knowing that her real win comes from the soul lesson of this experience.

Will He Call?

(Sent in by G. S.)

These two scenarios always stick out in my mind:

First: In a reading, you told me Pisces would call me that night (it was early days for our relationship, we were brand-new, and I wasn't sure what he was thinking . . . yet), and all night long I didn't receive the call. Not until the next morning! I realized that he *did* call, just as you said he would. I had my cell phone off, so he left a message. You were right on!

Second: You told me I will have an opportunity to move out of Minneapolis, but I didn't have any plans to do so. A week later, a major company called, asked if I would consider a move to where they were located. With the pay and promotion, I could not refuse. It was not the best experience, just as you said. ("It may not be the best move.") I did it anyway . . . for the money. I will never do that again!

Psychic diagnosis: Part one of the reading deals with whether someone will call or not. The client didn't realize it at the time, but her psychic connection to the boyfriend in the early stages of the relationship was so strong and most likely reciprocated by him that their thought vibrations intersected somewhere. The communication materialized as a phone call. Once the psychic connection between two people drops off, the materialization also drops off. Even if one party continues to exert energy vibrations toward the other, unless a similar thought comes along from the other party, the chances of physical manifestation become less.

This client eventually moved on from this relationship but holds on to the fond memories of the past. The trick is to not focus so much on past memories because that is not allowing yourself to have a clean piece of paper to draw on. Staying in the past-memory vibration will attract more similar types of relationships to the client. Recognizing where a past relationship went off track allows the client the opportunity to change the vibration so future relationships are better.

Part two of the reading shows how the client took a chance and moved, even though the psychic reading suggested that it may not be the best thing for her to do. Yet the experience was necessary for the client so she could see and learn that true happiness isn't always connected to money.

The best psychic prescription for this client would be to have an *astrological relocation chart* cast to see where in the world she would find both love and career happiness. A relocation chart is simply an ordinary natal horoscope moved to a different location. It's a birth chart cast for the person's moment of birth, but looked at from another location as if the person had been born there.

The House

(Sent in by D. D.)

I would like to share my experiences with you.

You told me that I would be getting this house. However, you also said they would give me a hard time about the pricing but if I just held on, I would get it. You were not too comfortable with the address numbers and even though I sent you pictures of the house, the address still bothered you. As of this writing, I just found out that the house has major water problems, and I am not too sure about taking on all of these existing conditions.

You also told me that my ex-boyfriend had become friends with a woman at work, and it was just a friendship. But by the new year I would find out that the relationship had advanced. During the early months of 2006, I caught my ex with another woman—his co-worker! You also told me that they would get married in a year and a half. They married in September 2007.

My sister M. spoke with you in 1999. You told her that by the end of the year she would be pregnant with a son, regardless of the fact that she'd had in-vitro five times and miscarried. You said her son would be born in the early fall. In October 2000, my sister gave birth to her son.

Thank you!

Psychic diagnosis: In the above examples you can see how this client used a psychic reading for guidance concerning the purchase of a house. She still stays in touch with her free will to choose even though I, the psychic reader, wasn't too comfortable with the address. The client did purchase the house and did get a better deal by holding out on the price.

Part two concerns the client getting confirmation that her old boyfriend was seeing someone else, and being told that he would wind up with another woman let this client freely cut the cords of the relationship so she could move forward instead of staying stuck in a memory. A memory is a multidimensional thoughtform that sometimes is like a favorite song: you play it over and over until something new comes along to push the original memory out of the way, to make room for the new creative processes that are always coming in.

Part three of this client's example shows how she was able to get some information concerning her sister because of the strong emotional ties that they share. Psychic readings can only pick up on other people as they relate to you.

Dealing with Jealousy

(Sent in by S.)

You've helped me with so many things. Should I tell you about my yucky neighbor, who you could tell so very much about and you were right? You told me I would sell my car and I did. You told me my son would get the job as a fireman that he applied for and he did.

You've told me so much about my husband's daughter-in-law, and you are so right about her. She's a terribly jealous person. His daughter is another story. You told me to be careful and not to trust her, and I definitely see what you mean and am very cautious.

You told me my husband had problems with his health. Actually, he went to the doctor this morning for his three-month diabetic checkup. He won't get any results for a day or two, however. Will let you know how that went. You've told me what will happen when he passes. You see a man whose wife has cancer and how he and I will be seeing each other because his wife will have passed away, too. If I remember right, you told me that he would ask me to marry him three different times and I will say no, because

I don't want to get married again and you would advise
me not to as all he wants is someone to take care of him.
I'm convinced that's all these older men want is a slave, to
do everything for them. You are right—I don't want to get
married again. You've told me how negative and jealous
my sister is of me and she is. I could go on and on.

Till later,

S.

Psychic diagnosis: This client is a very sweet, truly nice, and giving person, but she must learn how to close off people who are
jealous of her happy disposition. People who can't generate their
own vibrational light are attracted to people like this client, as the
moth is to the flame. Awareness keeps this woman from falling
victim to energy vampires. Knowing that there are jealous people
around her doesn't make her mean to them; it just allows her to
understand where they are coming from and move past them.

This client also was truly happy for her son to get his desired
job and very pleased about the information concerning the sale
of her car. This client operates with a lot of gratitude, and you
can hear it in her voice when she speaks.

Her husband is a diabetic, and I wonder if the vibration of
dealing with a man who is diabetic was attracted to this woman
who is truly very sweet?

This woman will have the opportunity to marry again, but she
realizes that what she wants to experience is the security of being
by herself and not the fake security of feeling that just because
someone is in the same house with her that she is not alone. She
has evolved to the point of finding out that her own company is
the best company.

Magic Carpet Ride

(Sent in by Kat)

It was the first time I had talked to you. You were a gift from a friend, the best gift I had ever received.

I was driving to a house that I was looking to rent and had never seen the house or location before, although I knew the area as it was my old neighborhood. I was nervous. You described the house before I arrived.

You said:

- Convertible parked outside (True: on the corner but an odd corner . . .)
- Three-way, strange intersection (True)
- Large green fence (True)
- Armed with protection (True: security camera at gate)
- White door (True: there was a huge white gate)
- The number four (True: address out front labeled 400 in plain sight)

But you alarmed me and said that I would live there for six months only to move east?! I liked the house so why would I leave it?

I did not believe you. I hated the thought of living on the East Coast. I only liked to visit. I had my job and I was moving permanently and signed a year lease.

I loved the house. I fixed it up and decorated every inch of it. I thought I would be there forever. That was last August.

In February I left my job, traveled to Europe, and moved permanently shortly thereafter to the *Middle* East. I lived in the 400 house for exactly six months and by May, the house was empty and I moved to the Middle East. That's what you meant by *east*!

You said that a Scorpio in a suit would be involved with me, and I am with him and moved here to Jordan with him. You knew! We are doing business together.

So, we signed a contract yesterday on the 26th just like you said. I am still in Jordan (East).

As I say, *Lisa called it.*

Psychic diagnosis: For the above client I was able to remotely view where she would be moving, because this client is psychically open and therefore I was able to reach further out into her astral field. This particular client has some developed intuitive abilities of her own and understands what a psychic reading is all about.

When dealing with this type of client, the psychic reader is able to be on the same vibration or wavelength, so to speak, and tune in to the client. The psychic reader acts as a *psychic editor* to make sure that the client is aware of necessary corrections, takes out mistakes, is aware of opportunities for expansion, and is encouraged to enjoy a well-balanced, creative, adventurous life. Some fine-tuning along the way has been necessary, but her life experience on a whole has been filled with many interesting people and situations.

Afterword

I hope the concept of this book conveyed to you the best way to approach a psychic when procuring a psychic reading. There are so many different types of psychic readers and also many different types of clients. I wanted to present some very complex metaphysical information about the world of psychic readers and psychic readings in an easy-to-understand, street-smart style so even a novice venturing into the multidimensional universe will have an understanding of what it is like to really deal with psychic energy.

Psychic readers are only as good as the energy that you give them to work with and tap into. Following the simple rules of grounding your own energy and approaching the psychic-reading session with respect and responsibility should land you, the psychic seeker, the ultimate psychic-reading experience.

Going to a psychic is more than just entertainment. You are venturing beyond the veil of the here and now. Quantum leaps into the vast universe are a road trip that you best prepare for. To get a good psychic reading, respect the fact that you are tampering with energy, and energy can be transmuted from one form to another. What you think, you shall also create. Make sure that the psychic readers that you allow into your very personal energetic space are clear and grounded. The laws of balance exist in the universe, and the way you approach something determines the way you will receive your results. The concept behind getting a good psychic reading is elementary and so very easy to follow. The elementary part or the four thoughtform vibrations are based on the elements of earth, air, water, and fire.

Psychic readings are unique, personal experiences. There is comfort in realizing that you have a future. The thrill of knowing what will happen next can become very addictive, but the responsibility of too much of a good thing lies with both the psychic reader and the client.

What spurs us on to seek out the unknown? Can curiosity about what lies ahead turn into an addiction? Maybe each and every one of us is a potential psychic junkie just a hairline away from making the transition from occasional, recreational psychic-reading user to full-blown addict. Once the desire for psychic readings gets out of hand, the preoccupation and anticipation of getting that psychic-reading high can cause dependence. The cravings for more psychic readings to satisfy the seekers inquisitiveness about their life can easily lead to psychic-reading binges in which contacting psychics actually makes the individual feel euphoric. There is a fine line between use and abuse.

Who are the psychic readers and where did they all come from? I guess the big question is: are we born with psychic gifts, or are they learned skills? The jury is still out on that one. I believe that who we are is encoded into our DNA, where the generations before us live on. There is no denying that the same information strands in the DNA of our great ancestors ultimately becomes part of our makeup, too.

In my own family I can see the predisposition to being a psychic. My mother and father are both highly insightful, my aunt Rose is an amazing tarot-card reader, and my three children all possess keen intuition, attesting to the fact that it must be in my

lineage. A look at my genealogy and family name of D'Amico confirms that a Giovanni Battista D'Amico, who was born in 1512, was
an astrologer and a philosopher.

I have had past-life readings from numerous experts, and there
is always a common thread making reference to an incarnation as
an Asian healer and also one as a medieval mystic. My interest in
the metaphysical field came naturally and was always a part of who
I am. As a child I would draw pictures, and after having a few past-
life readings I can see that what I was drawing were actually pictures of a past incarnation.

Society promises to always provide an abundance of people
who are lost or looking for answers and confirmation for a better
tomorrow. Who promises that there will be enough psychic readers to help all of these people looking for answers? Should psychics mate with other psychics to ensure that there is never any
shortage of psychic readers? Imagine the type of super psychic
that would be produced because of psychic inbreeding!

Psychic readings are useful tools in helping seekers realize
that there is a purpose, reason, and outcome to different events
in their life. People who get psychic readings are not crazy; if
anything, they are usually very together people who admit that
there is a force that drives our destiny. It is the arrogant naysayers who are really missing out on all that life has to offer, which
includes psychic knowledge.

Everyone seems to strive for one thing: happiness. Psychic
readers are often asked to see when the client will find happiness
or how the client should find happiness. Psychic readers help
their clients get through life's maze and obtain the ultimate goal,
which is happiness. Money can't buy happiness and you can't use
other people as a source for it; it can only come from within, because your soul has to earn it.

You come into this world with nothing, and you leave this
world with nothing. Everything in between is merely a test.

To Write to the Author

If you wish to contact the author or would like more information about this book, please write to the author in care of Llewellyn Worldwide and we will forward your request. Both the author and publisher appreciate hearing from you and learning of your enjoyment of this book and how it has helped you. Llewellyn Worldwide cannot guarantee that every letter written to the author can be answered, but all will be forwarded. Please write to:

Lisa Barretta
℅ Llewellyn Worldwide
2143 Wooddale Drive, Dept. 978-0-7387-1850-7
Woodbury, MN 55125-2989, U.S.A.
Please enclose a self-addressed stamped envelope for reply,
or $1.00 to cover costs. If outside the U.S.A., enclose
an international postal reply coupon.

Many of Llewellyn's authors have websites with additional information and resources. For more information, please visit our website at http://www.llewellyn.com.

Free Catalog

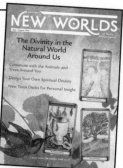

Get the latest information on our body, mind, and spirit products! To receive a **free** copy of Llewellyn's consumer catalog, *New Worlds of Mind & Spirit,* simply call 1-877-NEW-WRLD or visit our website at www.llewellyn.com and click on *New Worlds.*

🌙 LLEWELLYN ORDERING INFORMATION

Order Online:
Visit our website at www.llewellyn.com, select your books, and order them on our secure server.

Order by Phone:
- Call toll-free within the U.S. at 1-877-NEW-WRLD (1-877-639-9753). Call toll-free within Canada at 1-866-NEW-WRLD (1-866-639-9753)
- We accept VISA, MasterCard, and American Express

Order by Mail:
Send the full price of your order (MN residents add 6.875% sales tax) in U.S. funds, plus postage & handling to:

> **Llewellyn Worldwide**
> **2143 Wooddale Drive, Dept. 978-0-7387-1850-7**
> **Woodbury, MN 55125-2989**

Postage & Handling:

Standard (U.S., Mexico & Canada). If your order is:
> $24.99 and under, add $4.00
> $25.00 and over, FREE STANDARD SHIPPING

AK, HI, PR: $16.00 for one book plus $2.00 for each additional book.

International Orders (airmail only):
> $16.00 for one book plus $3.00 for each additional book

Orders are processed within 2 business days.
Please allow for normal shipping time. Postage and handling rates subject to change.

Discover Your Psychic Type

Developing and Using Your Natural Intuition

SHERRIE DILLARD

Intuition and spiritual growth are indelibly linked, according to professional psychic and therapist Sherrie Dillard. Offering a personalized approach to psychic development, this breakthrough guide introduces four different psychic types and explains how to develop the unique spiritual capabilities of each.

Are you a physical, mental, emotional, or spiritual intuitive? Take Dillard's insightful quiz to find out. Discover more about each type's intuitive nature, personality, potential physical weaknesses, and more. There are guided meditations for each kind of intuitive, as well as exercises to hone your psychic skills. Remarkable stories from the author's professional life illustrate the incredible power of intuition and its connection to the spirit world, inner wisdom, and your higher self.

From psychic protection to spirit guides to mystical states, Dillard offers guidance as you evolve toward the final destination of every psychic type: union with the divine.

978-0-7387-1278-9, 288 pp., 5³⁄₁₆ x 8 $14.95

Extraordinary Psychic

Proven Techniques to Master Your Natural Psychic Abilities

DEBRA LYNNE KATZ

Whether you are a beginner exploring your psychic abilities, or a professional looking to fine-tune your skills, this training guide will teach you to better understand your clairvoyant capacities and to reach your full psychic potential.

This is a no-nonsense, straightforward approach to becoming the clairvoyant you truly are, without apology or hesitation. The proven author of the popular title *You Are Psychic* motivates students along a path of self-discovery that begins with a fresh and concise breakdown of basic clairvoyant training techniques. Next, Katz provides in-depth answers to all your frequently asked questions about how to discover, harness, and apply your psychic skills through readings as well as healings. Learn how to get over the fear of doing readings. Discover how to remote-view objects and events. Katz also teaches how to employ the laws of attraction to overcome challenges and to build a career as an ethical psychic reader and healer.

978-0-7387-1333-5, 312 pp., 6 x 9 $17.95

Practical Guide to Psychic Powers

Awaken Your Sixth Sense

Denning & Phillips

Because you are missing out on so much without them! Who has not dreamed of possessing powers to move objects without physically touching them, to see at a distance or into the future, to know another's thoughts, to read the past of an object or person, or to find water or mineral wealth by dowsing?

This book is a complete course—teaching you step-by-step how to develop the powers that actually have been yours since birth. Psychic powers are a natural part of your mind; by expanding your mind in this way, you will gain health and vitality, emotional strength, greater success in your daily pursuits, and a new understanding of your inner self.

You'll learn to play with these new skills, working with groups of friends to accomplish things you never would have believed possible. The text shows you how to make the equipment, do the exercises—many of them at any time, anywhere—and how to use your abilities to change your life and the lives of those close to you.

978-0-87542-191-1, 288 pp., 5³⁄₁₆ x 8 $11.95